Re-Sisters

Musician and artist Cosey Fanni Tutti has continually challenged boundaries and conventions for four decades. As a founding member of the hugely influential avant-garde band Throbbing Gristle, as one half of electronic pioneers Chris & Cosey, and as an artist channelling her experience in pornographic modelling and striptease, her work on the margins has come to reshape the mainstream. Her first book, *Art Sex Music*, was a *Sunday Times*, *Telegraph*, *Rough Trade*, *Pitchfork* and *Uncut* Book of the Year, and was shortlisted for the Penderyn Music Book Prize.

Further praise for *Re-Sisters*:

'A compelling read.' *Big Issue*

'Fascinating.' *Choice Magazine*

'Cosey Fanni Tutti continues to explore her remarkable creative journey . . . *Re-Sisters* is an unapologetic account of artistic resilience from a boundary-pushing, unrepentant voice . . . Highlights the uphill battle that comes with being a woman in the arts — today, yesterday and six hundred years ago.' Riley Glaister-Ryder, *Hot Press* Music Book of the Month

'Full of active curiosity about the ways distant artists compel and ignite us. Some elements with which she weaves parallels are particularly fascinating, like Derbyshire's involvement in free love and the trauma of her childhood, while Kempe's rebelliousness and resistance in pilgrimage emanates an enthralling power. So does this book.' Jude Rogers, *Mojo*

'Passionate, original and fiercely defiant.' Rupert Thomson

'Tutti has proved herself to be as fearless, knowledgeable and incisive a writer of words as she has been a left field experimental artist . . . Each of these women's lives were their art, and their art their lives, and Tutti makes the case for a selfhood that must be expressed at all costs.' Kitty Empire, *Guardian*

'This engaging entwining of lives is about defying your place as a woman, the freedom to define yourself, and preserving yourself among stultifying societal norms and patriarchal belittlement and aggression . . . There is a wealth of detail here, including fantastic reflections on the working practices of both Derbyshire and Tutti's approach to creating music. Ultimately, what comes through, and is truly inspiring, is strength of character, strength of creativity – true fortitude, not least in the face of trauma . . . They all transcend those experiences, and are truly alive in this book.' Katrina Dixon, *The Wire*

'Awe-inspiring. This book is for anybody who wants to discover the work of three women who, without fanfare, have enriched our world.' Robert Wyatt

'A fascinating tale of the interlinking lives of three legendary trailblazers.' Salena Godden

'Cosey Fanni Tutti has lived the life and has the stories to tell: not just hers, but those of two other still unheralded female pioneers.' Jon Savage

———

by the same author

ART SEX MUSIC

RE-SISTERS

The Lives and Recordings of Delia Derbyshire, Margery Kempe and Cosey Fanni Tutti

COSEY FANNI TUTTI

faber

This edition first published in the UK in 2022
by Faber & Faber Ltd,
The Bindery, 51 Hatton Garden,
London, ECIN 8HN
First published in the USA in 2022

This paperback edition first published in 2023

Typeset by Ian Bahrami
Printed in the UK by CPI Group (UK) Ltd, Croydon CRO 4YY

A CIP record for this book
is available from the British Library

ISBN 978-0-571-36219-6

2 4 6 8 10 9 7 5 3 1

Cosey Fanni Tutti 1951–
Artist. Musician. Author

Delia Derbyshire 1937–2001
Musician

Margery Kempe 1373–1439
Mystic visionary. Author

Dedicated to *Self*hood

Contents

Author's Note

The past few years have been some of the busiest, most demanding and exciting I've had. A multitude of creative activities and unexpected opportunities have all contributed to a vast melting pot of ideas that have been gathering momentum, forming some semblance of collective purpose and coherence until the subject for writing this book emerged. The exploration of the lives of three women – myself, the electronic musician Delia Derbyshire and the fifteenth-century mystic and author Margery Kempe – through our 'recordings': my own as a multimedia artist, Delia's music and Margery's autobiography.

In 2018 I was commissioned to compose the soundtrack for a film about Delia, whom I had long admired. I became immersed in exploring her life and music through the Delia Derbyshire archive at the University of Manchester, discovering her work and that of the remarkable experimental musician Daphne Oram, and meeting many of Delia's surviving friends and colleagues – and for my own curious pleasure I was reading Margery's *Book* in between working on my own projects. I'd accumulated quite a stack of paperwork and books that I'd take with me on my numerous travels, so Delia and Margery both became a part of my life. Margery's bravery and audacity as a woman living in medieval times was remarkable. From her marriage onwards all stages of her life were unconventional. She didn't fit the female 'type' and wasn't willing to settle for a life lying low, hiding out of the sight and the judgemental aim of 'authorities'. But what made such a huge impression on me was her being the author of the first autobiography in English, making Margery Kempe and her 'recording' of monumental historical importance – as are Delia's pioneering experimental sound recordings from her time working for and independent to the BBC Radiophonic Workshop.

I was working on two film projects about female fortitude at the time, 'Delia' and one based on my 2017 autobiography, *Art Sex Music*. So when Margery's book turned up unexpectedly one day while I was out shopping, it seemed to announce her arrival beside myself and Delia – a trinity of the sacred and profane, sinners and saints of a kind. Three defiant women with our individual, unconventional attitude to life. Untameable spirits, progressive thinkers living within the inherent societal constraints of our times but finding our own ways to circumvent them in our pursuit of *self*-dom. We all pushed against restrictions, compelled by 'visions' of differing kinds and a deep sense of needing to rid ourselves of the unease we felt at being in the 'places' we were expected to accept without question, undaunted by both feeling and being treated as outsiders while embracing and staying true to the outsider in us. I felt a sense of connection with both Delia and Margery not only from unexpected coincidences but our like-mindedness, bloody-mindedness, our resistance to inequalities, albeit in differing circumstances, and our determination to retain our sense of *self* when undermined by societal pressures to accept our 'place', to play our 'part'. We all found ways to traverse the world on our own terms despite facing vilification, rejection and worse for our views, lifestyle and 'works'. Our 'recordings' played a vital role in sustaining us, making our lives meaningful, making us feel whole, ourselves – the processes adopted being the route to a sense of freedom. We weren't afraid to 'record' our presence in the world through our actions and to create something to share.

My work on the film soundtrack and this book coexisted. My composing the music provided, in part, a framework for the book. Our stories weave through one another, revealing the challenges we encountered as we shifted between 'places' within society and on the fringe. We all stepped outside the norm – Margery six hundred years before me and Delia – each of us driven by a feeling that coping with the demands we faced was sometimes too much, while simultaneously knowing that the life we envisaged and wanted for ourselves was about so much more.

This book is not simply about the likening of one person's life to another's. It's about individualism. What we choose to 'say', why and how, and when other less troublesome options are open to us, why we seek out alternative ways of living and expressing ourselves despite the difficulties. What's important is that we do it at all.

1

2017 proved to be a significant turning point in my life, firstly due to the exhibition of the art collective COUM Transmissions I co-curated, as one of the original key members, for Hull City of Culture. The show ran for seven weeks and was seen by over thirty thousand visitors, then deinstalled and all items returned to their assorted archives. It inspired the making of a BBC documentary film about the story of COUM. I and all the other surviving members were interviewed in turn. But over and above the COUM exhibition, what was key in changing the direction of my life was the publication of my autobiography, *Art Sex Music*. My first sixty-five years recorded for ever by my own hand, chronicling the controversial activities and challenges of my life on the fringes of society and my 'art is life, life is art' approach centred on equality, freedom of expression and breaking down notions of art, music, sex and gender. My art projects of the 1970s involved my working as a model in the sex industry, performing in pornographic films, appearing in hard- and softcore magazines and as a striptease artist. In 1976 questions about my work were raised in Parliament in response to the COUM exhibition *Prostitution* and I was subjected to public scrutiny by the press, who carried out a sustained and mainly vicious attack on my work and character. More recently, changes in views about art, sex and women have meant my artworks have been 'reappraised' and have found their place, often within a feminist context, in international exhibitions and prestigious collections. My appetite and reputation for pushing things to the extreme have brought gains and losses – my co-founding in 1975 of a new genre of industrial music as part of the band Throbbing Gristle was both. Music has always been my passion, especially innovative electronic music and all that I've created with my lifelong partner Chris Carter as Chris & Cosey, Carter Tutti and Throbbing Gristle, releasing over fifty albums, collaborating with numerous musicians and artists and performing across the world.

Writing my autobiography was a huge task, but with *Art Sex Music* out in the world I could rest assured that my voice was heard, that I'd spoken in truth about myself and my work up to that point and could now set it aside – that was 'then', that was 'me', and from here on I was free and more than ready to embrace what came next. I was quite content for my life to slow down and to take some time for myself. I had no expectations of any opportunities arising from the book or the COUM show. But it turned out that they laid the groundwork for what was to come.

The thirty-date book tour and promotional interviews for *Art Sex Music* began as soon as the COUM exhibition closed and would take up the majority of my time for the rest of the year travelling throughout the UK and Europe, and a brief trip to the USA. I made a rather special visit to the BBC studios in London to appear on Radio 4's *Woman's Hour*, talking about my book with Jenni Murray, who it turned out knew all about my early COUM art activities on the streets of Hull as she'd been studying at Hull Art College at the time. It was ironic and amusing to be on *Woman's Hour*, a programme that had always signified conventionality but was showing signs of becoming more representative of women's lives and open to a discussion of the unconventional aspects of my autobiography. A week later I was back in London for the official launch of *Art Sex Music* at Rough Trade East, a fitting venue considering our history. The Rough Trade shop had started its record label around the same time as Throbbing Gristle launched our own label, Industrial Records. We were both independent of the mainstream music companies and worked hand in glove to support each other. I was in conversation with Luke Turner of *The Quietus* and taking questions from the packed-out, enthusiastic audience, relishing the chance to talk with them. But there's always one . . . At the end of the Q&A a guy chirped up from the middle of the room: 'Did you write the book yourself? Or did someone else do it for you?' My hackles went up immediately. There was an audible groan from the audience. People seemed annoyed and offended on my behalf. Would he have even thought about or dared to ask a man that question? I should have told him to go fuck himself, but on second thoughts, and with some detectable disdain for his smirking cockiness and insulting question, I just calmly replied to confirm that I had written it all myself.

After returning from a book-related trip to Brussels I flew to New York for the US launch of *Art Sex Music* at McNally Jackson bookstore. It was a whirlwind visit, with the usual challenge of exhaustion from jet lag. I landed at Newark and took a cab to the hotel in Watts Street, SoHo. I was to have an 'in conversation' the next day with Lenny Kaye, the composer, guitarist and Patti Smith's long-time friend and collaborator. We'd emailed each other prior to my leaving for New York, so it was great to finally meet him and be able to chat about all manner of things over lunch before our public talk. He was perfectly wonderful, a gentle, fun person, and also jet-lagged having just returned from an Australian tour with Patti, so we were both adjusting to NY time. The evening was more like a party. A full house and jubilant atmosphere with the smiling faces of some of my friends who had travelled across the US to see me.

Before I set off back to Blighty I dropped by Rough Trade NY to sign their stock of my book. It had been an amazing trip and I was at Newark airport in good time to witness the level of paranoia over terrorism manifest itself in the form of a buzzard-faced old woman refusing to watch my bag while I went to the bathroom. I understood the security issues about luggage, but she was so hostile and accusatory even her companion gave me a sympathetic look. My mood wasn't helped by the TV screens everywhere feeding the audio of a Donald Trump speech through ceiling speakers at high volume. I was being rained on by Trump. The situation was an exercise in self-restraint. If I'd kicked off at her I could have been bumped off my flight, so I ignored her, but I felt it was well deserved when due to a logistical problem the two women's premium-class seats were changed to economy. I arrived at Heathrow at 6 a.m. and ran into Chris's arms. He'd set off from home at 3 a.m. and was full of praise for Toyota's cruise control as I lay in the back, snuggled into a pillow and blanket, homeward bound to Norfolk.

I wasn't quite feeling back down to earth, for a reason other than jet lag. I was on cloud nine. Before I left for New York I'd exchanged emails with my literary agents Matthew and Lesley. They had been approached by the director Andrew Hulme, who wanted to make a feature film based on my autobiography. I was pleased Andrew had also emailed me directly to introduce himself. As it turned out, we had a connection from way back, when we'd both performed as part of an ambient music weekend at the Melkweg in Amsterdam in the early nineties, him in the band O Yuki Conjugate and me with Chris. Andrew had moved on to film writing and directing, worked as editor on some of my favourite films, and been nominated and won awards. That was a relief – that he wasn't 'Hollywood', more arthouse, signs of possible compatibility. The idea of a film about me seemed fantastical, something I would never have thought could even happen. My initial reaction was to check that I'd read his email correctly, then a ripple of delight ran through me, verging on nausea. What a thrilling, once-in-a-lifetime opportunity. My mind was racing, visualising it complete, thinking of it in the abstract, as a project. Then as I started going over in my mind what it might entail, doubts started creeping in about what obstacles would crop up. What would the content be? How would I and others I cared for be portrayed? Would the idea even go beyond talking about it? Not questions that usually even cross my mind when the chance of a new experience presents itself. I took a leap of faith, and as is my way, pushed aside uncertainties and risks.

I agreed to an informal meeting at my agents' for me and Andrew to get a 'feel' of each other. I took the early-morning train to London, arriving at the offices in Gray's Inn Road in time to have a chat with Matthew and Lesley first about the whole process of optioning a book for a film. The meeting room was directly above the reception and had a glass floor, which meant I got a preview of Andrew before we met in person. I watched him enter and sit down, putting his bag on his lap, looking around as he waited for someone to come and introduce him to me. It was strangely voyeuristic. Snooping into his private space felt like I had an unfair advantage in sussing him out before we even made eye contact. As it happened, we got on really well. He felt the right fit for my story, someone who wanted to get to know 'me' and to work with me to that end, including my input. After numerous meet-ups exploring what we each expected to get from collaborating creatively, and if we felt it could work, I signed a contract. My first collaborative feature film project had passed the initial stage, with many more to go before I could be confident that it would be a reality. Until such time I had to keep a lid on the whole thing.

At the same time as discussing the film with Andrew I'd been working on a solo exhibition at Cabinet Gallery in London and on a deluxe vinyl edition of my first solo album, *Time to Tell* – which turned out to be a mammoth task, rescanning images, rewriting texts and remastering from the 1982 originals. It seemed like the elements of the Cabinet show were part of the autobiographical continuum, not least my film *Harmonic COUMaction*, made for Hull City of Culture 2017, which was composed entirely of images and sampled audio from my life. It was installed in the basement of the gallery, a low-ceilinged cement space accessed by lift from the ground floor. As the lift doors opened you could hear strange noises from the installation speakers below. When the doors closed the lift shaft had the effect of a sound tunnel, funnelling reverberating rhythmic thrumming upwards, making your feet buzz. It was like being confined within an audio chamber, the sound increasing in volume as you descended into the depths of Cabinet Gallery – until the doors opened into the space, delivering a full-on blast of music in synergy with the visuals. Everything felt like it was gelling. Andrew and the *ASM* film producer, Christine Alderson, had come to the opening of the show. A few weeks later they wrote to tell me that the British Film Institute (BFI) had given their keen support to the film.

The year was taking on a celebratory theme. Soon I was back at Rough Trade East for another talk and Q&A, this time for a different celebration – the fortieth anniversary of Throbbing Gristle's first LP release, *Second Annual Report* – and to announce TG's re-signing to Mute Records. Chris had performed a solo improvised set. We were both in conversation with Daniel Miller of Mute Records and then made our way to sign albums. As I stepped down from the stage into the audience I recognised the actor Caroline Catz, who was looking at me with a 'hello' in her eyes and a big smile. We moved towards each other and made our introductions. She congratulated me on my Cabinet exhibition, saying she'd been twice to watch *Harmonic COUMaction* and how much she loved it. I'd heard that Caroline was making a film about Delia Derbyshire's life, and we had a brief chat about whether I'd be interested in being involved with the music. I'd known and loved Delia's music for years, so much so that Chris and I had recorded and released a ten-inch single in her honour called 'Coolicon' (the name of a metal lampshade that was her favourite sound source).

I met up with Caroline over the next few months whenever we both had some free time. The rapport between us was immediate, as was our mutual enthusiasm, curiosity and love for everything about Delia. We'd talk and talk for hours about the film, about what Caroline wanted it to say and how she envisioned it would look. Her passion was infectious. Our exchanges of ideas about Delia's life and our feelings for her contributed so much to how I eventually decided to approach creating the music, the sound sources and methods I used. They had to work together as companion elements to Caroline's 'vision' and sit comfortably for me as part of a collaborative representation of Delia. Those intense meetings led to my accepting the commission to compose the soundtrack. I couldn't have been more thrilled.

With so many exciting proposals arriving, a whole new world was opening up. For the first year working on my contribution to the 'Delia' film I dipped in and out of my research on her while I consulted with Andrew on the *ASM* film and continued with an increasingly busy schedule, promoting my autobiography, travelling far and wide for readings and talks. I spent my sixty-fifth birthday at Crossing Borders literature and music festival in The Hague, taking part in a book talk with my friend John Grant. It was the first time I'd spent my birthday apart from Chris since we'd met, but Lee, my editor, surprised me with a delicious cake and a rendition of 'Happy Birthday' from the audience. John made it a special day too, treating me with fine food and a birthday gift from our inspiring visit to the Escher museum.

I wasn't at home for any extended periods, usually just a week or less, and began to feel disconnected, returning from trips and replenishing my travel case as necessary, ready for the next excursion. I was fully focused on the escalating demands surrounding my book, which had been a factor in the renewed interest in my work, and in curatorial discussions with my gallerist Andrew Wheatley and a wonderfully insightful curator, Gallien Déjean, about an exhibition at Le Plateau FRAC Île-de-France gallery in Paris. The exhibition was titled *A Study in Scarlet*, after my 1987 video piece and encompassed all aspects of my work in relation to a wide range of other artists who also subverted stereotypes (including that of the 'artist'), using various strategies to address issues of gender, pornography and the male gaze. I took the Eurostar to Paris for the opening and to take part in a panel discussion, staying at the aptly named Scarlet hotel. Seeing how all the exhibits together seemed to roar the same message of individualism and freedom of self-expression, I felt a surge of vindication and also privilege to be amidst like-minded artists. The bringing together of artists whose work was centred on issues of self-representation and identity through infiltrating and subverting 'institutions', fracturing established conventions through art, music and actions, felt in keeping with the issues of identity and the *self* that were at the core of my approach to my work on the music for the 'Delia' film – her struggles with liberating herself while working within and against the confines of an institution.

Initial development funding for the *ASM* film had been approved by the BFI. I was ecstatic, and although it was still very hush-hush it fuelled my sense of purpose as I read through the script Andrew had written and answered his questions about aspects of my life via emails and long phone calls. I was well and truly in the 'film' zone, whether on behalf of myself (which was weird) or on the trail of Delia – which led me to London.

When you're not used to attending concerts at the Royal Albert Hall, finding your way to the relevant entrance can be a bit tricky. Chris and I walked all the way round and then halfway round again before we came across the designated door for the Elgar Room, where we were to watch a special anniversary concert by the Radiophonic Workshop. The workshop had been set up in 1958 by the BBC to produce sound effects and tunes for TV and radio, and there had recently been a resurgence of interest in and respect for its progressive music. The workshop was no more, but original and new members had formed a band and, no longer with the BBC, they simply called themselves the Radiophonic Workshop. It turned out that Chris and myself were Mute Records label-mates with them. Chris's EP *Chemistry Lessons Volume 1.1 Coursework* was due to be released on Mute, with remixes being planned, and his list of possible remixers was topped by the Radiophonic Workshop. Paul Taylor of Mute approached their manager Cliff Jones on Chris's behalf, and Cliff cordially invited me and Chris to the show and afterparty. I in turn invited Caroline. Our interest was all about Delia, as the majority of her music had been created during her time as a hugely influential member of the BBC Radiophonic Workshop.

The room was full to capacity and a cheer went up as an all-male line-up took to the stage – original members Dick Mills, Peter Howell, Paddy Kingsland and Roger Limb, and new collaborators Mark Ayres and Kieron Pepper. The music was not quite what I had expected. The stage was jam-packed with electronic gadgets and equipment, synthesisers, keyboards, computers and musical instruments, with a large projection screen at centre back. It was a well-co-ordinated and professional audiovisual presentation to a very appreciative audience, including two former BBC Radiophonic Workshop members, Glynis Jones and Elizabeth Parker. Elizabeth had literally been the last to leave the workshop in 1998, and had wept as one of the engineers asked for her keys, escorted her out and locked the doors behind her.

I have to admit to being disappointed that Delia's name was mentioned only fleetingly, considering the content, and the 'star' of the performance (for me and others) was her *Doctor Who* theme tune. She would have felt gratified by the ecstatic response of the audience when the opening sounds started up. Chris, Caroline and I cast glances towards each other, acknowledging Delia being so noticeable by her absence. Half an hour into the gig I moved to sit at the back of the room on the platform where the mixing desk stood, watching the video feed on the small monitors but mostly closing my eyes just to focus on the music. People were nudging elbows and nodding in our and Caroline's direction as they recognised us, catching glimpses of others' puzzled expressions, wondering why all three of us were there together. An unlikely alliance of industrial musicians, a *Doc Martin* actor and *Doctor Who*.

At the afterparty various people gave speeches about the BBC Radiophonic Workshop, including Delia's dear friend and collaborator Brian Hodgson, who clearly adored her, saying how talented and wonderful she was. Then to our surprise he mentioned

Caroline's film and how he hoped it would reflect just how amazing Delia was. Before we left, David Butler, one of the researchers and curators of Delia's archive, kindly introduced me and Chris to Brian. We spoke for quite some time and arranged to meet at his house. Peter Howell came over to talk to Chris about the remix he was doing of one of his album tracks, and in exchange Chris agreed to do a remix from the new RW album. It had been a fruitful evening in many ways: hearing the music in a different setting, being part of the celebration of the RW and witnessing the enduring enthusiasm for it. As we left to start our long walk to the tube station there was an almighty crack of thunder and flashes of lightning, followed by torrential rain that danced off the ground and quickly formed deep puddles, drenching us through in minutes. The squelching sound of our sodden feet accompanied us as we dashed up the road to flag down a taxi. What an end to the night and so redolent of Delia, as I would later find out.

The weather on our visit to Brian Hodgson's home couldn't have been more different to that stormy night in London when we first met. It was one of the hottest July days of the year. Chris and I met Caroline at King's Lynn train station and headed east across the agricultural flatlands of west Norfolk, driving down narrow country lanes surrounded by vast expanses of golden wheat and sugar beet, making our way towards the Norfolk Broads and Brian's impressive and enviable eco house. He was so warm and welcoming. We sat together on the patio by the small pond in his garden paradise, sipping cool drinks and eating raspberry cheesecake as he recounted tales of Delia, her joyous, mischievous ways, and the darker stories of the effect her personal life and alcohol had on her work. I was struck by how gentle and unassuming he was. So clearly fond of her and their times together. It was the first time I'd talked to anyone so closely connected to Delia. Listening to him and seeing the look in his eyes when he spoke about her lit a spark in me. I felt I needed to find 'Delia' before I could immerse myself in making music for her. When we returned home I sat and wrote down all I could remember of what Brian had said in my red 'Delia' Moleskine notebook. I took a new box file from the cupboard in my office, dropped the book inside, printed out a large 'DELIA' label, stuck it on the spine, closed the box and placed it prominently on my desk. A marker of Delia's presence, awaiting further developments and additional notes from forging my way through all available information on her – starting from the beginning.

2

Delia Ann Derbyshire entered the world on Wednesday 5 May 1937, two years before the Second World War broke out. She and her younger sister Benita (who died in childhood) were born in Coventry to devout Catholic working-class parents Emma (Emmie) and Edward (Ted) Derbyshire. The family home was 104 Cedars Avenue, clearly marked on the canister of Delia's government-issue gas mask, a relic from her first eight years lived in the shadow of war. With all the disruptions that brought to everyday life, obeying orders was imperative. At times it could mean the difference between life and death. Maintaining daily routines and optimism for the future was vital for morale. Her upbringing was all about precision and order, secular and religious. The old mantras must have been drilled into her – cleanliness is next to godliness, a tidy house is a tidy mind, a place for everything and everything in its place. That included children. Parenting was nothing like now for Delia and myself. Our parents weren't our 'best friends', children didn't have lots of toys, and jumping on sofas or noisy play indoors wasn't allowed. Physical games took place outside, and even then weren't permitted to disrupt set routines, annoy neighbours or get out of hand. Bad behaviour wasn't tolerated. So children grabbed opportunities and found places to let rip well out of sight of their parents. Children's feelings were repressed too. Crying or those involuntary squeals of excitement I love to hear didn't always meet with approval. I remember being told to stop crying, stop acting 'up', stop acting 'out', calm down or simply shut up and 'behave', or else . . .

Delia and I both had an aptitude for the arts and science. Delia's first love was music and she started learning to play the piano at the age of eight, but the educational system viewed the arts as secondary to academic subjects. When she was eleven years old she started at Barr's Hill High School for girls. One period a week was allocated for music, and that was for either singing or learning to play the violin – which she hated. Her request to switch to the piano was refused, so she took it upon herself to make sure she got what she needed and continued with private lessons, supported by her parents, who bought her a piano. By the time she was thirteen she'd reached a high level of proficiency, performing at festivals, entering and winning competitions, and joining the National Youth Orchestra. I never reached the same levels as Delia, but we shared a love of Beethoven's sonatas, my favourite being 'Für Elise', one of very few pieces I would play voluntarily for my own pleasure. I was eleven when I took my first piano lessons. Our piano was against one wall of the dining room, next to the table where my mother would often sit after work, crunching numbers for the workers' wages on a big Burroughs adding machine while I did my piano practice, her 'playing' the big adding machine, punching away at the keys, setting in motion the rhythmic ker-chunks as the internal metal mechanisms did their reckoning. It was like a duet – mathematics in audio motion accompanied by my piano chords and occasional outbursts of expressive, informal, off-script whacking of random ivory and black keys.

Although much of Delia's time was taken up with practising the piano, she had a boyfriend, Graham Harris. They had been born a few weeks apart and got to know one another through their parents' friendship and frequent visits to his home. Their childhood affection changed to something deeper when Delia turned up to Graham's sister's birthday party looking like a goddess in her pale blue dress. Graham was smitten and the two fourteen-year-olds entered into a 'love affair', exchanging letters – with Delia's always written on blue Basildon Bond and delivered to Graham by her friend Lois, who caught the same bus home as him. In the summer months they would meet up and play tennis together, then go for ice cream. Much to Graham's delight, Delia would ride her bicycle to meet him outside the school gates. Even in her school uniform of blue-and-white-striped dress, navy blazer and straw boater she was captivating. Delia made such an impression on Graham, he carved her name in twelve-inch letters on a quarry wall when on a school trip.

Delia's schooling instilled in her a rigorous approach to everything that affected her for the rest of her life, creating an obsession with accuracy. She used mathematics as a route to (near) perfection in her music. Yet, much like myself, she was resistant to certain rules from an early age. We shared a need to 'get out', not wanting to be swallowed up by the system and family pressures, an unwillingness to accept limitations that stood in the way of our own plans. I had no rigid plan but Delia did, and she knew what was important in order to fulfil her ambition of going to university, being involved with the arts and working at the BBC – where everyone spoke so 'very very' well. She needed to get the 'fit' right, and her Coventry accent would have flagged her as being from up North, which in snob circles would have had a negative effect on her status and credentials. She took elocution lessons and built on them to eradicate or at least conceal any traces of her accent – incorporating 'golly gosh' and 'tickled pink', among other typically polite quips, refashioning her voice into the very distinctive, rather posh one everyone knows her by. You could say her first sound project was her own voice.

Delia excelled at mathematics and unusually for a working-class girl was awarded a scholarship at Cambridge University, the most prestigious place for the study of mathematics. I was only five years old and starting school for the first time when Delia was enrolled at the all-female Girton College in 1956. She was over the moon but her elation didn't last long. The misogynistic attitudes she experienced were bad enough to cause a third of her fellow students to drop out in the first year. Delia wasn't going to give in. Ironically, so many women leaving the course presented her with an unexpected opportunity to switch subjects, from reading mathematics to music.

> I wanted to do music; to me that was a forbidden paradise. They eventually realised that I had a natural instinct for music and allowed me to enter the course . . . There were only a few women at the university at that time and so we were treated terribly. But I had the solace of my music.

Having finally gained access to the place where she could increase her knowledge, she found the course boring. Much to the disapproval of her tutors she strayed away from the syllabus, which focused on the period 1650 to 1900, to investigate the theory of sound and a broader range of medieval and modern music. Delia had an open mind when it came to music: the term covered a very broad spectrum. For her it included the ancient and modern, physics, mathematics, harmonics and acoustics. She also knew music could be a free and adventurous creative field to work in, having had such a fun time abroad when she toured Europe providing sound effects for the Pembroke College Players' performances of *Julius Caesar*.

Just before her graduation in 1959 Delia and her music student friend Jonathan Harvey (whom she'd first met when in the

National Youth Orchestra) took a trip to Brussels to visit Expo '58, the World's Fair. They went specifically to see *Le poème électronique* at the Philips Pavilion, a symbol of post-war progress in technology, designed by Swiss–French architect Le Corbusier and Greek architect and composer Iannis Xenakis, with its light show and music by the French composer Edgard Varèse. It was so much more than a building. It was an experiential space that was itself the embodiment of the 'poem', as Le Corbusier was eager to point out: 'I will not make a pavilion for you but an Electronic Poem and a vessel containing the poem; light, color image, rhythm and sound joined together in an organic synthesis.' The building was dynamic and impressive, in the way people in the 1950s imagined the future would look – what we now refer to as retro-futurism. The structure was composed of nine hyperbolic paraboloids, resembling the shape of a 3D waveform similar to one generated by an oscilloscope.

Delia and Jonathan entered the pavilion to be greeted by an eight-minute, seven-part audiovisual show of projections and electronic music on the theme of the history of humankind. They sat on the floor of a stomach-shaped space, surrounded by walls and surfaces designed with mathematical precision relatable to the theme itself, and with a control tape that routed sound to 350 speakers. The whole audiovisual and physical effect of sitting on the floor and feeling the sound vibrating was an immersive experience and undoubtedly a huge influence on Delia. The meeting of geometry and sound must have been music to her ears. After the war people could once again afford to look to the future, and there in the Philips Pavilion was the future of visual art, music and mathematics in all its blazing glory, awaiting Delia's 'call'. By the time she'd left Cambridge the Philips Pavilion, which had likely helped to light the spark of her lifelong love of the alternative approach to music and visuals, had been demolished, just a memory of the possibilities of what sound, light and space can evoke.

When Delia graduated from Cambridge with a BA in Music and Mathematics my focus as an eight-year-old was on enjoying my childhood, having fun exploring the world to my heart's content. I was wilful, disobeying my father by going places and doing things a (his) daughter should not do. I strayed way too far from home, miles away into the countryside with my friend Les, being trespassing nuisances to farmers, chasing each other through their fields and damaging their crops, stealing apples from orchards and using derelict and bombed-out buildings as adventure playgrounds. Inevitably I got into trouble and had to face my father's wrath and the punishments he chose to inflict on me to teach me a lesson: beating me, grounding me, restricting my activities and putting a stop to the simple pleasures of watching TV, listening to the radio and reading comics and books. As I sat confined to my bedroom, seething at the injustice, occupying my time with drawing and painting, Delia was focusing on finding work which could offer her the opportunity to further explore sound. She was seething at an injustice I was yet to face.

In 1959 she applied for a position at Decca Records and was turned down, dismissively told that women were not employed in the studio and there was no intention to start now. It took her some years and various jobs to finally achieve her goal. She left the country, taking a job at the UN in Geneva teaching the children of diplomats mathematics and piano – including showing them the inside workings – and in the evenings she'd listen to experimental music. Much to her relief she was moved from teaching to something more suited to her interests, working at the International Telecommunications Union as assistant to the Head of the Radio Conference. The new post was a step closer to a job at the BBC.

She sent a deluge of letters pursuing employment there, not letting up until she finally succeeded.

It may seem peculiar that Delia was so obsessed with the BBC, but BBC radio had been a hugely important influence on her as the main source of information, music and drama throughout her childhood. I remember listening to it every day as a child and teenager, as most households owned or had access to a radio. It could transport you to other worlds, feeding the imagination. Delia's relentless pursuit to join the BBC was central to the plan she'd devised to put an end to music being her 'forbidden paradise'. It would enable her to live and breathe music openly in an environment that encouraged sound experimentation and composition.

3

As I grappled with finding 'Delia' it made me wonder how, from what we leave in our wake, we expect people to have any understanding of who we really are or the reasons behind our life choices. How our true selves or how we may want to be perceived could intentionally or inadvertently be conveyed or misconveyed through our 'recordings'. Also just how important 'recordings' are, not only in the purpose they serve in our lifetime but as imprints of our presence in the world when we are gone.

I'd stumbled upon Margery Kempe when I'd been rummaging through the second-hand section of a bookshop in King's Lynn, the nearest town to where I live. I found a small, faded paperback book about the life of Margery, a visionary mystic born in King's Lynn in 1373 who was persecuted for her unorthodox ways, travelled extensively abroad on pilgrimages, and fiercely defended herself when arrested and charged with heresy – no fewer than seven times. I bought the book and read it over the next few days, then went online to see the British Library's digitised original version and translation. I was riveted by Margery's life story, by what she'd done, the consequences of her queer behaviour, and how she'd made sure it was documented, leaving her mark on the world, with her 'recording', *The Book of Margery Kempe*. I thought that I wasn't unlike Margery, with her being called the 'Madwoman of God' and me being denounced by a Member of Parliament as a 'wrecker of civilisation' – which continues to be used as a kind of badge of honour, often by way of introduction in articles, programmes or talks.

To think I could be comparable to Margery, a woman from over six hundred years ago, may seem a bit of a stretch, but the more I delved, the more things mounted up. I felt an affinity with her resilience, what drove her, our revisionist approach to life despite the opposition we came across and the hardships it entailed, coping with doing what was expected of us when it felt so wrong. And that insatiable, quivering, restless energy that refuses to go unanswered, living the best we can, maintaining our presence and strength of will, handling all the bad things thrown our way. I've long believed that things happen at the right time. What precedes that moment feeds the inevitability of things presenting themselves at the appropriate time, bringing a rich intensity to a work or experience. The timing of Margery's arrival in my life seemed so relevant.

When I read Margery's book it really did feel like I was entering another time and mindset I couldn't hope to lock into, especially as religion was at the heart of her story and had no place in my own. Fifteenth-century England was a world apart from what I know, but one that's always fascinated me, more so since my move from London in 1984 to live close to King's Lynn, where so many buildings from when Margery lived there are still standing. I discovered that I shared something familial with Margery – that centuries ago one of my maternal grandmother's ancestors, Henry Chinnery, had, like Margery's father, been Mayor of King's Lynn and was buried at St Margaret's Church. I also realised that my home town of Hull had direct links to King's Lynn through trade, both being part of the powerful Hanseatic League – a select group of towns and cities across Europe that protected the commercial interests of its members.

I often walk out of the modernised town centre to the quiet old town. I stroll around Purfleet Quay and cut through to King Street via one of the many alleys that lead to the river. They were once noisy public thoroughfares, with people moving goods back and forth stacked onto wooden carts and trundled across cobblestones, pilgrims disembarking on their way to the holy shrine at Walsingham – and, scarily, press gangs would prowl here too. Now the alleys are quiet, used mainly for access to the converted medieval merchants' homes and warehouses. One house still has its tower, where a merchant could look out to see his ships coming along the Great Ouse river.

I've met people for interviews and lunched so often in the vaulted undercroft of St George's Guildhall coffee shop down King Street and visited exhibitions in its adjoining old warehouses, not knowing that this was where Margery and her merchant family lived and worked. I love the atmosphere of the undercroft, its stillness (there's no background music), and I always sit at the far end near a huge heavy wooden door that once opened onto the quay where ships unloaded their cargo. Running parallel and now sealed off are tunnels that once opened onto the harbour for small boats to bring merchandise securely ashore, as well as being a discreet place for sexual activities. Beneath the Tuesday Market Place further along the quay is a warren of medieval underground tunnels. The first market was in Saturday Market Place, adjacent to and dominated by the twelfth-century St Margaret's Church, where Margery worshipped daily, and very close to where most ships anchored.

I could imagine what it must have been like when Bishop's Lynn, as it was then known, was a bustling and important trading port. Ships were coming and going, exporting and importing goods through the League's trade links. The town would be crammed on market days with traders, foreign merchants, musicians and villagers all buying and selling at stalls and shops, with inns doing a thriving business. Margery's father John Burnham was a big part of that, holding high official positions in the town as a merchant and Mayor of Lynn five times, as well as a Member of Parliament. Being born into such a privileged bourgeois family, one of the most powerful in Lynn, gave Margery a great start in life. She lived a materialistic lifestyle, dressing in the latest fashions, proud, vain and boastful about her social status and associations with the nobility, influential businessmen and Norfolk gentry. How she went from that and from being a wife, mother and failed businesswoman to the holy, chaste visionary mystic she wanted to be perceived as is what her book is about. It's a testament of her spirituality and individual form of piety. The 'recording' of her process of *self*-transformation, with all its trials and tribulations, exposes misogyny, absolute male entitlement and female subjugation on a level difficult to relate to from a twenty-first-century perspective.

I had the additional issue of trying to avoid a degree of confirmation bias. How was I going to prevent my own beliefs influencing how I 'read' Margery? I had to keep reminding myself to set aside any knowledge I had that contradicted or challenged certain aspects of medieval life. Whenever I sat down to write about Margery it was like travelling back to a time when life was simpler than now, but harsh and judgemental in so many other ways. I felt like I was watching her battle her way through. At the end of each writing day my mind replayed the events from her book that I'd been working on, and as I drifted off to sleep Margery would enter my dreams. Sometimes the answer to the question about her that had been bugging me would emerge and I'd wake suddenly, grab my pen and scribble it down as quickly and coherently as possible – followed by a sense of satisfaction as I drifted into restful sleep.

Delia left us so much material, but all there is of Margery is her book. It is difficult to know what's true. I investigated life in the fifteenth century to determine what was plausible as far as Margery's life and actions were concerned, to help me reach some

23

understanding of her, particularly what it could have felt like and meant for her always to be regarded as lesser than men. Something problematic for us both and Delia – the idea of which I will never accept but from necessity have learnt to get around in various ways, not allowing it to undermine my autonomy. Refusing to accept inequality is an essential part of who I am. It's the only way I function. As I discovered the depth of what being lesser than men meant for Margery, the extent of the physical, mental and social impact it had on her and how she dealt with it, my admiration for her grew. She had so much more to contend with than me or Delia. The fifteenth century was pre-Enlightenment. God was everything. The font of all knowledge. A man. He held all the answers. He held all the power. There was no science to explain the physics behind what people believed to be God's wrath or grace, only a very crude 'knowledge' of the biology of the human body and disease – nor (God forbid) the existence of the notion of individualism. Women were believed to be inferior beings, perverse 'versions' of men, our genitalia internalised, inverted male organs hidden from view, mysterious, dark, and our sexuality seductively 'dangerous' – a site of sin. Women were the devil's temptresses, according to the Church, which blamed women (Eve) for the fall of man.

The level of religious fervour was high in the fourteenth and fifteenth centuries, not least because of the Black Death, which had killed over thirty per cent of the population of England in the 1340s and 50s – forty per cent of the inhabitants of Bishop's Lynn – and set people praying to God for forgiveness of what they feared they'd done to cause such a horrifying disease. Any such scourge was perceived as a judgement and punishment from God. Growing up in the 1370s and 80s, Margery was indoctrinated into the Catholic Church, the veneration of the Holy Trinity and the

Virgin Mary. Women were especially encouraged to focus their religious efforts on Marian virtues, and told of the importance of confession, chastity, humility, doing penance and the veneration of other virgin saints like St Katharine and St Margaret. The Marian cult was endorsed and promoted by the Catholic Church, and could seem to have been tailor-made for women. Mary, as mother and protector of Christ, was in a privileged position, having a 'direct line' to Christ to appeal on behalf of women who prayed to her. As such she was the most popular go-to saint for women. The cynic in me thinks that the Virgin Mary was not only necessary as Christ's mother but also a useful 'token woman' to make female followers feel included and under an obligation of conformity – with Mary used as a virtuous, unattainable example of womanhood. Margery readily identified with and followed the practices of the Marian virtues, and as a reward Mary 'visited' her during her meditations to comfort her.

Living in Lynn, Margery would have seen and met people of different nationalities coming and going through trade. But also, for a relatively small town, it was a throbbing religious hub, with many monastic houses espousing the doctrines of the Church: Dominican (Black), Benedictine, Carmelite (White), Franciscan (Grey) and Augustinian. There were priests and other clergy, as well as anchorites withdrawn from society, convents, priories and hospitals (providing hospitality for poor travellers and pilgrims). If Margery travelled just outside Lynn the landscape was the same. The surrounding villages and those near where I live, just six miles from King's Lynn, still bear their fifteenth-century religious names – Wiggenhall St Mary the Virgin, Wiggenhall St Mary Magdalene – with other areas named after saints offering protection for mariners or farmers. Over twenty churches within a ten-mile radius of the town were dedicated to St Mary the Virgin or St Mary

Magdalene – and nearly nine hundred different religious houses in Norfolk. The old pilgrim path to the shrine of the Virgin Mary at Walsingham runs past my house. Each year I still see groups of pilgrims lugging a heavy cross down the centre of the road as they make their way there.

Every direction Margery turned, whether locally or across the country, she was reminded that her life was centred on her faith in God and revolved around her adherence to his word. Her religious devotion was reinforced in her home life, sex life, how she and her husband made a living, in the church itself. The Catholic Church had a lot going for it with its seductive trappings of extravagant, colourful costumes, ritualistic theatre and music. As a package they played to and heightened the senses of the congregation, seducing them through awe and wonder into a state of submission and obedience. The preachings and teachings continued in the streets too. *The Digby Mary Magdalene Play* is believed to have been written for and performed to people in Bishop's Lynn and Norwich. No doubt, if Margery had watched any of the numerous performances she would have been inspired to follow Mary Magdalene's path to redemption through her public displays of piety, reassured that Mary had also fought and overcome her sins of lechery and pride. Weeping being the driving force behind Margery's defining style, she mimicked Mary Magdalene's 'gift of tears'. It's easy to see why. The tears were a feature of the mystery plays about Mary Magdalene's life. These plays with their all-male casts were dramatic and spectacular, with special effects like containers full of animal blood for the gruesome acts depicted and demonic possession portrayed by smoke pouring out of actors' mouths as their bodies convulsed in torment. Due to Mary's total commitment to Christ she is traditionally known as 'the bride of Christ'. Bride or not, painting her as a reformed whore would have suited the Church well in getting women to adhere to certain rules. It seemed to have worked with Margery, who was obsessed with becoming the bride of Christ too.

Margery had her work cut out for her. Women's status and rights, rich or poor, were defined by whether they were married, single, widows or virginal nuns, and whatever the assigned label, it was dependent on and controlled by men. It could also be reassessed and updated while men's status stayed the same (barring exceptional circumstances). A medieval woman's life was mapped out for her. She would spend her life in service, in worship, and as a commodity with a 'market' value dependent on her being pure, fertile and faithful to her husband and God. Margery appears to have met all the necessary criteria. There was immense importance placed on a woman's body as being essential to reproduction, to secure the next generation. Infertile women were viewed as faulty. Virginity had spiritual value and was a required condition of marriage to make sure the blood line was true, with virginity tests carried out and folklore surrounding the proving of a woman's purity. The tests varied from physical examinations to signs to look out for. A show of blood from a broken hymen or a clear golden shower of urine was good – but a loose bladder or loose tongue suggested loose morals. The fluids under test also included tears. A woman unable to stem the flow of tears or chatter (like Margery) was looked upon as wicked. Women found ways around the tests, helping each other out when they could with tricks including potions of nettles, nutmeg and alum to shrink the skin and give the impression of a tight, unviolated vagina.

The Church and the Crown ruled. That was accepted, if not always 'acceptable', particularly to Margery. She found the religious and social rules imposed on women restrictive. She flouted them, bending them to her own individual needs, not complying

27

with the behaviour expected of a woman, especially one of her status. Nonconformity was not tolerated. There was an emphasis on discretion, especially when at prayer, and Margery's loud and exhibitionistic style of worship was far from discreet. Neither was her manner of dress. She broke strict dress codes that made her conspicuous as 'other'. The behaviours Margery adopted to find her*self* and her 'place' were regarded as improper and became the source of her notoriety and numerous difficulties that at times threatened her life. It's against this backdrop that Margery's story is so extraordinary.

4

My first visit to the Delia Derbyshire Archive was with Caroline. Following Delia's death in 2001 her partner of the last twenty-one years of her life, Clive Blackburn, discovered 267 reel-to-reel tapes in her attic and over a thousand documents. He gave these to Brian Hodgson, who entrusted them to the Radiophonic Workshop archivist, Mark Ayres. They were subsequently digitised by David Butler and Louis Niebur and are now safely housed on permanent loan at the John Rylands Library at Manchester University as part of their special collection. I sat with Caroline in the far corner of the reading room, at one of the long workbenches that lined the walls, next to the floor-to-ceiling window that overlooked the wet streets of Manchester. We had our notebooks and pencils at the ready, plugged in our headphones and started to go through the audio files, casting wide-eyed glances at each other in response to pertinent works and sonic surprises, making notes of file names, with descriptions for reference later. Caroline was called away unexpectedly, so I carried on. There was so much to get through. As I listened I smiled at the playfulness of some of Delia's pieces, in awe at the ingenuity of her incongruous combinations of sound and the simplicity that belied the complex techniques involved in achieving them. I heard great swoops of white noise, rumblings, Kodo-type drums, ethereal voices, and Delia's own voice clearly relaying instructions about where to locate the audio sections in the programme she'd been working on. It felt so intimate and personal listening to her through my headphones, her soft tone giving way to one which suggested she was a little rushed and frustrated. The extensive range of her library of sounds was phenomenal, some similar to my own recent recordings in mood, melody and frequency. Her music defied time.

After lunch we met with David Butler to listen to and discuss more of Delia's audio recordings, relocating to the Victorian neo-Gothic John Rylands Library itself, a magnificent and imposing memorial to John Rylands, built in his honour by his third wife Enriqueta and opened in 1900. We were led through the Historic Reading Room, which had been purposely placed thirty feet above street level to maximise natural light and minimise distractions from the noise of the horses and carriages clattering along the busy cobbled streets outside. The vast space with its forty-foot-high carved stone vaulted ceiling felt both ecclesiastical and collegiate, with an open central section resembling the nave of a church that immediately brought to mind images of grandiose religious processions. Facing each other across the length of the room, as if standing guard over the library, were life-size matching white Seravezza marble statues of John and Enriqueta on granite plinths. John the nonconformist stood under the huge stained-glass Biblical Window depicting twenty prophets and other biblical figures alongside medieval and Protestant theologians. Enriqueta was beneath the equally impressive Secular Window portraying twenty famous figures of art, literature and philosophy from across time, many of whom had been important to Delia. The designer of the windows was Charles Eamer Kempe, which seemed a rather nice nod to Margery. Not that he necessarily had a genealogical link to her, but I took it as a good omen, along with John Rylands's mother's maiden name – Pilkington – being the same as my paternal grandmother's. Oak bookcases lined the walls and the gallery above. They were divided into study spaces by stone column arches with centrally placed statues of luminaries from the arts, science, theology and philosophy, looking rather like the statues of saints you see in churches. Enriqueta project-managed the construction of the library with a firm hand and meticulous attention to detail, especially in her selection of the people represented throughout the building. It was well thought out and progressive, an insightful, clever mix of arts and crafts and religious themes that was a perfect representation of both Enriqueta's and John's spiritual and secular interests.

We moved on to the Bible Room, a special place where John and Enriqueta's precious collection of Bibles was kept safe and protected from the elements. It was like entering the inner sanctum, and I felt rather privileged to be allowed inside. The first thing I saw was a bust of Dante sat beneath the twin arched glass windows. There was carved wooden panelling on the walls, and tall glass-fronted cabinets made of Polish oak, all crammed with the Bible collection. Dating as far back as six hundred years, it included illustrated medieval manuscripts, sacred texts and Bibles of various religions written in over four hundred different languages, as well as almost one hundred editions of the Vulgate (the official Latin version of the Bible). On seeing that John Wycliffe's works sat among the orthodox scriptures, I immediately thought of Margery. They were there because Enriqueta had moved from being Catholic to Congregationalist Christian. The origins of this branch of Christianity were derived from John Wycliffe, whose criticism of Catholicism led to the Lollard movement in Margery's time, which was one of the reasons why her unconventional behaviour attracted accusations of heresy.

The Bible Room was square, with sandstone arches arranged to create an octagonal inner space and vaulted ceiling. In the middle of the room was a beautiful, ornate, bronze art-nouveau-style light hanging down above a large worn wooden table where the original octagonal desk had once stood. I couldn't help but think, given Enriqueta's attention to detail, that the octagonal theme was of special significance. The number eight often appears in the Bible as a symbol of renewal, representative of heaven and earth, resurrection, eternal life. After all, the building was a memorial to John. But also knowing Delia's fastidious approach to mathematical and musical theory, in which the octave was considered to be 'the basic miracle of music', I felt the Bible Room was a fitting setting for listening to more of her music.

The library building was rich in diverse connections to Delia and Margery, being constructed of pink- and red-hued sandstone from Cumbria, where Delia lived after leaving the BBC. And the finest oak used throughout came from Gdańsk (formerly Danzig), where Margery travelled on her last journey and pilgrimage abroad in 1433. I sat in one of the original high-back wooden chairs with my feet firmly planted on the Gdańsk oak parquet floor, cocooned by warm Cumbrian pink sandstone. All associations that somehow strangely sat comfortably together in the small, contemplative, chapel-like space. It felt like my, Delia's and Margery's worlds had converged. The scent of the dusty tomes hung in the air. It was warm and welcoming, with Delia's music filling the room through the speakers David had set up for us. Caroline, David and I huddled around the table, discussing in detail the likely sound sources of particular sections of works relevant to the film script and the original timelines and programme briefs, to further understand Delia's techniques. That was crucial for me, not only in engaging with a different era but also with Delia's unfamiliar kinds of musical groupings. I was going to have to take a step sideways, move away from my own practice to Delia's, then return to merge the resulting similarities and differences. It was an incredibly enlightening and useful meeting for us all on many levels, exchanging opinions and information. The pages of my 'Delia' red Moleskine notebook were filling up fast.

As our meeting came to a close I enquired as to where the toilets were. I was directed to a large door in the corner. I turned the brass handle on the heavy wooden door, which swung open to reveal a grand boudoir with subdued, flattering, decorative lighting, complete with dressing table, large mirror, black marble hand basin and a huge coiled fire hose with brass fittings mounted on the wall like an artwork. On the far wall facing the door was the toilet itself, the size of a very big armchair with a massive oak seat and cistern – which turned out to have an idiosyncratic flush technique that left water drips all over the seat, looking like you'd peed on it. I had to step up to take my seat and sat down feeling rather regal, as if I was on a throne. I never expect to be overawed by a restroom, but this one was something special. It was no mere water closet, offering a different experience to normal. It turned out that practicalities had dictated the room's size: it had to accommodate the Victorian ladies' sizeable bustles.

The library had been a source of unexpected delights. I left the Rylands building with the thought that in memorialising her husband by constructing a library open to all, filled with hundreds of thousands of books, manuscripts, maps and texts, Enriqueta had also created her own monumental 'recording', a secular cathedral for study and learning. She had left instructions for all her personal letters and papers to be burnt after her death, and I wondered if that deliberate act of erasure was intended to ensure she would be remembered for the library alone. But in naming it after her husband, she allowed it to be thought of as his lasting legacy, which somewhat overshadows her own. Enriqueta, much like Margery with her book, had left her imprint, which would stand as a personal statement for how she wanted to be perceived. She was a strong, determined, religious woman, intelligent, philanthropic and charitable, who had achieved some acknowledgement by being the first woman to receive the freedom of the City of Manchester.

5

I was told in no uncertain terms that the BBC does not employ composers and so it was only by kind of infiltrating the system that I managed to do music.

In 1960, when Delia turned twenty-three, her strategy of infiltrating the BBC to find a way to compose her own music began to pay off. She secured a job at the BBC, as trainee assistant studio manager on a programme that reviewed classical music, and moved to London. She was 'in', and determined to work her way into the Radiophonic Workshop. She spent her spare time going to sit and watch the RW at work and learning about tape manipulation. In 1962 she asked to be transferred. That was unheard of – no one requested to work in the RW. She had to prove she was capable of using the equipment to create musical works and highly competent at recording and editing on tape. Delia passed with flying colours and was given the position of studio assistant. At last she had got her dream job and had the means to begin working on composing her own music.

—⁓—

It's fair to say that if it hadn't been for a woman, the pioneer of electronic music, composer, musician and inventor Daphne Oram, the BBC Radiophonic Workshop would not have been in existence when Delia arrived at the BBC. And as Delia intimated, if Daphne had been the one in control, the RW would have been a very different place to work in. Daphne was the prime mover in making the RW happen, despite having to deal with sexism and with indifference towards electronic music. She was eighteen years old when she joined the BBC as a programme engineer, sound-balancing for radio. It was 1943, and the Second World War had provided unusual job opportunities for her and other women at the BBC as stand-ins for the male engineers and technicians who had been called up to serve their country. As part of her job Daphne also worked at the Royal Albert Hall, where she used her considerable record turntable skills (what we'd now call 'beat matching') to smoothly cross-fade from the live orchestral performance to a 78 rpm recording of the same piece at exactly the same point, should an air raid interrupt the live broadcast. While people headed for the bomb shelters, Daphne stayed on, always worried as she sat under the huge glass dome of the Albert Hall that it could shatter at any moment and come raining down on her.

Daphne's experience with orchestras and her turntable skills were key elements in her 1949 work *Still Point*, composed almost a decade before the RW was founded. The thirty-four-minute piece was written for two orchestras, five microphones and prerecorded sounds that she manipulated live using three turntables. It was a radical, groundbreaking electroacoustic work conceived when the experimental works of Pierre Henry and Pierre Schaeffer were just emerging and Karlheinz Stockhausen's had yet to begin. It's phenomenal to think that Daphne was anticipating the real-time manipulation and mixing of sound we see and hear so much of today and that *Still Point* could fit easily in many contemporary music festivals. When she presented the score to the BBC for possible entry to the Prix Italia the Corporation rejected it outright, saying it was too weirdly abstract. They utterly failed to understand the purpose or concept of the innovative live manipulation techniques of pre-recorded sounds or accept her unorthodox structuring. Her score was tucked away and left to collect dust, never to be heard as Daphne had originally envisaged it. More than six decades later the piece finally got heard in a reimagined version by Shiva Feshareki and James Bulley, performed with the London Contemporary Orchestra in 2016 at St John's Square, London, and again in 2018 (fittingly, at the Royal Albert Hall).

Like Delia, Daphne was a classically trained musician and accomplished pianist, as well as a composer and engineer. She was confident about her abilities and about what the BBC could offer both her and the progress of electronic music. To that end she applied for different positions in the music department but was turned down time after time. The same rejection of advancement that Delia faced later. But also like Delia, Daphne was steadfast. From 1952 she kept on pressuring the BBC music department to create something similar to the experimental electronic studios she'd visited in Paris, Cologne and Milan. They had inspired her and made her even more determined to continue with her sound experiments, and she bombarded the BBC with technical information and examples of the music she envisaged making. She stuck at it, and once the BBC had accepted the need to produce experimental sound for radio, finally in 1958 the workshop opened on, of all days, 1 April. Maybe that wasn't an intentional reference to April Fool's Day; it could just have been a financial decision, April being the start of the new tax year.

Daphne's knowledge and first-hand experience of avant-garde music made her an obvious choice as one of the RW studio managers. Crucially, her widely acclaimed 1958 score for Jean Giraudoux's play *Amphitryon 38* was the first piece of radiophonic music used in a BBC television programme. She'd already proved that she was a great source of advice on what equipment would be needed to set up the workshop and the people best suited to work there, including the sound engineer Desmond Briscoe from the special effects department. Daphne and Desmond are both cited as co-founders of the RW, but Daphne was regarded as the unofficial head, rightly so considering her vital role in pushing so hard for it. They were very different personalities and their objectives differed too. Whereas Desmond was content to make music to accompany radio and TV programmes, Daphne wanted her music to stand alone. She was artistic in temperament, much like Delia, whereas Desmond was great at managing but also had a personality trait that Daphne and some others had to contend with. As a former colleague, Ray White, put it, 'Desmond was very clever at ascribing things to himself, often saying, "I thought of that."'

After all the effort of putting her heart and soul into fighting for the RW, Daphne didn't stay there long. Her visit to Expo '58 alongside other sound pioneers including Stockhausen, Luciano Berio and John Cage (and unbeknown to Daphne, twenty-one-year-old Delia) contributed to her decision to leave the BBC. She found the extraordinary work taking place at Expo '58 invigorating and realised that the RW wasn't what she'd hoped it would be. Not only did she want to create music ungoverned by scripts or directives, she was also frustrated by the BBC's health and safety rules, which imposed a fixed term of three months for staff working in the RW, due to the suspected ill effects on mental health of prolonged exposure to extreme frequencies. The short working period played havoc with the training of new recruits to the RW. By the time assignees had familiarised themselves with the workshop's equipment and techniques, their three months were up and the whole process had to be started again with a new set of people.

The stop–start approach defeated the RW's objective of achieving progress and had a massive negative effect on Daphne, who would be faced with having to abandon work to take her 'rest' period. She also felt that being a woman affected how she was treated. Once she asked a senior engineer if she could use equipment and have technical assistance for a piece of music she wanted to make. He belittled her: 'he reduced me to a very small height, and finished by saying – Miss Oram the BBC employs 100 musicians to make all the sounds they require thank you.' She wasn't put off, and developed her techniques on the quiet. But working at the RW had turned out to be an obstacle to developing her ideas. She gave up, worked her three months' notice and left the BBC in January 1959, having been at the Radiophonic Workshop for less than a year. Desmond Briscoe took over as studio manager.

Leaving the BBC was a very brave move for Daphne as a single woman at that time. In preference to her compromised and uncomfortable position in the RW, she trod a precarious path, giving up a regular income, easy access to equipment and contacts for work. Her going it alone under such circumstances is a measure of how much she valued her integrity and her freedom to experiment with sound. She moved to Kent to live in an enormous converted oast house which she called 'Tower Folly' and installed her own studio there, making her the first woman to set up an independent studio. In many ways it echoed the RW, with old equipment and the parts of what became the great project of her later life, the Oramics electromechanical sound-generating machine, which also made her the first woman to design and build an electronic instrument. The machine looked rather Heath Robinson with its metal Dexion framework bolted together DIY-style and the Oramics controller that housed four small cathode ray tubes and circuit boards built into an old wooden dressing table. Daphne had the entire oast house wired to facilitate her work in the studio, using the huge steel water tank under the forecourt as a reverb room.

Daphne had started developing her Oramics machine in 1957, but the concept had been initiated when she was seven years old and spoke of imagining a machine that would make any sound she wanted, even a sound that an orchestra would find impossible to make. Then in 1944, on a mandatory BBC engineering course, she looked at the waveform patterns of sound on a cathode ray oscilloscope and asked her tutor inquisitively whether it was possible to make the shape first and then use that to create a sound. He cut her off sharpish with a clear 'No'. Further discussion was clearly unwelcome, and lateral thinking like Daphne's was not to be indulged. But it was like a red rag to a bull for Daphne and she started thinking, 'Why not?'

That BBC engineering course paid unexpected dividends in sowing the seeds of ideas for what she referred to as 'graphical music'. It was the start of her move towards creating non-acoustic sounds, dispensing with musical scales, switching to a form of pure synthesised sound generated from graphics drawn by hand onto blank 35 mm film strips. Effectively the hand of the sound artist determined the sound via the image, much as a visual artist determines the nuanced shapes when painting or drawing, creating a unique 'language'. Daphne's technique involved optically scanning her hand drawings to generate sounds with her Oramics machine. The film strips were mounted onto motorised reels and run past a cathode ray tube (the type of display which had set Daphne's original idea in motion). The modified light was projected onto light-sensitive receptors, which in turn controlled a tone generator. Her Oramics machine can be described as a very early type of sequencer and tone generator in one – a huge beast. It's now part of the London Science Museum's permanent collection, its original objectives more conveniently met by either computer software or a phone app.

Daphne's work was revolutionary, of key importance to the development of electronic music, and immensely influential. Experimental music would have been all the poorer had it not been for her tenacious dedication and unique approach to the concept of sound, whether as a composer, engineer, performer or teacher. She felt it was especially important for children to be introduced to and make experimental music, to find their own way of expressing themselves and not to follow other styles – including her own. She was an individualist like Delia, with individualistic attitudes to life and music.

Delia and Daphne met through their connections with the BBC and remained long-term friends. They shared many skills, but I'm not sure they would have been compatible as collaborators, going by their personalities and the singular processes they used to create music. Whatever differences they had, they were kindred spirits, both bent on forging forward into unknown sonic territories. Daphne, the electronic sound pioneer who had founded the RW, had provided Delia with the opportunity to indulge her love of making new sounds.

—◊—

Delia wasn't the only woman when she first joined the RW. Maddalena Fagandini was already there but soon left to go into production. She noted a great shift in the workshop's approach once Delia joined. Delia was more adventurous and enthusiastic about as yet unexplored possibilities that would add extra elements to the music, all due to her knowledge of harmonics and the application of mathematics in relation to structuring the sounds.

The workshop environment had rules. A lot of the ones that had been a problem for Delia's predecessor Daphne were still in place, including a military-style hierarchy. As men had returned to their jobs after the war the women who had competently filled in for them had been dismissed, a case of collateral damage. Gender (and thus status) trumped skill. Delia had no real status, being the most junior, even though she was the best-qualified musician. There were additional protocols for her to deal with in the male-dominated world of electronic music, especially as an assertive woman working in an institution like the BBC. It was regarded as unbecoming for a woman to voice her opinions freely, so when Delia did, it usually provoked sarcasm and condescension from many of her male colleagues. She was a 'novelty' female among many males. Directors would come to see her work and comment on how attractive she was, or remark that she must be there because she was a feminist. Why else would a woman want to do 'men's work'?

Unlike our male counterparts, Delia and I have both been subjected to being referred to in terms of our physical attributes rather than our skills – as desirable women, tall, slim, attractive, sexy, vivacious – or by our marital status, with our intellect and artistic abilities appearing to be secondary. I can't recall instances when the same measure has been routinely applied to men I work with when their art is under discussion. If it was, where would anyone begin? At his body shape, hair, weight, good looks, the size of the bulge in his pants? When reversed it sounds like what it is – absurd and demeaning. The whole issue of placing women's physicality and personal situations before their work continues to rankle with me. I understand the need for context in a review or article on my work, but the emphasis on my being 'other', referred to as someone's girlfriend or 'ex', and portrayed domestically time and again, is mostly irrelevant and wouldn't be used in the same way when writing about a man. It must have rankled equally for Delia to be either not mentioned in reports about the 'men of the Radiophonic Workshop' or referred to as an abnormal 'feature'. As if, as a woman, she had a role as an oddity within an odd, predominantly male music studio.

This attitude prevailed in the RW and caused similar discomfort for other women, like Elizabeth Parker, who worked there after Delia had left. In May 1981 Elizabeth presented her proposal of music for the TV series *The Living Planet* to a large room full of grey-suited men, bar three women. It was an unnerving atmosphere as her fifteen-minute video tape was played to everyone. The tension was broken by David Attenborough standing up and announcing his approval. The series was broadcast in 1984 and received BAFTA and Emmy awards.

Sexism was endemic in the BBC during Delia's time there, with just a few women, such as producer Verity Lambert, occupying senior positions. This is still a problem today, with inequality disputes and criticism of the difference in the way the BBC treats its female and male staff – women being more harshly punished for 'stepping out of line' and paid less than men doing the same job. But like most women have done and still do, Delia took it in her stride as best she could, working within the rules, and surreptitiously bending them to suit her own aims whenever she got the chance. It must have been an oppressive and intimidating environment in which to work creatively. We all find a way of alleviating difficult situations, not only in order to cope but also to enable us to forge on with our own objectives and not allow prevailing attitudes and rules to deter us from what is of primary importance to us. And for Delia that was creating music her way, by any means necessary.

One thing in Delia's favour was that opinions about electronic sound within the BBC had shifted since 1959, when Daphne had left and William Glock had become Controller of Music. Glock was into avant-garde composers, which proved to be opportune for Delia. He'd set up the Dartington Summer School of Music, and in 1961–2 she assisted the composer and conductor Luciano Berio when he gave classes there. He was a gifted pianist like Delia but had changed to studying composition because of a hand injury he suffered as a conscripted soldier during the Second World War when his rifle exploded. Berio was exploring electronic music and also had an experimental and innovative approach to notation and composition which would have appealed to and perhaps influenced Delia – like his rebellious spirit, having joined the partisans against fascism at the end of the war. That rebel in Berio was inherent in his music as it was in Delia's, both in the sounds she chose and created, as part of her process and techniques, and in her sometimes playfully cynical sense of humour. They had traits in common that had led them both to Expo '58.

In the early 1950s, prior to the inception of the Radiophonic Workshop, Daphne Oram and Desmond Briscoe had a keen interest in sound experiments and were aware of the work taking place in Paris and Cologne. Electronic music was getting more attention with the establishment of dedicated experimental music studios in Europe, and with works such as Bebe and Louis Barron's award-winning soundtrack to the 1956 film *Forbidden Planet*, the first entirely electronic film score. There was some rivalry between the various avant-garde musicians of the government-funded studios of France and West Germany. Unlike the BBC, these studios didn't have to justify their funding. The European studios were more like research laboratories and the musicians were free to experiment without time constraints, specific goals or the pressure to release sound suitable for public consumption.

Delia knew about the European studios, and when she first joined the RW she visited the French studios to see how they operated.

> I joined in 1962 and the first thing that I did was to go off and tour around our European colleagues' studios like the ORTF [Office de Radiodiffusion-Télévision Française at Radio France] to see how they worked. I was so brave – just marching in like that!

One of the studios that ran on similar lines to the BBC RW during Delia's time was the Bauhaus-style Funkhaus (*Funk* being German for 'radio') in the former East Berlin, designed by Franz Ehrlich under the orders of the East German government. Its construction began in 1951, the year I was born. Strange to think that I ended up there recording new Throbbing Gristle material some fifty-five years later. The BBC and the Funkhaus were both sources of public entertainment and information, but the Funkhaus was on a much grander scale. It was the largest radio broadcasting studio complex in the world, employing up to three thousand people at its height. It also had a sinister function. It was used as a facility for spying by the Stasi, the East German secret police. Behind every clock in the building sat wiretaps recording and monitoring people 24/7, which made it a stressful environment of a different kind to Delia's BBC studio set-up. At least she didn't have to contend with being spied upon on top of the time running away from her.

The BBC RW worked as a service and most of its commissions were from programmes for schools. Those radiophonics were burnt into the psyche of children like myself as we listened to BBC radio and watched the TV programmes that were accompanied by the extraordinary 'music' of the RW, priming us for accepting preternatural sounds. Delia, having taught children in Geneva and briefly in Coventry on her return to the UK, had an understanding of what would be interesting for them, what would grab and keep their attention. Her track 'Dance from Noah', made for a 1972 BBC radio drama series for schools, was a prime example. It recently came to light again and was lauded as the forerunner of the rhythmic rave tracks that people danced to decades later, tranced out for hours on end. It gained her another accolade as the Godmother of Techno. With my label as the Godmother of Industrial Music, we'd both apparently achieved some recognition as heaven-sent music pioneers.

Delia's obsession with numbers and how the Fibonacci sequence affected the body springs to mind when I think of her 'Noah' track – the rhythm speaking to the body. People thought the rediscovered track was a hoax and found it hard to believe that such a musical composition was possible with the technology of the 1970s, that musicians were even thinking like that back then . . . Delia most certainly was. She was way ahead of her time and often went beyond her remit, venturing outside the BBC, investigating other people's work, seeking additional knowledge centred on her love of creating music.

6

In early summer 2019 I was back recording in our studio. The view out of the window gave a glimpse of neutrality, no distractions, just peaceful tranquillity – nature going about its business, with birds nesting in the tree, its branches scraping against the glass as they flew in and out, foraging. The pheasant clucked his arrival as he approached the opening into the garden from the riverbank, then like Roadrunner speedily made his way to the feeding station to join pigeons, doves, sparrows, blackbirds and blue tits all happily sharing the bounty. A pair of ducks flew across the fields and settled on the roof. I could hear them quacking before they descended, the male keeping a watchful eye, guarding the female as she devoured seeds like a vacuum cleaner.

The studio is where moments of great exultation and despondency occur, depending on whether inspiration is firing on all cylinders or frustratingly absent, or because of a mismatch of personalities, changes in mood or the external pressure of targets to be met. These can all be 'instrumental' in affecting the outcome of musical compositions as well as physical and mental health – as is the case for many musicians, including Delia. The importance of the studio environment shouldn't be underestimated: it has a direct impact on the creative process and can hinder or assist the ability to connect on the emotional level needed to free the imagination. Uninvited interruptions destroy imagination. The smallest distraction causes a disconnect, stopping the flow in its tracks. And getting back to that 'moment' can be nigh on impossible. It's an intense state of concentration that has no space for extraneous interventions. I'm not sure non-creatives fully understand the nature and difficulties of entering and staying in the creative zone. Delia spoke of being interrupted in her work by 'petty bureaucracy', perhaps to be questioned about her expenses claim for a sixpenny bus fare. And she wondered why some people seemed to think composers' inspiration came from God. She and I both know otherwise. It comes from a deep state of concentration that requires discipline. For her it was the discipline of numbers, closely linked to music as far back as the Greeks' simple harmonic series, and the Fibonacci sequence, which is used in not only mathematics but science, echoed in nature and art. She consistently if not obsessively used and referenced these, and always had at hand her own book of logarithm tables, the Pythagorean scale, the mean tone scale. One of the first things she did when she joined the RW was to correct mistakes in a book of tables and frequencies that she saw on a shelf during a workshop meeting, disrupting the proceedings by shouting out, grabbing the book and chuntering away as she fanatically made her annotations. She also believed that the imagination transcends worldly thoughts and earthly practicalities – much like John Keats had said.

I mean Negative Capability, when man is capable of being in uncertainties, Mysteries, doubts, without any irritable reaching after fact and reason . . .

Keats's concept of negative capability in relation to writing is easily applicable to artists and musicians. Certainly to myself – it's chalked up on my studio blackboard. I have a free-association approach to life and my creative works – suspending 'knowledge' to liberate creativity, letting all the elements fire off one another, go into free fall, crash and burn; then ultimately some coming together is sure to happen, but not always when or how I may want or expect it to. Zoning out and into the 'third mind', as I call it. The workshop was a vital space for Delia.

—◇—

The BBC studios at Maida Vale had been converted in 1933 from the Maida Vale Roller Skating Palace and Club, a huge art nouveau building that now housed most of the Corporation's music studios. Initially the Radiophonic Workshop was allocated Rooms 13 and 14, plus the interconnected, very small Room 15 for recording in isolation. The rooms were all located along the balcony that looked down on the old ice rink. Another studio was soon built in Room 12. When Delia first arrived at the RW she expected to see gleaming new equipment and people in white lab coats but was disappointed to be confronted by men in suits looking like bank managers and a shabby studio kitted out with old surplus equipment. There seemed to be a very limited budget for anything new. (Some time later the RW received an internal memo listing old and obsolete equipment and requesting that it be given to the new 'Engineering Museum'. The list included almost all of the workshop's equipment.) A pair of huge synchronised Motosacoche tape machines had the appearance of a 1950s enamelled metal washing machine, with lids that opened up to reveal the tape spools. Another tape machine, the green EMI BTR2 used for mastering, resembled a cooker with doors at the front like an oven. Recording apparatus dominated the room, with numerous reel-to-reel tape recorders, including a Ferrograph, three free-running Philips recorders, a Reflectograph variable-speed recorder and a stand-alone Leevers-Rich eight-track, one-inch tape recorder. These were used not only for recording sounds but for other unconventional applications – effectively used as instruments.

The making of tape loops was common practice in the workshop and hundreds of them dangled from the walls, with further miscellaneous objects used to make 'noise' scattered around. Different spaces in the building were mic'd up and used to get varying echo and reverb effects. Other sources of sounds and effects included twelve Jason valve oscillators with a keying unit (keyboard), sine and square wave generators, a white noise generator, an oscilloscope, reverberation plates, filters, ring modulators, limiters, equalisers, a Tempophon (for adjusting pitch without affecting the tempo), a beat frequency oscillator known as the Wobbulator (a testing device for other equipment, but used by the RW to create new sounds), record decks, a twenty-channel mixing console, even a gunfire effects generator, and a video playback machine for syncing sound to TV programmes. There were also musical instruments at their disposal, including the Multi-colour Tone Organ specially ordered for the music department, pipe and electronic organs, and a harmonium made in 1887 and certified as having 'mouse proof pedals'. But the conventional instruments were mostly used unconventionally, such as the contact-mic'd and customised auto-harp and guitar, and the prepared piano – as were other everyday objects, including Delia's go-to favourite, the battered green Coolicon metal lampshade. All that sound-making equipment is now available 'invisibly' as part of virtual software and banks of samples and effects, but back then it was all in physical form that took up whole rooms with its auxiliary equipment and massive monitor speakers.

Rooms 13 and 14 had been knocked together and became Workshop 1, about twenty-five feet long by fifteen feet wide, but an awkward shape due to a beam that ran the full length of the space and two wide, imposing concrete pillars. The ceiling was quite low, with two frosted windows facing onto Delaware Road providing little daylight. The studio got hot and stuffy pretty quickly, due to the lack of ventilation, the heat generated from the many valve machines and the number of people smoking. The ventilator fan let in too much outside noise, so people would stuff rags into it. When the lack of air became unbearable they'd remove the rags and throw open the door.

Sturdy workbenches ran along the edges of the room, laden with old BBC equipment previously used for testing and calibrating broadcast gear but now repurposed to generate tones that were then treated and modified to create 'electronic sounds'. It looked more like an engine room than a conventional studio. Everything was on view: the jackfield with its tangle of connecting cables, the metal trunking for electrical cabling that ran along the ceiling and down the walls, the chunky metal junction boxes and the peg boards that held cables, tape loops and notes. The pictures and descriptions of its industrial vibe, low ceiling and poor light and ventilation put me in mind of Throbbing Gristle's old factory basement studio in Martello Street. Once in there with no clock it felt like time was suspended and the outside world didn't exist. The TG studio had its downsides, like damp, mould and being freezing cold all year round. The RW at least had carpet tile flooring but it also had its own distinct drawbacks. With muted lighting from pendant lamps with Coolicon shades and a few small desks and chairs for paperwork, it was very much a 'work' area. It was dusty and rather claustrophobic and had a reputation for driving people crazy. The oppressive atmosphere was heightened not only by the physical discomforts of being so confined but by the intense concentration of people focused on recording and processing, whether working in isolation or huddled together, all putting in hours of work to create relatively short pieces of music.

Although it's inspiring, being engrossed for prolonged periods is exhausting. I've sat at my studio desk for hours, head down, deep in concentration, sampling, tweaking and modifying sound after sound, building up either tracks or a library of sounds for a project. When I finally surface it feels like I've got a crash helmet on; my whole body and brain are numb and all I'm fit for is sleep – which is impossible until my mind has gradually wound down from internalised creative processing.

Because so much of the RW equipment had seen better days the workshop technicians were very adept at making the most of their limited, decrepit resources. That limitation proved to be advantageous as it led them to discover ingenious ways of making new sounds. It was all part and parcel of the intention behind the workshop: to create 'special music', not music per se. That was in part to appease the BBC Music Department and the Musicians' Union, who were worried that their established role could be threatened by 'non-musicians', who would then be entitled to be called 'composers' – a convoluted reasoning that also prevented the RW musicians receiving personal (composer) credit for their work. Conservative, traditional, 'proper' music needed to be protected against subversive, electronic, 'non-standard' music. Sound could only be defined as music if it could be notated, and the main work of the RW had been to provide sound effects (SFX), which couldn't be.

I remember getting the first notated sheets of music from our then publisher for some of the Chris & Cosey album tracks. That was really strange, seeing our music in written form, as neither Chris nor I could score music. Considering some of the weird sounds on the album, it was quite an achievement, and it probably wouldn't have fitted the criteria for music set by the BBC Music Department of Delia's day. Neither would we have cut the mustard as 'musicians', according to the view at the BBC that experimental electronic musicians hid behind their pseudo-music because they hadn't the skill to play 'proper' music. Consequently Delia and the other RW assistants were viewed as subordinate to the Music Department, which is ludicrous considering Delia's qualifications as a musician. She herself regarded what she did as music: as she told Jo Hutton in an interview, 'It was music, it was abstract electronic sound, organised.'

The difference between the Music Department and the RW was clearly stated in the 1963 BBC Engineering Monograph No. 51, *Radiophonics in the BBC*: 'The term "radiophonics" is taken (in the BBC at any rate) to mean the production of sounds from natural or artificial sources to convey the mood of a broadcast programme, but not the creation of musical compositions as such.'

The monograph also quoted from Francis Bacon's utopian vision of music in *The New Atlantis*, first published in 1627:

Wee have also Sound-Houses, where we practise and demonstrate all Sounds, and their Generation. Wee have Harmonies which you have not, of Quarter-Sounds, and lesser Slides of Sounds. Divers Instruments of Musick likewise to you unknown, some sweeter than any you have.

It was Daphne Oram's favourite quotation, which she printed out and pinned to the wall of the workshop in 1958. Chris also printed it out and pinned it above his electronic gadget workbench in Crouch End in the early 1970s, and it now resides on our present studio wall. Their proud display and use of Bacon's visionary notion of new 'Musick' to describe the type of sounds produced in the workshop rather contradicted the BBC's policy of not defining their work as 'music'. That policy resulted in the workshop staff being defined as 'assistants', 'technicians' or 'engineers', and not credited individually by name but collectively as 'The BBC Radiophonic Workshop'. This meant many of Delia's ingenious works were not officially attributed to her and caused her problems when it came to receiving royalties.

In 1963 the jazz musician and composer John Baker joined the RW. As a member of the Musicians' Union he was au fait with the system and applied successfully to the Performing Rights Society (PRS) to claim his authorship royalties, having learnt that apparently the BBC were paying the PRS but not claiming the money back. His actions resulted in the credit rules being changed and the RW composers' contracts amended, including Delia's, giving a boost to their bank accounts and morale.

The Music Department's insistence on hierarchy led to the RW assistants and engineers being seen as second-class, while the studio managers and producers were first-class. A rather inequitable and inappropriate value system to apply to jobs that all demanded great skill. It put me in mind of the satirical 'Class Sketch' from the BBC's *Frost Report* in 1966, with John Cleese, Ronnie Barker and Ronnie Corbett standing in order of height and social status, describing why they look up to or down on each other. There was a lot of looking up to and looking down on in the BBC, and being a woman made it doubly hard for Delia, on top of the lack of respect for her chosen style of music.

Even after the success of *Doctor Who* was established, I still had to fight prejudice against electronic music . . . But there was still a lot of resistance to my work at the BBC. I remember bounding into the canteen and saying to my boss, 'This producer's just listened to my music and he's going to use it!' His reply was 'You call that stuff music?!'

The industrial music of TG at its inception was not considered 'music', just as Delia's work wasn't. Both defied description or categorisation. TG was usually denounced in derogatory terms as failing to be 'music' of any known description, until much later, when 'industrial' became acknowledged as a new musical genre and other artists embraced the concept and took it in their own direction. Delia's was labelled as 'special effects' or 'special sound', even though she included elements of musique concrète, which *was* regarded as 'proper' music.

People seem to think I'm just working with funny noises, that it isn't quite serious or something. I think a lot of people have a sort of block about electronic music, they think it must sound frightening and oppressive.

TG has been and still is regarded as frightening and oppressive, but the purpose of the TG sound was different to Delia's. What connects us is our drive to discover a way to evoke a specific emotion or experience. In the case of TG this could also induce a physical effect because of the frequencies we experimented with in the studio and at live gigs – something Delia was well aware of from her own studies and experiments.

I find myself much more bass-sensitive than most other people, as other people have more sensitivity to certain frequencies. We did an experiment about sensitivity to high frequencies. All of us had an extreme sensitivity to a frequency which was nine hundred and something cycles. One girl had a fantastic peak at something over two K and we eventually had to put that down to the fact that she had just recently had a new baby and she was really sensitive to this particular high frequency which was probably the frequency of the baby's cry.

Having your own studio in the 1960s and 70s was unusual, and commercial studios weren't set up for experimentation. Their primary use was for recording instruments and vocals onto tape. (One exception was Peter Zinovieff and Tristram Cary's EMS studio, a purist electronic space with very little acoustic work.) Certainly Decca, had she secured a position there, wouldn't have given Delia the unique options offered by the RW. Studios were expensive and musicians booked time in them only after the music had been written, rehearsed and was ready to be recorded. To most musicians back then the recording studio was just that. And it was a very mechanical process, with no visible representation of what was going on, unlike now, with software that makes readily available images of waveforms and spectrograms on computer screens. That invisibility made the process seem like a 'black art' to those not familiar with studio engineering. The RW was a totally different animal, operating in many ways as an instrument itself. The only other comparable studio was that of the musician, engineer and record producer Joe Meek. He had his own small-scale version of a commercial studio, equipped with home-made and modified gadgets, including oscillators. But there was nothing as experimental as the RW. It was at the centre of Delia's world, where she spent so much of her time, working all day and many nights.

When the working day came to an end and everyone had gone home the RW studio would fall eerily silent. That was how Delia liked it when she had an intensely demanding project to explore. She had the run of the place – literally running tape beyond the studio walls, along the corridors, trailing it past the tape heads and back again. She's said to hold the record for the longest tape loop.

Yes! It went out through the double doors and then through the next pair; just opposite the ladies' toilet and reception. The longest corridor in London, with the longest tape loop!

Each little snippet of tape, each cut and splice angled to perfection to achieve the sound she envisaged. But she was also open to and intrigued by the mystery element that only revealed itself on playback. Even Delia's fastidious attention to precision tape-splicing couldn't eliminate surprises. As she said, 'It was a magic experience because I couldn't see from the music how it was going to sound.'

Delia's working hours had been extended soon after she joined the workshop. Night working meant that she escaped the restrictions imposed on her during the day, when she'd have to beg to use certain equipment. With no one there she was free to plug in all the equipment she wanted in Room 12, which had been allocated to her. Alone in the workshop, the space became her own and she felt free from the condescending attitude of some of the male staff, who were bemused by an attractive woman doing the work of a man. At night she had no one constantly watching over her, supervising or questioning her methods. The incessant focus on meeting deadlines was a hindrance. She was well aware of time, actually obsessed by it. Timing was everything; it's the rhythm that speaks to the beat of all living things. Mathematically proven, and expressed in our bodies through circadian rhythm. Music and mathematics.

Some nights she'd fall asleep either slumped over her desk or against the door of the studio, to be woken the next morning by the cleaners or her colleagues trying to push their way in. The porters thought of her as a curiosity, this tall, stick-thin, elegant woman with her supply of cheese and tipples. Her behaviour was regarded as eccentric, and there were rumours of her sometimes working naked during her late-night stints. For Delia and some of her colleagues alcohol became a compensatory habit for the inconveniences and frustrations they had to put up with. Empty bottles of Chianti, Sauternes, Beaujolais or cider got incorporated into their bank of tools, used to make sound, either empty or containing differing amounts of liquid to vary the results.

The perpetual expenditure of energy to counteract the negative influences, and the late hours in the studio Delia endured in order to work in her own way, contributed to the onset of her long-term problem with alcohol. She'd sip wine throughout the day and into the night, using it as a kind of medication, as many functioning alcoholics do. It began during the nights working on commissions, when she'd take a bottle of wine and some snacks and settle in for a long session, and became a real problem by the mid-1960s. By the time she did the music for Ron Grainer's play *On the Level* in August 1965, her RW colleagues were seriously worried about the amount of alcohol she was consuming – up to two bottles of wine a day, not counting what she may have drunk at night. When they mentioned it to her she got very upset. She tried to give up but her moods changed dramatically for the worse, and she became so difficult to be around, prickly and manic at times, that after six weeks her colleagues suggested she take up drinking again.

By then she'd acquired another habit. After going to see an old doctor friend to get advice on her constant irritating sniffles, she came out, crossed the road to the bus stop and stood in the queue, sniffing away. The old man next to her asked if she had a cold. 'No, it's not that,' she said, 'I've just been told I have vasomotor rhinitis.' 'Aaah – here, luv, try a bit of this, it stops sniffles,' and he gave her a pinch of his snuff. True to his word, the ground tobacco gave Delia instant relief and a clear head – essential when working in the studio. That was it for Delia. She very quickly became addicted to the hit of nicotine and always stuck to a particular brand that she ordered in bulk, J&H Wilson SP No. 1. It now comes with a health warning: 'This tobacco product can damage your health and is addictive.' At least snuff countered the soporific effect of alcohol, which was helpful when she was working at night, just so long as she could get the balance right.

I'm not sure if Delia's mental state at this time was purely down to being overworked in the oppressive atmosphere of the RW or her attempt at abstaining from alcohol and her snuff habit, or whether it was a combination of those and what she was dealing with on a personal level. In the late summer of that year she received word from her mother that her father was terminally ill. She told her mother she would be home as soon as she could, but that she needed to fulfil her professional obligations first. Because her work was so entwined with her own methods it would have been very difficult for someone to step in and finish a commission for her. Her father died before she got the chance to go back to Coventry and be by his side to say farewell. It's sad to think that her colleagues at the RW were totally unaware that her father was dying or that she may have needed time off to be with her mother. Delia was an essentially private person who kept up appearances and hid her emotions well. Maybe she didn't feel able to share something so painful and personal with the RW team, who in fairness possibly found her complex emotions hard to read.

Even with all its pluses in providing Delia with what she needed as an experimental musician, the RW studio was not the best place for people of a sensitive nature like herself. It offered little time or opportunity – whether due to the incompatibilities of some personalities or the oppressive and misogynistic environment – for her to feel comfortable enough to confide in anyone about the personal demands of life outside or problems within the workshop. 'Sharing' was rigidly focused on the work. And it wasn't about to get any easier.

7

2019 started with a bang. I received the first draft of the *Art Sex Music* film script. It had been sent simultaneously to the BFI in the hope of securing script development funding, so I was doubly trepidatious about reading it and Andrew was holding his breath awaiting my reaction. I printed it out and read it straight away. It's hard to describe how I felt reading about myself being 'acted out' – my voice, my physicality, my emotions, displayed and 'played'. My main problem was accepting it as Andrew's interpretation of my life and reconciling it with my own need for it to be representative of 'me'. I had to put those thoughts to one side and wrestle with them later. Chronological discrepancies and some small details troubled me, being someone who likes things to be accurate. I needed to let them go and give way to artistic licence, allowing my story to unfold in a different way. I went through it over and over and sent Andrew my comments, followed by long phone and face-to-face conversations tunnelling down into the details of dialogue, atmospheres and the very personal. It was like reliving my life, being asked questions about certain events, my actions and feelings. But Andrew's interest had a different slant and purpose to it, which was interesting for me and vitally important for the film. From our brainstorming sessions it was obvious to us both that the film wasn't going to be a typical biopic. The film project was becoming rather like my magazine actions, submitting myself to someone else's vision of me, which I could then reclaim to create my own artwork. It was Andrew's film, but it was important for me to 'own' the project – it was essentially a part of me and it had to feel right – which he was sensitive to and understood from the start. It was going to be a long haul and the realisation of the film was totally dependent on funding. This, in addition to my tendency to think the worst so that things can only get better, helped to keep my excitement in check.

I was going through a period of welcomes and farewells, what with all the new projects, the upcoming final Chris & Cosey live performance and the release of the final Carter Tutti Void album. A new era was emerging. Six weeks of preparation went into putting a Chris & Cosey set together to perform at Subliminal Impulse electronic music festival, during the Manchester International Festival. Chris and I had agreed not to do any gigs for a while, but Alan Hempsall's idea behind the festival made it impossible for us to refuse. The objective was to provide a public platform for the wealth of lesser-known and unknown talent, those on the fringe, by holding a weekend of free performances by over forty artists from a broad spectrum of electronic music and visual arts. The shows would take place across the Northern Quarter – Manchester music central. Just a couple of better-known artists would hopefully act as a draw and support. We were more than happy to be part of it.

Our designated venue was the legendary Band on the Wall and we asked Maxine Peake to DJ for us. I'd met her a year before, when we did an artist talk together for Radio 4, and we'd got on so well. We met again when she came along with her partner Pav to a book talk I did with Elizabeth Alker for Hebden Bridge Arts Festival. It was a special night for me. We arranged to meet Maxine and Pav in the small bar of the White Lion Hotel, where we were staying, not far from the Trades Club, where the talk was being held. They arrived with friends from theatre and film, filling the room within minutes. All such down-to-earth, fun people.

No artsy-fartsy pretentiousness – with someone shouting out, 'Oh look, it's only Carol fucking Morley!' cheerily announcing Carol's arrival. The atmosphere was so animated, a blast of exuberance, with lots of introductions, from handshakes to hugs to a surprise kiss on my lips. I hadn't been in the company of so many women for years. Being surrounded by their energy and the sound of their voices was balm for my soul. Chris and Pav sat to one side while the life force of femaleness thrummed away, charged by our collective energies. The talk at the Trades Club was all the richer for having them all in tow with their whoops and cheers.

It was an evening full of warmth and smiles, made even better by the mischievous grin of the comedian Lucy Beaumont as she stepped up to have me sign her copy of my book. 'We're connected, you know,' she said with that familiar Hull drawl. I gave her a curious look. 'Your aunty Barbara is my godmother,' she said. It was a WTF!? moment for me. We went on to chat about Barbara and Hull. I was aware that others were waiting behind her but I wanted to know more. She'd had the guidance and mentoring that I'd missed out on because of my dad ostracising Barbara and the rest of our family. I'd never been told my aunty Barbara was into art and music or that she taught at Hull Art College. I could have had the benefit of her shared love of the arts and her support when I really needed it. My father never encouraged my artistic tendencies. He thought they were self-indulgent and a waste of time, so he had no qualms about depriving me of the opportunity Barbara could have provided in nurturing my creativity. It was funny to think that although Lucy, Maxine and I had all done our bit for Hull City of Culture, our paths hadn't crossed for various reasons. Somehow Hebden Bridge had turned out to be the place that brought us together, with all the other women I'd met through Maxine who made that night so memorable.

Chris and I made a pragmatic decision, based on our physical limitations and the amount of work we had to do, that the Subliminal Impulse gig would be the last time we'd perform our Chris & Cosey songs. It didn't really hit me what that meant until near the end of our performance. The evening was so joyous, with people in gay abandon, answering the call of the music, all with blissful beaming faces, swaying, dancing, jumping or just standing watching our every move. I was sad at the thought of not sharing those songs live again. When the opening bars of 'October Love Song' rang out, the audience's response was explosive – as one person put it, 'The roof nearly came off.' It made my heart flutter and my eyes fill with tears. I was caught between rapture and sadness as people sang along with me and couples embraced, singing the words 'our hearts together, beating forever, forever together' to each other. I was overcome by immense waves of love washing over me. I thought of Delia's reflection upon how she and so many others had been touched by that moment of beauty and emotion while listening to her piece 'Blue Veils and Golden Sands', that it 'melted' you. I felt utterly 'melted', emotionally disarmed in the most wonderful way.

I walked off stage to be hugged by Maxine and Pav. That day's rehearsal for her role as Nico in *The Nico Project*, a theatrical collaboration with Sarah Frankcom, had finished early so she'd managed to catch some of our show and was ready to do her DJ set. Earlier in the day we'd taken turns to talk with Mary Anne Hobbs on BBC 6 Music about what we'd be doing for the festival. I'd chatted about my book and the gig with Chris, and Maxine had said she would be focusing on Nico's music and identity in a theatrical reimagining of her solo album *The Marble Index*. It was in the same spirit as TG's version of Nico's *Desertshore* album and similar to what I would be doing with Delia's work. Now Maxine's

DJ spot beckoned. She stepped on stage, put her pint of beer on the console and spun the first record.

I set about the post-gig packing away of equipment and talking to people who had travelled from far and wide. One person was introduced to me as Annie Ryan's son. I'd written about Annie in my autobiography, describing how much she meant to me when we knew each other back in 1969. And here was her son stood in front of me, a bit younger than my own, telling me that he'd read my book and how pleased he'd been to discover a part of his mother's life he'd known nothing about, and thanking me with all his heart. I was happy I could genuinely say to him that she was a beautiful person, loved by everyone who knew her.

Chris tapped me on the shoulder to tell me our equipment cases were all packed. It was time to go back to our hotel and face the familiar post-gig feelings of just the two of us in a small, quiet room, having only minutes ago been in the company of so many in a vast space filled with music. It's a bit like a come-down from an out-of-body experience, when you're left staggered by the enormity of the emotional impact, wondering how to resolve the dichotomy between it and earthly reality. The sanctuary of sleep always helps – downloading and assimilating by way of busy, colourful dreams – and then the journey home, an opportunity to talk through and ponder over the gig and what's next on the horizon. It was a long drive back from Manchester. The road to the M1 wound its way through Saddleworth Moor. The vastness of the landscape against the dark grey cloudy sky was stunning, as was the extent of the damage from the wildfires of the previous year, acres and acres of charred black moorland – like dark shadows reflecting what the moor had become known for and what had struck fear into myself and others. The horrific Moors Murders. The subject of one of the first TG songs.

8

Since childhood I've been fascinated by things that aren't of my world, different cultures, the past, the future. As a child I wanted to be in the future as my adult self. I'd have make-believe conversations of being interviewed about my life, my work, my association with others. Maybe just daydreams or possibly premonitions of what my life has eventually become, the course I took, the avenues I explored so recklessly at times, not knowing why the temptation was so irresistible, no matter what the risks. I have a need to get the most I can out of the present. Whatever I do, I have to do it to excess, to explore it to the edges, step over into the unknown, affirm my existence.

I'm told I overthink things, taking the mundane up a level or more, until the once simple view of a road sweeper struggling with a blocked overflowing drain has escalated into the possible end of the world from an unforeseen danger that lurks behind the problem. Overthinking can be a positive thing too. Thoughts shooting off at tangents lead to all kinds of inspiring imaginings, like simply lying in the garden on a summer's day, looking up at the sky, wondering about the meaning of life on earth, visualising myself being transported into space in search of other life forms. I once had a dream in which I orbited the earth. I could feel myself smiling in my sleep. I was in a spacecraft but also out of my body, hovering above the planet. The view looking down was like NASA's photo of Saturn. I was looking at myself sat in the spacecraft within a golden globe that in my dreamlike state was a representation of earth in the cosmos. From my position in space I watched a small ball circling in orbit – then it entered space, out of earth's gravitational pull, and I relayed an affirmation of its trajectory back to myself in the spacecraft.

I've always felt outside the world as much as within it. I still do, sometimes feeling as if I live on a different plane. I have a deep connection with it, with a simultaneous sense of disconnection. Like traversing two parallel dimensions in the optimistic view that they will coalesce in the most positive way – the best of both worlds. Sometimes that's what seems to happen. The inexplicable has a special place in life and the act of creating. There's something quite wonderful about the seemingly ordinary being uninhibitedly expanded into a fantasy, into something new, in another form, and then placed into the real world. That's what's so thrilling about sampling sounds from everyday objects, reshaping them and re-presenting them.

For Margery Kempe, it was her fantastical visions that she 'made real' by bringing them into the material world in her own customised form to facilitate the redefining of her*self*. She refers to her 'spiritual eye' and 'physical eye'. I read this to mean she felt she had the ability to occupy 'other' worlds, whether in the past, present or future. Margery was about twenty years old when she had her first vision. It occurred following the birth of her first child, within the first year of her marriage to a merchant's son, John Kempe. Her confinement was horrendous. She doesn't say what she was suffering from but she was seriously ill throughout the nine months, feeling near death at times. The birth was long and traumatic, leaving her in the condition most mothers experience of feeling physically battered and in an intensely heightened emotional and psychological state. She and her son John survived, quite a feat in itself. Still thinking that she was going to die, she called for a priest, desperate to get absolution for a past secret sin that had hounded her and would see her condemned to hell. When she began telling her confessor about her 'small' sins, his reaction was so scathing she didn't dare tell him the real reason she needed him.

She tried to think of a solution, torn between confessing to God 'privately', by a kind of self-prescribed penance through prayer and fasting, or going through the normal channel of her Catholic priest, who should (but, as it turned out, didn't) guarantee customer satisfaction. Neither way to absolution had worked for her and she was left with her (unknown) greatest sin still on her conscience, both confession and penance well overdue. Her guilt and fear tipped her over the edge into 'madness'. Distraught and hysterical, believing she was being tormented by the devil, she flailed about, cursing her family and friends, clawing at her heart with her fingernails, biting deep into her hand, scarring herself for life. Her husband had her tied down to protect her from herself. After nearly three months of delirium, being restrained and confined to her bedroom, she had her first vision: Christ dressed 'royally' in deep purple silk robes, standing at the end of her bed and uttering reassurances that everything was going to be all right – a familiar image from the Bible of Christ's adornment in sovereign-coloured silks prior to his crucifixion and being mocked as 'king of the Jews'. She 'miraculously' recovered.

There are many contemporary theories about Margery's first vision. It could have been a case of post-partum psychosis or a spiritual crisis caused by the dilemma she faced over that damnable sin. Both could have been contributing factors. She may well have been suffering from an infection that caused fits of delirium, which is known to trigger hallucinations, ranting and aggressive behaviour. What we see and hear when in an altered state of mind can seem so very real. Waking from hyper-realistic dreams can leave you feeling like they actually happened. I've experienced the hallucinations associated with sleep paralysis when trapped between sleep and consciousness, when I swear I'm awake but can't move or speak, no matter how much I try. I can feel an evil presence close by, a terrible sense of impending danger, but I'm paralysed, unable to protect myself or call out for help. Panic sets in, then fear of suffocation as the bedclothes are too close to my mouth and nose. I try and jolt myself into full consciousness or scream but nothing happens. The only way 'out' is to drift back into sleep and reawaken with my body and brain in sync.

Whatever the cause of Margery's vision, it was real to her and planted the seeds of change that eventually led to her altering her lifestyle. But that was all to come. After her recovery she defaulted back to her old ways, carrying on with life as before – as a wife and mother many times over, dressing ostentatiously, putting a big dent in the family's funds. Instead of moderating her indulgent lifestyle as her husband suggested, she started up brewing and milling businesses to pay for her expensive clothes. It was all about keeping up appearances for Margery at that time. When both businesses failed, people said she was cursed, but Margery, thinking back to her vision, took her failings as a sign that God wanted her to mend her ways.

In 1409 she began a three-year period of fasting, praying and weeping in penance. She no longer paraded her wealth and status, moderating her clothing, spending the best part of every day devoted to God and resenting any sexual approaches her husband made towards her. I was curious as to what the significant moment was that instigated Margery's seismic shift from her exhibitionistic ways to her being a fully-fledged obsessive penitent seeking chastity. It turned out to be music, an auditory hallucination that was her awakening. While in bed with her husband on the eve of St Margaret's Day, 19 July, she heard a 'Melody so Sweet', like nothing she'd heard before, the harmonic sounds of heaven, played by angels. How beautiful that 'otherworldly music' was, her signal call to her new life of spirituality.

Delia kept numerous quotes about music scattered throughout her school workbooks. One that seemed so apposite to Margery was Edward Bulwer-Lytton's 'Music, once admitted into the soul, becomes a sort of spirit, and never dies.' The effect of music is so powerful. Delia's recognition of that as a teenager was written large in her notebooks, as if her mind would wander to her favourite subject during her assigned studies. Moving away from academia, she would put down her pencil and pick up her fountain pen to write in beautiful script quotes by Thomas Carlyle, Percy Bysshe Shelley, Henry Wadsworth Longfellow and others, all expressing the beauty of music and its effect on and importance to people. Delia put her own spin on Shakespeare's line, 'If music be the food of love, play on . . .' She wrote, 'If music be the screen of love I will play on,' giving it pride of place in the centre of the page, penned in blue ink over her graphite-grey notes on protoplasm and within a rectangular box – like a rubber stamp.

It was the saying 'Music is the real universal language of mankind' that jumped out at me as being key to Delia's attitude and understanding of music, that it took precedence over everything else for her. Maybe that's why she also gave it prominence using the same rectangular box as her version of Shakespeare, placing it over her essay on the Earl of Shaftesbury and the Popish Plot of 1678. The concerns of Catholicism 'rubber-stamped' as secondary to music.

For Margery, music and religion were mutually inclusive and formed a bond between her and the spiritual world. From her revelatory musical moment onward she endured sex with her husband on sufferance, begging him not to violate her, to allow her to be chaste. It was a constant topic of her prayers, as well as the sobbing in penance for that mysterious unrevealed sin, asking God over and over to stop her husband helping himself to her body, which she found not only abhorrent but very painful. She had so far endured more than ten pregnancies but hadn't gone off sex, just off John. She had adulterous thoughts of having sex with other men she fancied. Her lust for forbidden fruit became a dark cloud of guilt that hung over her, and it's not surprising that she directed her sexual desires towards Christ – a safe port of call in testing times – secure in the knowledge that she was following in the footsteps of St Bridget and St Katharine. Choosing Christ as her lover was far less physically painful, even if her anxieties and feelings of guilt proved torturous at times. The Catholic Church forbade sex at certain times, which offered Margery some breathing space: during pregnancy, the time before her church cleansing after childbirth, saints' feast days and holy days. Sex was also banned during menstruation, when women were 'unclean', unfit for sex or church. A woman bleeding from no visible injury could only be explained as yet another punishment from God for Eve's sin. Even too much or too little menstrual blood was judged negatively.

Margery had little autonomy, but her ambitious plan to forge a path to chastity had other benefits besides keeping her husband away from her. It also gave her a degree of liberation that was meagre compared to what women take for granted now, but to Margery it brought opportunities that meant she didn't have to settle for being an obedient wife and mother, or having to be pawed, prodded and poked at the whim of her husband. Her goal was sainthood and the key prerequisite was chastity. But she could regain her virgin status through mysticism and penance – dependent on the authorisation of the Church, of course. Celibate marriages weren't uncommon and the wife benefited by gaining more respect and independence. As a married woman Margery was on the bottom rung as far as status went with the Church. Becoming celibate and being perceived as spiritual meant her social position could be re-evaluated, elevated from unsuccessful merchant's wife to holy woman.

Margery's family's good reputation had started to decline from the early 1400s, around the time she began the first stages of her road to redemption. A holy woman was seen as having a meaningful life, an alternative to being a wife. Another benefit was that by professing to be Christ's bride she could reclaim her body. Only Christ had access to it, which of course wasn't physical – and it was up to her what 'contact' she had with him.

Margery's church was the main church in Lynn and was just yards away from where she lived. It was dedicated to St Margaret of Antioch, St Mary Magdalene and all virgin saints – an all-woman space and one that seems perfect for Margery, not only because her name was a derivation of Margaret. The Church throwing in 'all saints' for good measure pretty much covered women as they went about their devotions and prayers for mercy and forgiveness. St Mary Magdalene, a non-virgin, was principally the patron saint of women who were persecuted or ridiculed for their piety, who were penitent about their sins, and who struggled with sexual temptation – all issues that applied to Margery. She may not have been a virgin but she fitted the profile for St Margaret, the patron saint of pregnant women. Death in childbirth was so feared that the Church recommended women confess their sins beforehand and pray hard to St Margaret for protection. Any failure to deliver successfully at full term was put down to the woman not praying enough and miscarriage was seen as proof of sin. Women were under a lot of pressure at a time when infant mortality was high, as well as contending with the threat of their own death or serious injury and infection from giving birth. Margery's survival after fourteen births must have suggested that spending so much time praying to St Margaret had worked wonders.

I found it strange that she only wrote about her first son, John, and none of the other thirteen children. After so many pregnancies with no pain relief, and the trauma of who knows how many children she may have lost through miscarriage, stillbirths or death in infancy, I thought she'd have something to say about the emotional impact and all the time it took up during her childbearing years. She must have wondered how many more times she'd have to risk her life and how many more children she'd lose. It's not surprising she wanted to end sex with her husband. It was a matter of life and death.

Margery was doing penance for not being chaste and for that lingering sin by fasting and long spells of praying, starting as soon as the church doors were opened by the Benedictine monks in charge. They celebrated Latin mass, praying and chanting in the chancel eight times a day, starting at 2 a.m. and finishing at 6 p.m. They stood the whole time – well, I say 'stood', but they had misericords ('mercy seats') to lean on, giving the appearance of standing. The chancel was a 'monks only' part of St Margaret's, but Margery could listen to them and say her own prayers in the space allocated to lesser mortals. Or she may have been allowed into the exclusive Trinity Chapel, being the daughter of one of the members of the merchants' guild of the Holy Trinity, which helped pay for the upkeep of St Margaret's. The Trinity Chapel was very close to the chancel and only separated by a carved wooden screen.

Most people attended mass every day, but Margery was like a fixture at St Margaret's, praying and weeping the best part of every day to 'wash' herself and others of sin. She was persistent and dedicated over the years, taking her sexual urges as tests of her faith seriously enough that she wore a coarse and itchy hair shirt concealed under her clothes, never taking it off, even when she was pregnant.

During her prayers one day in 1412 Margery received (in her head) a command from God that she must undertake pilgrimages to Jerusalem, Rome and Santiago de Compostela. This was all very well but Lynn to Jerusalem was a six-thousand-mile round trip, arduous and dangerous, not least because it involved the phenomenal challenge of crossing the Alps, and all done by foot, donkey, ship or cart. Pilgrimages abroad were also expensive and Margery's finances at that point couldn't cover the cost, so it was very convenient that the 'command' wasn't to be acted upon with immediate effect, giving her notice to get her affairs in order. In the meantime the shrines in England would suffice until she could save enough money to fund the trip and obtain the permissions she needed.

9

On 26 April 1413, as Margery knelt in prayer in St Margaret's Church she got an answer from God and a possible solution to her problem with her husband. She was 'told' that if she fasted, he would 'slay' John before Whitsuntide. A pretty extreme and specific declaration of intent – maybe because prior to Whitsuntide sex was permitted, so a command from above was a way for her to keep John at a distance during his authorised 'access' time. Margery was happy to fast if it meant John would be struck impotent or dead. A few days later John rolled over in bed to have sex with her. She screamed out, 'Jesus, help me!' – presumably calling for him to keep his promise. It worked. John was so afraid he'd be struck down, he crawled off Margery and didn't go near her for sex for weeks.

1413 was a year full of special events for Margery, significantly around Easter and Whitsuntide, when the focus was on religious devotion and sex was forbidden. Holy Week being a very sacred and important time for Catholics, Margery's passion for Christ and Mary would have been in full flow, leaving her very receptive to any hints of revelation. As usual she took the short walk to St Margaret's to attend mass. As she knelt in prayer she heard a loud noise above her. She didn't dare look up, thinking it was a sign of God's disapproval that her critics had warned her about. A second later a large heavy stone and part of a wooden beam fell from the rafters, landing on her head and back, hitting her with such force the pain made her scream out, 'Jesus mercy!'

Miraculously the pain went away . . . and conveniently (because all miracles require a witness) a merchant, John of Wereham, saw it happen and helped her, saying it was a miracle she hadn't been killed or severely injured. A local friar was also impressed, as were a few other onlookers, but most of the locals took it as a sign of the punishment they'd said would happen, and thought that she'd just had a narrow escape. It wasn't accepted as a miracle, one of the prerequisites for sainthood.

After Whitsun Margery set off with John on pilgrimages to various shrines around England. She needed both his permission and protection. Travelling by foot and donkey, they stopped off at various shrines on the 120-mile journey to York, where they took in the Corpus Christi mystery plays. When they left York to go to Bridlington, Margery was presented with the opportune moment she'd been praying for. It was Friday 23 June 1413, '*Fryday on Mydsomyr Evyn*', the summer solstice, a night associated with partying, fertility and sex. Margery and John were strolling along when they stopped for a drink and something to eat. He'd done as she'd wanted and gone eight weeks without approaching her for sex. Now he asked her if it would really be so bad for her to let him fuck her. Would she still say no even if he were to be threatened with having his head chopped off unless he did it? Without a second's thought she said she'd rather he were killed than have him humping on top of her again. He called her a 'bad wife' and continued to badger her for sex. They struck a deal. He'd make no more demands for sex on condition she settle his debts, end her fast and eat with him again on Fridays. This was all to be done before she went on her pilgrimage to Jerusalem.

Margery wanted official recognition of his relinquishing his rights to sex, for both of them to take a vow of chastity, and for the Bishop of Lincoln to grant her permission to wear the traditional mantle and ring that signified it. It was usually only given to widows, but to Margery it must have symbolised the death of her marriage. It would put an end to the rumours that she was still having sex with her husband and was not in fact chaste as she claimed to be. To emphasise her chastity, she also wanted the bishop to sanction her wearing white. Quite a list of 'asks', but she needed the permission of men – her husband and a bishop – to progress further in her mission. With some satisfaction that her plan was beginning to come together nicely, Margery and John set off to see the bishop and then went to Canterbury to visit the tomb of St Thomas Becket. The visit turned out to be unexpectedly adventurous. It was the first time Margery's indiscreet loud weeping and praying led to accusations of heresy, of her being a Lollard.

The name Lollard was given to followers of John Wycliffe who were critical of the power and corruption of the Catholic Church, disputed some of its practices and believed that the Bible should be available in English so that everyone, not only clergy, could read it. The Church and locals in Canterbury were on high alert for would-be Lollards, and Margery's boisterous sobbing all day long in the monastery not only raised suspicions but antagonised many, including monks and priests. Their attitude towards her got so fractious that John made himself scarce, leaving Margery to face the music on her own. As she left the monastery after prayers one evening she was followed by people screaming, 'Take her and burn her!' They shouted that they had a barrel to shove her into and enough kindling to set her alight. She kept walking away from them until she reached the gates of Canterbury, stopping just outside, shaking and panic-stricken, with no idea of what to do next or where her hostel was – or John. The crowd had grown and the cries to burn her started up again. Two men came to her rescue after she assured them, '*No, serys, I am neither eretyke ne loller,*' and took her back to her hostel, where she found her husband sat safe and sound.

The episode in Canterbury and the hateful things that had been said about her in Lynn made her dread what might happen to her and set her off into more prayers and weeping. She was caught in a feedback loop – a vicious cycle of being rebuked for her 'ungodly' penitent praying, which caused her to offer more 'improper' prayers of contrition, causing further rebuke. She was worried about wearing white clothing; she knew it would annoy people because it symbolised virtue and purity, the very attributes she was accused of lacking. The Bishop of Lincoln had witnessed her and John's vows of chastity, but after talking with his clerks, who couldn't abide Margery, he retracted her rights to the mantle and ring and to wear white, saying it might be better to wait until after she'd been to Jerusalem. He suggested that if she wanted these things sooner she should go to the Archbishop of Canterbury, Thomas Arundel, to get his permission for the bishop to grant her wishes.

She knew Arundel was fiercely against Lollard heretics and had overseen the heresy trial and burning at the stake in 1401 of William Sawtrey, a priest from her own church, St Margaret's. She knew she'd be inviting more trouble for herself if she wasn't very careful about how she worded her requests – and what she left out, like white clothing. It meant another journey for her and John. She was received by the archbishop, speaking with him until dark, telling him all about her conversations with Jesus and visitations. He granted her the right to live how she'd asked. What that meant or included she doesn't say. But his acceptance and sanctioning of her visions and way of life gave her some satisfaction – though whether her vow of chastity ever received this final approval is unknown. She and John returned home.

Her visitations and over-zealous weeping continued to cause her much criticism and upset now she was back within the Lynn community. Margery was slandered by so many, she desperately wanted and needed support from the Church authorities to confirm that she was sincere in her belief and that her visions were genuine. Bishop's Lynn was then under the control of the Bishop of Norwich, and so it was in Norwich, far from Lynn and Margery's controversial reputation, that she would find the right important people to help her.

Everything about Margery's method of piety had to ring true to make sure she was believed, and attention to detail was crucial. Around springtime in 1413 she headed off to Norwich, not in any old clothing, and not in white either, but dressed head to foot in black, a colour symbolising both mourning and chastity – as if she was outwardly signalling the death of her sexuality and birth of her chastity. That must have made the right impression when she visited and talked at length to her friends, the vicar of St Stephen's Richard Caister, White Friar William Southfield and the anchoress and Christian mystic Dame Julian of Norwich. They all vouched for her and reassured her that her visions were genuine, acting as shoulders to lean on as well as defenders against her detractors. She knew she was speaking to the converted really. The friar and Julian had visions like hers, and Richard was receptive to the idea of women being spoken to by God. He became her long-term confessor and defender. Julian reassured Margery, saying, 'Set all your trust in God and do not be afraid of what people say. Patience is necessary for you for in that you shall keep your own soul.' She was an inspiration to Margery. Her visions of Christ and Mary had first started when she thought she was on her deathbed, as had Margery's during her near-death experience. Having their encouragement and blessings, and those of her Dominican anchorite confessor in Lynn, Margery felt validated. Her mind was set on going to the Holy Land, and now that she had her letters of approval she was ready to prepare for her epic journey abroad.

Thanks to her father, who possibly set up a family trust for her, Margery had an income stream to draw from. That helped to change everything for her. She could choose to use what money she had at her disposal to travel, to broaden her horizons by going on pilgrimages overseas. It was an exceptional thing for a forty-year-old woman of her status to do – and to leave her husband and family behind for such a long time. Her surviving children were likely to have been independent by this time, either having married or found positions of employment. But Margery had specific reasons for going. She knew pilgrimages abroad were highly valued in terms of piety, over and above the English shrines, and were a major show of devotion and sign of commitment in terms of financial and personal risk. Going to Jerusalem, the site of the most sacred Christian places, earned you total absolution: all sins were forgiven, purgatory was avoided. A journey worth the money and the 'hell on earth' a devout Catholic had to go through to get there.

There were other possible motives for her leaving Lynn at that time. Her standing in the community was tarnished, not only by her own misbehaviour but also by controversies over the suspected mismanagement of the town's affairs by her father and other aldermen. The allegations her father faced were very public, and with Lynn having a population of not much more than five thousand, everyone knew about it – and about her husband, and her own businesses having failed. Margery's status meant so much to her. It commanded respect from her peers and from those above and below her. It gave her confidence to go about her life, socially and in business – and to act inappropriately. To be publicly shamed and vilified was a terrible thing for her.

The 'command' for a pilgrimage to Jerusalem that she eventually obeyed in the autumn of 1413 had coincided with difficult events in Margery's life. There were good reasons for her to get out of England, even though she was also possibly pregnant for the fourteenth and last time. '*In the time that this creatur had reuelacyons, owyr Lord seyd to hir . . . Dowtyr, thow art with childe.*' Her father had died and many of her friends had deserted her because of her bad reputation. But the most glaring reason that she was wise not to ignore was the very real fear of her being accused and tried as a Lollard heretic again. The Lollard leader John Oldcastle (a follower of Wycliffe's teachings) had been threatening a rebellion against the Church and king, and this took place in January 1414, just months after she left for Jerusalem. The revolt was unsuccessful and had dire consequences that affected Margery on her return to England.

10

I was getting to know Delia through talking with those who knew her, through her music and through spending time at the archive, listening to so many audio files, reading and holding papers she'd written on and touched. Those relics of her life were something other than mere objects and music. They were tangible, accessible entry points to her world, affirmations of her presence. I began to connect with her on a deeper level. The more I found out about her, the more I wanted to know. Not only her musical output but about herself and how she felt, being a woman among so many men during her years at the BBC Radiophonic Workshop, when electronic music was viewed as a masculine domain – which regrettably still holds true today. I was drawn into Delia's world of sound, a sense of her within the music she created. The smaller, more personal things about her loomed large, and in part displaced the academic writings I'd read that focused more on her technical achievements.

I was charmed by Delia's childlike, playful sense of humour. Two instances in particular made me smile. One was when her cat had kittens and she jokingly suggested the BBC give her maternity leave. Another time, while working at the BBC she received a letter from the Inland Revenue querying her declared income because of payments from theatre commissions she'd done. The taxman made the assumption that she was an actress and informed her that she must declare all sources of money. The letter included an estimate of what she'd earned and must pay tax on, a ridiculous amount which far exceeded her BBC salary. There was an option to appeal, so she wrote back, 'Dear Sirs, Further to your recent letter, I am not an actress but I am appealing!' She had a low tolerance for and a cynical attitude to officialdom that extended beyond the BBC.

I wanted to find out how much of Delia resided in her 'recordings', how much of herself she put into them, and ultimately how the emotion, knowledge and energy she brought to her work sadly ended up being exploited and appropriated, exhausting her. When I read and listened to interviews Delia had done later in her life I discerned different tones in her voice when she made comments or answered questions. It came across to me as if, because she hadn't enjoyed appreciation for her work for so long, she felt some pressure to accept and live up to how she was perceived by saying the 'right' things. Her voice seemed more alive when she talked about herself, how she felt about her music, how she'd been treated and what she got up to outside the BBC. I wanted more of those *self* moments, her laughter and flirtatious remarks, but there were times when her words faded away or stopped abruptly, abandoning a personal anecdote in favour of getting back to the topic of the interview and leaving 'Delia' unspoken.

It's never easy to be part of the establishment when you're driven by self-preservation to push against it. Delia's boldness and self-confidence helped. Some people have said she could be unpredictable, contradictory, feisty and difficult to work with. Up one minute and totally enthusiastic, with floods of ideas, then down and unmotivated the next, bereft of inspiration during periods of depression. Her mood swings suggest the possibility that she had bipolar disorder. Oscillating like a sine wave from positive, above the zero baseline, then plunging down into negativity – ironically, as demonstrated expertly by Delia herself for a BBC film using one of the RW oscilloscopes. She seems to have had many of the experiences that are believed to be potential triggers for bipolar episodes – a traumatic childhood, stress, the pressure of work and alcohol abuse. That may have been the case, but I could also understand why she may have come across that way for other reasons: having to work within the limitations of the equipment and technology, difficulties with her colleagues, sexism and other prejudices, whether blatant or unintentional.

Her patience must have been sorely tested at times, and I'd hazard a guess that her changes in mood and sudden outbursts could also have been a way of releasing the frustration she felt. She'd sometimes close herself off, not speak to anyone, which was flippantly referred to as 'sulking' or giving people the 'silent treatment', 'sending them to Coventry'. I know myself how seemingly innocent offhand remarks can be upsetting, insulting and infuriating, and the anger they cause can be hard to ignore and contain. The tone of voice and delivery of a simple comment can differ when a man speaks to a woman, rather than man to man. Some years ago my suggestion of adding a sound to a mix got the reply, 'We can do that later.' But it was spoken with such a dismissive, curt tone it made me take it as meaning, 'Shut up, woman, I'll let you know when I want your input.' Being spoken *of* and not *to*, as if you weren't there, especially if there's a technical problem. It's assumed that as a woman you know little about such things, so you must be to blame. This happened at TG gigs when PA crew (always men) came on stage to resolve tech issues, messing with my gear as they joked about it between themselves and the rest of the band, not talking to me, only to discover the issues were actually nothing to do with me and that someone else (a man) had done something dumb – but it was brushed off, not criticised or mocked, with no apology offered.

It's demeaning and annoying to be publicly treated that way. Sometimes circumstances dictate that it's best to suppress your feelings – which then sets in motion an act of self-appeasement by way of what I can only describe as an internalised controlled explosion of built-up emotions. An outburst could lead to saying something you may regret, quickly followed by more judgemental comments fired your way about the oversensitivity or hysteria of women – or, for Delia, getting fired from her job. Her withdrawals into silence would avoid that and also provide some protection for herself by 'closing the door' on people who were disrespecting her or her work. Or maybe it was just so she could refocus. I've done it myself in response to similar situations. Trying to make yourself understood but being seen as difficult or obstructive, when really you're reeling at the obstructiveness of others, their attitude towards you, their inability or unwillingness to empathise. Or you're simply deep in thought. I retreat inside myself: it's a place of comfort where I can get some relief from a world that can seem so alien to me, when I reach the point of overload, feeling that what's happening is wrong and doesn't relate to who I am or who people seem to think I am. It's a way of protecting the self. Inside is where no one can get to 'you'. Other times I make my feelings known in no uncertain terms. It's a case of what or who is the priority.

Delia was exacting and didn't tolerate imperfection in her own work, presenting only what she deemed perfect. Perfection is subjective – what I think is perfect, Delia may not have, but the works are our own and that decision lies entirely with us. Consequently she was affronted, angry and immensely resentful of the male–female hierarchy, when some men pulled rank on her and overruled her on creative decisions, talking at and down to her, disregarding her expertise with an air of authority about things they knew little about, certainly less than she did. To Delia they weren't qualified and had no right to interfere with her music. She was no shrinking violet and she'd put them right, often in public at a meeting or a party – much to the annoyance and indignation of the men she corrected. It was part of her character to correct inaccuracies – she couldn't help herself. Needless to say, her impropriety wasn't appreciated. Being pretty upfront and outspoken myself, I know how it can be seen – not as you being confident in your competence but as 'trouble', a sign of being uncooperative, whereas we're just not willing to be silenced or seen as a doormat to be walked over.

One of the ways Delia found relief from the relentless stresses was her sense of fun, which she got to indulge when she had to come up with witty and cheerful intros. What she called her 'jolly', more trivial works, like 'Door to Door' for a BBC Radio Leeds talk programme, made from recordings of door bells and door knockers, the abstract sounds extracted from objects relating to the subject of the brief. 'Oranges and Lemons' was made from the Greenwich time 'pips', processed and arranged to form the melody of the nursery rhyme. The pun was completely missed by the presenter who interviewed Delia for a radio listeners' Q&A about making electronic music. The exchange is typical of the prevailing attitude to women in the early 1960s, and it's infuriating to hear her, as a twenty-eight-year-old woman, being spoken to in such a patronising way. What's so admirable about Delia is her dignified demeanour and self-control, her consummate professionalism, when she must have been fuming inside as the man introduced her as 'a very versatile girl who has a good technical knowledge combined with a musical training and a sense of dramatic ability'. It's all rather jokey, and I couldn't imagine him introducing one of her male colleagues as a 'versatile boy', using the same belittling tone of voice. It would be assumed that a man already had the required skills to be working in the workshop in the first place, and considered insulting to assume otherwise. I doubt that a demonstration of a man's skills would have been treated in the same way either. Maybe the comedic ending of putting the pre-senter's voice through a ring modulator was suggested by Delia as subtle payback, a way of demeaning him by 'turning him into a fish'. Overall her work was presented as a jolly jape, trivialised, the opportunity for a fun way to end the interview.

Because of the demands of her work, Delia had little time for socialising. There were parties she went to, or premieres, if it was something she'd been involved with, but she wasn't a party animal or particularly comfortable in large groups of people. She found these occasions stressful and compensated by adopting a gregari-ous persona, announcing her arrival loudly with an affected 'Hello, darlings!' and flouncing about, playing to the room in her party role. Alcohol helped to loosen her up so she could cope, but she never went over the top or became uncontrollably drunk. After a few drinks she would happily mix with everyone and flirt with the ladies. Both men and women found her irresistible. Bisexual, like myself, she embraced the liberal sexual freedom of the six-ties. Following her strict Catholic upbringing in Coventry, leaving home had been liberating and exciting for her. She'd had a fair number of boyfriends during her time at university, followed by a string of casual sexual adventures with various composers once she moved to London. She was incredibly beautiful with her long auburn hair, 'Titian', as Brian Hodgson described her. She enjoyed an adventurous social life with a large circle of friends. And yet despite her openness she was difficult to get close to and people's opinions of her varied depending on the relationship they had with her. Brian said of her, 'I only saw certain aspects of Delia. It's often said that she was like a diamond and that it depended on what angle you shine the light from.' But the consensus among both men and women who knew her was that she was charismatic, with an air of confidence, and cut an imposing figure wherever she went, whether at parties or walking down Portland Place looking the epitome of sophistication in a huge hat, with her cloak flowing behind her.

Whenever possible Delia took the opportunity to holiday abroad, most often with Brian. Their relationship was platonic, although Delia had propositioned Brian once. He sweetly declined, saying his boyfriend wouldn't like it at all. After one particularly tough period of intense work they decided to get away for a while, to escape the stress and relax. Brian had been working with the television director Philip Saville, who was living with Diana Rigg at the time. Philip offered Brian and Delia the use of Diana's farmhouse on Ibiza. In the mid-1950s Ibiza had become *the* place for actors like Errol Flynn, Elizabeth Taylor, Ursula Andress, Maggie Smith, Denholm Elliott and Laurence Olivier – joined in the 1970s by other artists and celebrities including Nico, Joni Mitchell and Syd Barrett. The local people welcomed them and their beach parties and liberal lifestyles.

Brian and Delia set off for Ibiza, taking a British Airways flight from London to Barcelona. The flight, which was supposed to leave at eleven in the morning, didn't set off until ten at night. Delia was withdrawn and wouldn't speak to Brian. He couldn't fathom why, what he could have said or done. Even as they arrived in Barcelona, having endured the most horrendous thunderstorm Brian had ever experienced, with the plane dropping suddenly in the extreme turbulence, Delia remained silent. When they'd finally landed, safely disembarked and boarded the coach for the next leg of their journey, Delia turned to him and said enthusiastically, 'Isn't the sound of thunder wonderful!' The first words she spoke since leaving London were about the sounds generated by the electrical storm. Then she went silent again. The coach deposited them at the side of the vehicle access road to the farmhouse and they stepped out, to be confronted by two-foot-deep rain-water rushing down the middle of the street. As they looked round in shock, they spied a delightful-looking little bar. Brian picked up their cases and they headed straight for it and ordered desperately needed coffee and brandy. They eventually reached Diana's farm-house. It was large, with basic amenities and a sink in the corner of the kitchen. The local farmer came each day to clean for them, always shouting '*Hola!*' at the top of her voice from a safe distance at the end of the lane leading up to the house, as she knew Brian would be sunbathing naked and wanted to give him time to cover himself up.

They enjoyed a great holiday together, Brian recalled. He spent the days sunning himself on the large flat roof, while Delia stayed indoors out of the sun because of her sensitive complexion. She'd be working on ideas for music, constantly scribbling away on heaps of paper, with a bottle of wine at her side. As the sun began to set one evening, Delia called up to Brian to put some clothes on before she brought a tray of gin and tonic up to the roof for them to share. She swanned onto the roof like a glamorous film star, in a long diaphanous chiffon gown and over-large hat, which she non-chalantly dropped onto his naked crotch. They were going out for the night with Brian's friend, who lived in the old city. He arrived around 8 p.m. to drive them all to town for dinner and fun times.

A car was the most convenient way for them to get around because the farmhouse was on a hill and the only road to it wound around San Carlos. There was an alternative footpath, but they'd had an adventurous experience using that route when they'd returned from a night at Denholm Elliott's house. They'd had a great evening and were the worse for wear when they embarked on the journey home. It was late at night, with no lighting, so they sensibly got a cab as far as the driver could take them. Then, in the eerie pitch blackness, with only the sounds of nature's nightlife, they attempted to climb back up the track to the farmhouse. They were oblivious to any danger and thankfully not totally legless as they scrambled their way up the hill, giggling and shouting words of encouragement to each other, which set the local dogs barking. Delia kept losing her footing and one of her shoes. It was only the next morning, when Brian went to retrieve her shoe, that he realised what they'd done. He was horrified to see it wasn't a path at all but a 'fucking canyon' where the rainwater ran down. Somehow they'd managed to clamber over rocks and through mud, and had been lucky not to have ended up falling and killing themselves. What with the thunderstorm during the flight and their rock-climbing adventure, it began to feel like they'd escaped death twice on their getaway trip to paradise.

Delia returned to London recharged, but she was re-entering a lifestyle and work routine that would lead her to make some dramatic decisions.

11

It's always fascinated me that I can be working in the same or similar fields and ways to others I'm not aware of, be they near or far away across the world, and whether the simultaneous activities can be explained in some way through concepts like six degrees of separation or psychogeography. The music for David Lynch's 1977 film *Eraserhead* seemed to mirror the grinding, bleak sounds I, as part of Throbbing Gristle, was making around the same time. In 1948 Tōru Takemitsu and Pierre Schaeffer had both simultaneously conceived the idea of electronic music, based on the method of musique concrète. And the American composer Suzanne Ciani worked in a similar vein to Delia Derbyshire and Daphne Oram, but only discovered later that they had all been creating electronic music at the same time. When you do finally 'connect' it's a moment of joyous validation – you're not crazy or 'other' at all.

I once described the activities of innovative, radical individuals and groups of people as 'pockets of resistance'. Similar to the butterfly effect, their new thinking, unorthodox actions and ideas somehow filter through all the noise of the bustling world at large. As if by magic, there's a space for the 'echoes' of these 'others' to slip through like infiltrators, undermining norms, revealing and inspiring new fields to explore. Their echoes can take many forms and consequently evoke different responses. A sound, an image, an event, a criticism, a personal trauma can be loaded with murmurings of 'unfinished business' – that there's more to be done, more to discover. I think of them as contributory and determining factors, integral parts of my 'recordings'. The murmurings from the past rise to the surface, above the quagmire of anonymity and superficiality, the mundane, seasoned, tired experiences, and take on a new meaning and invigorating purpose. This is what the sirens of wartime did for Delia, becoming the inspiration for much of her audio palette. A welcome shift in instinctive response. Little fragments of the world making themselves heard in peculiar and particular ways, as abstract sounds, as music, as opposed to charging the body with a sense of fear. The abstract sounds that influenced me as a child were benign compared to Delia's. They were the wailings, bleeps and whooshes from the radios my father built by hand. Familiar sounds in our home, so that when I was twelve and first heard Delia's music on the TV and radio, what had once been weird and 'non-musical' had become 'music' to me, innovatively formed into tunes. Such audio curiosities of my childhood via Delia and my father turned out to be a fundamental element in my musical output.

I see myself, Delia and Margery as 'pockets of resistance' – despite often being targets for derision, striving for and actively seeking the as yet undiscovered, to try and find a solution to the restless, unquantifiable passion and emotional expression we call creativity. I'm not alone in my notion that people who feel 'other' play a part in society as a means of achieving their goal to be them-selves. Nathalie Léger describes it perfectly in her book *Suite for Barbara Loden* as 'putting on an act in order to break free'. I've lost count of the times I was told as a child to stop 'acting out' or 'acting up'. In other words, get back within the right parameters and down from your high horse – how dare you assert yourself by trying to step outside and be more than you're supposed to be? I've certainly had to operate within my societal 'place'. At times

I've used it to my advantage, finding ways around the rules to gain access to what I need. The struggles that happen along the way to uncertain 'places' can be exhilarating as well as enlightening – whether for better or worse. Unmapped territory is my place of choice. From a young age I had a sense that there was more 'out there', that I wouldn't and couldn't accept or conform to what seemed to be agreeable enough for everyone else. I still feel the same. It's who I am and I've never given much thought to trying to find out why being this way is important to me; that's never been as important as following my intuition, maintaining my inner 'spirit'. That's as spiritual as I get these days. I used to be interested in the mystical and magical, even religion. It was all new to me in my youth and I researched belief systems, looking for a place that felt mine rather than the place I was expected to take – but none of them ever felt right. I pushed it all away as irrelevant. The unconventional was always more appealing for me, as it was for Delia: 'I've never wanted to be on the inside of the music world, I've always wanted to be on the fringe.'

We both sought and found some degree of refuge and affirmation by, at times, being part of like-minded groups which advocated autonomy, freedom and an unconventional, creative approach to life. It's good to be among people who share your sense of otherness, who struggle to fit in and be the person they never were. We can fall apart trying to play a part within a society that views you as alien, a threat to be ignored or silenced, at the very worst eradicated. Being 'other' in a collective of 'others' helps. It gives you the freedom to be who you are and helps relieve the sense of remoteness, of difference. It eases the everyday pressure of handling prejudices and provides reassurance that we're not crazy but just people with a different view and expectation of what life is about and our active role within it.

Living on the radical fringe can be amazingly thrilling and at times a nightmare. The reaction to so-called 'radical behaviour' is a curiously love/hate, negative/positive thing. By stepping out of line and meeting with disapproval and contempt, you're faced with attempts to break your spirit, so you're consequently in a permanent state of repairing and reinforcing your defences to ensure any precious new discoveries of *self* can't be violated. Whenever I've hit resistance (as did Delia and Margery), whether in the form of criticism, being reviled and maligned, or attempts to hold me down in my so-called place, I've harnessed the surge of energy from the anger I've felt and used it to fuel my resolve. Sadly, life in a collective can also have challenges that necessitate the same defensive approach – as I found out way back when I was part of the COUM art collective.

My ex-partner and lover Genesis would criticise me for not being fully committed or willing to follow his instructions and accept whatever extreme physical, psychological and emotional discomfort that involved. He would say that letting go of my doubts, fears and 'hang-ups' was part of becoming a better person – that his method of deconditioning would give me a sense of freedom and autonomy. He made it clear to me there were certain conditions to our relationship, that our artistic and musical collaboration and 'sharing' extended to sex, and that my body was accessible to him as and when he saw fit. This was not what I expected of an alternative to the conventional lifestyle I was seeking to avoid, nor my understanding of autonomy. It was just replacing one set of conditions with others that didn't sit well with me and seemed to be a 'fringe benefit' for him. Another of the many mindfucks a lot of women faced in the 'liberated' counterculture of the 1960s and 70s.

One summer's day the group's van was parked in a quiet side street. Myself, Genesis and COUM member Gary were going to give it the usual checking over before we all set off on our journey. The other members were still sleeping in the house. It was a box van with a bed in the back. Genesis opened the back door and we all climbed inside to make sure everything was good. I was stood by the bed straightening the covers when I heard the door being closed behind me, blocking out most of the light. Quite matter-of-factly Genesis suggested that I let Gary fuck me on the bed.

'That's what it's there for,' Genesis said.

'I don't want to,' I said.

My reply prompted an awkward silence and an air of intimidating expectancy. The space closed in on me, suddenly claustrophobic. Then words of encouragement broke the atmosphere. 'Gary has always fancied you,' Genesis told me with a lopsided grin in an attempt to lighten things up. Gary looked a little tentative and coy, hopeful, sort of scoffing with anticipation. I felt the emotional pressure from Genesis to concede – an arched eyebrow and that look that always accompanied the refrain, 'It's part of our group ethos to be free and push yourself if you hit some resistance,' and I had. I didn't want to have sex with Gary. But Genesis's simmering anger at my refusal was palpable and worked its way deep inside my psyche. My unwillingness to please him was being taken as a betrayal. The emotional pressure he exerted on me worked. I took my place on the bed and assumed the position, while Gary fumbled to get his cock out of his trousers, half laughing at his good fortune to have a fuck laid on for him. I lay there, impassive. Genesis took hold of my hand, saying over and over again in my ear, 'Do it because you love me,' 'It will make you stronger,' 'Sex is powerful,' all of which was supposed to make me feel better and reinforce the reasons why I should let this happen to me – because I loved Genesis and because sex magic was an important part of my role in his life and as a member of COUM.

I turned my head to one side, as if not seeing the act itself could make it less real. But it heightened the physical sensations of Gary's hot cock as he tried to find entry, then the penetration, the clumsy thrusting and the smell of male sex and sweat. My attempt to disassociate myself from the vile reality didn't work. I felt tears roll down my cheek as I heard Genesis's continuous words of encouragement, saying he loved me, holding my hand, encouraging me to overcome my resistance to the waves of repulsion I felt and cope throughout the time it took for Gary to come. Thankfully it was over quickly. As soon as he climbed off me I swung my legs over the side of the bed. As I stood up the spunk trickled out, the hot, disgusting residual evidence of what had just happened, what I'd tried to deny to myself. I wanted the foul poison out of me; it didn't belong there. They both looked at me in a way that made me realise they saw me as compliant. The two of them smiling about what a special moment it had been, both ignoring my having refused and being coerced into it. Their sense of entitlement had enabled them to take me under the pretence of testing my loyalty and adherence to the 'rules' Genesis imposed on my relationship with him and his dictatorial group ethos. Genesis's face with his triumphant smile is imprinted in my memory: how proud he was of me for allowing myself to be violated, overcoming the challenge . . . he had won another battle using his methods of 'persuasion'.

I needed to be alone, to get away. I felt hurt, betrayed and angry. Throughout the ordeal I must have managed to achieve a degree of disassociation because I remember at one point I seemed to be looking down on myself from the ceiling of the van. It didn't freak me out. It had happened before, sometimes unexpectedly, and at other times when I practised in order to try and acquire the ability to achieve an out-of-body experience at will. I'd had no idea it would come in useful for something so abominable, never anticipating my watching myself in a scene saturated with sadness and insidious cruelty. I'm sure the ordeal played a part in my being able to do sex work, to detach myself emotionally when necessary. But nothing in the pornographic work I did compared to the violation I felt as a result of what happened in the van. Those who defiled me and broke my trust became lesser to me. Their continuing belief that they had power over me may have kept them happy in feeling superior, but that was inconsequential to me, nonsensical. Unknown to them, their actions had fortified my resistance and willpower.

Within the so-called 'free and alternative' relationship I was in, there was an assumed contractual obligation, an unspoken debt, for me to surrender my body on the command of my partner. It flew in the face of the awakening of women's sexual freedom in the 1970s, and later it struck me as a version of Margery's 'debt' experience with her husband John. My own recounting wasn't far from her descriptions of repulsion at having to accede to her husband's sexual demands. Within medieval marriage (and sadly in some cases today) the 'conjugal debt' was part of the deal. Margery was under contract to allow her husband to use her body for sex whenever he wished. It was her duty as a wife, even when she had no desire to. She had no choice. She was his property. Regardless of Margery's motivation to be seen as suffering for her would-be saint-hood, her descriptions of how dreadful she felt during the assaults on her body and the awful situation she was trapped in paint a very graphic picture. Her own words in her book (speaking in the third person) give a very clear idea of her feelings of violation:

> . . . the dette of matrimony was so abhominabyl to hir that sche had levar, hir thowt, etyn or drynkyn the wose, the mukke in the chanel, than to consentyn to any fleschly comownyng saf only for obedyens.

[The conjugal debt was so abominable to her that, she thought, she would have rather eaten or drunk the slime, the muck, in the gutter than consent to any sexual contact, except out of obedience.]

Margery had pledged herself to Christ, to live a life of chastity. There had been a time when she really enjoyed sex with her husband, but things had changed. Becoming chaste was required for her to be accepted as Christ's bride, not her husband's, so the sexual violation and pain inflicted by John was physical and spiritual – she felt disloyal to Christ. The power God had over her was her reality, even if it didn't always feel right. She didn't want to do some of the things God expected of her – no more than I did with Genesis. The difficult demands he made of me and God made of Margery were presented as 'tests' of our love and loyalty. When God 'told' Margery to wear white, she knew she'd be vilified and mocked, and she voiced her resistance, like I had with Genesis. All she got in 'reply' was, 'The more mockery you get for my love, the more you please me.' That has echoes of how Genesis justified what he imposed on me – 'Do it because you love me' – no matter how awful the personal effect and price of repercussions. I should have read more into him naming himself Genesis. Maybe he thought he was a modern-day Godhead.

Margery's reaction to her lot probably had much to do with the hypocrisy she witnessed among the clergy, who could take the moral high ground but bend the word of God to suit their carnal or political needs. God's word was supposed to remain inviolable, not be open to convenient reinterpretation. Margery, Delia and I share the same intolerance of inaccuracy, especially the rewriting of truth, replacing it with falsehoods. A different kind of creativity, malevolent and manipulative – the bending of rules to secure conformity for dubious, cruel purposes.

Margery's account of sex with her husband is a description of rape within marriage, of non-consensual sex. The crime of rape was so very different in the 1400s. Its definition defies logic and biology but provides an inventive way out for anyone accused. Sex was for procreation only, and the belief was that pregnancy was a result of the female orgasm, at which point the mixing of the female and male seeds took place. In marriage it wouldn't matter if a woman conceived having orgasmed or not. But if she was raped by anyone other than her husband and got pregnant, the understanding was that she must have had an orgasm and enjoyed the sex – therefore, regardless of how brutal the sexual assault, the sex was deemed consensual and not rape. There was another way out for rapists. Women were regarded as lecherous temptresses – the still-familiar refrain of 'It was her fault.' The prettier and more irresistible the woman, the less guilty the man, because he was only acting on his natural instinct. I can see why Margery was so scared when she travelled the world, and why she held little respect for some clergy who visited prostitutes (regulated by the Crown and Church). The temptation of the attractive women in the brothels was so great, a man just couldn't help himself – which allowed the clergy to rationalise violating their vows of celibacy by blaming women for their own sinful ways, following up with a visit to their bishop to get absolution.

It was the rape incident that prompted me to further protect my*self* and focus on finding 'my place' – like Margery did after years of her husband's carnal abuse, and Delia after her heart and trust were broken by some of her lovers and some of those she worked with.

12

The search for a sense of *self*-contentment is uplifting but can also be dispiriting, as it's fraught with unforeseen obstacles, complications and disappointments. Some events experienced in relation to involvement with the 'alternative' scenes of the 1960s and 70s proved to be problematic for both me and Delia. When Delia rode her bicycle to Putney and knocked on Peter Zinovieff's front door in 1966, itching to tell him about her exciting idea, she couldn't have known it would set in motion a series of events that had a huge impact on her life. She had met Peter before and knew about his impressive studio in the huge garden shed at the back of his large London house. She loved his exploratory approach to music and his collection of unconventional sound-generating equipment. And him having a studio for her to work in, freed from the rigid practices of the RW, meant she could pursue additional commercial projects that were more her cup of tea. But importantly she could feel some sense of 'ownership' of a creative space.

Delia proposed that she, Peter and Brian Hodgson go into partnership to make and promote electronic music for the theatre, film, the arts and advertising. At first Peter, knowing her from her work at the BBC, thought she was asking on behalf of the Radiophonic Workshop, but she was interested in forming their own unit. They talked through ideas and the practicalities and debated what they would call themselves. They settled on Unit Delta Plus (UDP) – a name that runs easily off the tongue yet was much more than just an on-trend title for a group of avant-garde musicians. It was very much a sign of Delia and her analytical mind. Each of the three words and their arrangement had a specific meaning. 'Unit' represented the three of them together. 'Delta', being central, was the core of the project and also a symbol for Delia – not just in her initial 'D', being the fourth letter of the alphabet as delta was fourth in the Greek alphabet, but additionally in reference to her love of mathematics and how she married that with music. The mathematical symbol of upper-case delta is a triangle and, most significantly at this stage in Delia's life, mathematically symbolises difference or change. The lower-case delta they also used as a graphic signified a change of mode in music. 'Plus' simply represented the two men in addition to Delia. The name of her first independent music group also subtly hints at her sense of autonomy and *self*-empowerment.

Exciting as UDP was, the BBC still loomed in the background. As studio manager of the RW Desmond Briscoe may have been a stickler for the BBC rule book but he also knew that there was value in giving his assistants some leeway and freedom off the premises, thinking that they would benefit from their moonlighting. However, with the BBC in general being so strict about its employees working on outside projects, Delia and Brian decided to adopt pseudonyms. They took themselves off to a setting conducive to contemplating suitable aliases, the softly lit, midnight-blue cocktail bar of the Cumberland Hotel, cogitating while sat at the white alabaster bar drinking copious amounts of vodka and tonic, finally choosing names that held little significance – Li De La Russe for Delia and Nikki St George for Brian. The names were fun alter egos that provided welcome distance from the RW, and also by appearing in print and on records they were a declaration of Delia's *self*-chosen identity.

Names are like signifiers of who we are, how we're first introduced to people, as well as a means of representing ourselves for reasons like Delia's and Brian's chosen aliases. Most people are comfortable with their given name and can 'own' it without question. That isn't always the case. I changed my name in my teens, just prior to my leaving the family home. My given name wasn't 'me' and represented everything I wasn't to my father too. Right from birth I was chasing his affection – reserved for a son, but I turned up instead. I needed to shed the negative associations that reverberated every time I was called Christine or Carol. I'd moved on and become Cosey. But Delia never officially changed her name. Both Delia Ann Derbyshire and her younger sister, Benita Catherine, were named after Catholic saints, not one saint's name each but two, like doubly ensuring their identities were firmly anchored in their religion. The Catholic Church has long accepted the legend of St Delia as being one of the virgin companions of St Ursula who were all martyred for their faith while on a pilgrimage to Rome. The name of a Christian virgin martyr murdered by heathen Huns for her 'difference' has sinister connotations I wouldn't want to impose on my child, but whatever symbolism can be drawn from St Delia is of less significance when compared to the origins of Delia's name in Greek mythology. It seemed all roads led to ancient Greece rather than Catholic Rome. And as Delia has said numerous times, the Greeks were everything to her in relation to her music:

> I go back to first principles when it comes to music. I go back to the Greeks and the original, well, the simple harmonic series. I think that's a very healthy thing to do for anyone.

It's easy to see why she embraced her name, not only because she loved its alliteration and warm, sensual sound, but also because its origins, like music in her view, went as far back as the Greeks. She thought the name Delia was gloriously wonderful. It was her to a T, and she dropped her middle name. 'Delia' was the epithet of the Greek moon goddess Artemis, twin sister to Apollo. It means 'woman from the island of Delos', in the Aegean Sea, the home of Apollo and Artemis. And how wonderful it is to discover that those who lived on Delos were called Delians. Artemis is known as the goddess of contradictions, which seems rather apt when thinking about what people have said about Delia's moods.

—ɯ—

Delia wasted no time in utilising her studio management skills and set about organising events for UDP. The unit began delivering lectures on electronic music and presenting concerts that were a cross between demonstrations of their techniques and audio 'experiences' – much like the Throbbing Gristle gigs, when we used selected sounds that created physical responses by way of a shared experience rather than just an exposition. TG music was also about enjoyment, or 'entertainment through pain', as we dubbed it. The 'pain' that comes from being jump-started out of your comfort zone by a kind of music you'd never heard before, with the overpowering volume levels and physical effects of the frequencies we generated. UDP were highbrow, presenting technical statements about their work. TG took a similar approach in communicating our objectives, more tongue-in-cheek but no less serious about our music. Taking an officious tone, like a business 'annual report' delivered by our own label Industrial Records, made it clear that what we did was not a frivolous venture but a means to break free of musical genres and expectations. Not unlike Delia and her unit.

In 1966 Delia organised a UDP evening of electronic music at the Watermill Theatre in Bagnor, Berkshire, with a light show by lecturers from Hornsey College of Art. It's said to have been the first British electronic music show, but there were other audio-visual concerts around then too. The London avant-garde scene had been active for a while and was rather incestuous. Everybody knew someone via somebody else, most linked up one way or another. That's how Delia came to meet Paul McCartney. He was living in London, involved with setting up the Indica Gallery, and went to one of Berio's lectures at the Italian Institute in February 1966. In a roundabout way this led to him seeking out Delia at Peter's studio in Putney to listen to her music and talk about her methodologies and the unusual phrase lengths she'd been working with. She reconnected with him for 1967's Million Volt Light and Sound Rave at the Roundhouse in Camden, which featured taped music by UDP and McCartney's fourteen-minute experimental music piece *Carnival of Light*. Paul apparently chose to be elsewhere that night, and the chaotic organisation had Delia and Brian heading for the pub straight after their set. The event was again a mix of sound and visuals, with twenty projectors casting colours and shapes onto sixty-foot screens. Screens that size were a real draw, especially for those tripping on acid. The huge projections onto buildings today were a mere fantasy half a century ago.

Delia's aesthetic was eclectic, reflecting her personality, encompassing musical styles from abstract musique concrète – from her knowledge of and work with Stockhausen and Berio – to more conventional and melodic pieces. She had a penchant and a real talent for melody that, along with her other tasteful sounds and playfulness, challenged preconceptions of electronic music, whether for the BBC or her outside commissions. She was an innovative multimedia artist who loved working with visual artists, not only creating musical accompaniments for the works of Goya, Picasso, Henry Moore and others for BBC programmes, but frequently collaborating with contemporary artists, including those from Hornsey College of Art's Light/Sound Workshop. Her and my paths and interests focus on our love of all creative media. The cross-pollination of ideas that takes place when you work across platforms enhances and expands on existing works in ways you don't expect, as well as informing and inspiring new work and avenues to check out with new people.

Delia's extracurricular pursuits went way beyond the parameters of her work at the BBC. They must have influenced the sounds she made in the RW, and vice versa. She recycled some of her BBC music in other activities, like the 1967 soundtrack she provided for students at the Royal College of Art for their ICI-sponsored fashion show. It was the first fashion show to use electronic music. In my mind's eye I imagine it being quite a spectacle of crazy designs promoting new materials developed by ICI, trying to make the wonders and delights of Terylene, Crimplene and Bri-nylon look appealingly stylish as the student models sashayed along to a futuristic Delia soundtrack. When I was fifteen Crimplene was seen as being for grannies, while Bri-nylon non-iron shirts, although all the rage, tended to smell of stale sweat, as did the nylon sheets, which were also so slippery you could slide out of bed if you jumped in too quick.

It's clear Delia always thought elements of her music had a place and function beyond their original purpose for the BBC. Her music for the 1967 Brighton Festival on the West Pier was to accompany experimental multimedia experiences alongside performances by an old acquaintance of mine, Bruce Lacey, and the then up-and-coming psychedelic band Pink Floyd. Of course, a lot of the events were fuelled by LSD and other drugs that were considered 'mind-expanding' rather than taken solely for hedonistic indulgence. As far as the Brighton Festival was concerned, they certainly would have enhanced the effect of the music and visuals, and other environmental experiences laid on for people to participate in. The intriguing Dream Machine sounded like a trip in itself, with fantastical images projected onto the inside of a darkened seven-foot-diameter cylinder while the viewer lay on a slowly revolving turntable staring at the dreamlike moving projections. Their merging and shifting and the turntable constantly moving evoked a feeling of being within the visuals. A mind-bending experience, whether on acid or not.

By the beginning of 1968 UDP had come to an inevitable and amicable end. The last lecture they did was at the Royal College of Art. Peter had changed the programme from a lecture to a 'happening' without telling Delia or Brian. They were really put out, and Brian walked off the stage and sat in the audience in protest. The following day Delia and Brian went to Peter's house and told him they wanted to end UDP. He agreed it was time to go their separate ways. Peter's workflow and musical direction was so different to Delia's and Brian's. He was into computers and against using tape, while Delia and Brian were still very much into it.

UDP had introduced Delia to the avant-garde scene, and she was now at the epicentre of the swinging sixties, hanging out with the London 'in crowd', going to Paul McCartney's birthday party dressed in her vivid magenta jumpsuit, a stunning vision of beauty with her red hair piled high. She had no idea that she was about to embark on one of the greatest challenges of her life after an encounter at one of the last UDP events.

At the end of a UDP lecture at Morley College, a hip young physicist and musician came up to Delia and introduced himself as David Vorhaus. He'd been on his way to orchestra practice when he was told there was a lecture in the next room on electronic music techniques using tape editing. He gave his practice a miss and went and sat through the whole talk. He'd recognised the name UDP from the Roundhouse event poster and knew Delia and Brian were with the RW. Delia and David had a lot in common. They both loved to play the double bass – that got them talking. Delia told him she'd always longed to play the double bass, laughingly commenting that it suited her very large hands and long arms more than the violin her school had insisted she learn to play. She confided that she'd once gone with a friend to Buckingham Palace and measured the length of her arms against a Coldstream Guard's, to reveal hers were actually longer than his. She enthused to David that she'd taken double bass lessons in her lunch hour when she moved to London, and how much she loved the sound of it, that she felt as if it 'spoke' to her.

At high school she'd written an essay called 'Little Willie's Sneeze'. 'Little Willie' was a double bass, so named because he was self-conscious about being bigger than his friends in the music shop, the violin, flute, music stand and metronome. He was teased relentlessly and made to listen to the same familiar sounds they always played. Desperate to hear something different, he sighed so deeply in annoyance that he blew clouds of dust everywhere, then sneezed so loudly that 'everything in the music shop wakened up suddenly at this noise'. They'd never heard the double bass make that sound before. A new sound. As they scuttled about to avoid the dust they also made all manner of unusual noises they'd never made before, with the metronome donging and ticking totally out of time and the flute hiccoughing, making Willie laugh uncontrollably – emitting another new sound. Delia ended her essay: 'You did not know a double bass could laugh? Then listen carefully when you next hear an orchestra. You might hear the "POM, POM, HA, HA, POM, DOM, HO, HO" of Little Willie the double bass.' It's hard for me not to draw analogies between this character and Delia herself as an overly tall fourteen-year-old schoolgirl, prone to sneezing, frustrated in her desire to take up the double bass, and thinking about the joy of creating alternative expressive musical sounds, straying from the rules.

Delia and David immediately hit it off, with Brian looking on at two people who appeared to be madly in love, flush with lust. Within a week of the break-up of UDP Delia, Brian and David had formed the Kaleidophon studio and a new group called White Noise, with similar aspirations to UDP but also planning to release commercial records of electronic music. David moved in with Delia and they took to inviting friends round to dinner. Delia was never really cut out to be a homemaker. Her attempt to make zabaglione for their guests one evening ended with it splattered all over the walls of the flat after her first try at using an electric whisk. It wasn't long before Delia and David moved and set up their love nest at 281–283 Camden High Street, renting the two floors above what was at times a gay porn shop. The Kaleidophon studio was on the top floor and their bedroom above the shop was decorated in bright colours using unconventional materials, with a pink parachute draped across the ceiling, tin foil on the kitchen walls, the other walls covered in striped brown wrapping paper and the floor carpeted in soft blue felt. It sounds similar to my home in Prince Street, Hull, a reflection of the personalities who lived there.

For Delia domesticity took a back seat to her music. She had neither the time nor the inclination to do boring housework and was also rebelling against her mother having been so fastidiously house-proud. The flat was dirty, and her cat was always getting fleas, all of which probably had some part in inspiring the White Noise album track 'Here Come the Fleas' – for which Delia did the intro of electronic flicks and boings that sound like fleas jumping around. Their flea-ridden summer months were relieved by spending what time they could relaxing on the rooftop, looking down at the crowds of shoppers on Camden High Street.

Meeting, working and entering a relationship with David marked a big turning point in Delia's life. She'd come from such a strict Catholic background and was experiencing her first taste of living with a partner and a very alternative lifestyle, as well as working on an album of music free of any ties, *An Electric Storm*. Or so she thought. They had to gradually buy equipment for their studio set-up but started writing and recording for the album straight away, sneaking into the BBC at night to use the RW equipment. With the kind of music they were making, largely improvised and involving endless hours of experimenting, tape-splicing and re-recording, there was no way they could afford to use a commercial studio. The volume and types of sounds they produced drove their neighbour crazy. It was a battle royal between their neighbour indulging his love of traditional steel drums and their screaming, orgasmic vocals and offbeat electronics. He had a big problem with them making a racket at all hours, and they thought he was a pain in the neck for always complaining to the police about their music being so loud, making them waste time responding to legal letters and going to court. Then they got a lucky break. A friend of Brian's put David in touch with someone in the A&R department at Island Records, who gave them a hefty advance to record their album. Now they could afford to properly equip their studio and even buy a drum kit and a battered old Mini to get around in – which ended up costing a fortune in fines after they displayed a fake tax disc made from beer mats.

David's attraction to and fascination with Delia exasperated him at times. He found her fiery and a bit crazy, bordering on genius and insanity, especially when she'd go off on tangents, then more and more tangents, losing people in the process, until eventually she returned to the point she was making at the start. She could have just been verbalising her thought processes, logically coming to some conclusion. Maybe it was her 'fiery' character that influenced their co-written song 'Firebird'. The lyrics seem to reflect their relationship as well as the typical hippy ethos of 'no ties'. 'Firebird, fly high, fly free. I can't hold you down. You're too wild for me . . .' Delia was wild and didn't want to be held down but she did want to be shown some consideration and respect for what they had together as two people supposedly in love. David was into the 1960s idea of 'free love'. It was part and parcel of the hippy lifestyle. Relationships weren't regarded as monogamous; couples could spread their wings and have casual flings. Delia had gone along with the swing of things, the loose morality of the time, taking lovers as and when she felt an attraction, many of them younger than her, as was David. But she had a deep affection for David, they travelled abroad on holiday together – 'we were as one', in his words – so his many liaisons weren't easy for her to deal with. She'd entered into a loving relationship with him as two like-minded musicians. David was her willing protégé and she his mentor, teaching him tape manipulation and cutting and splicing techniques, among other things. She had a profound effect on the direction his life took, opening his mind to physics being used creatively, encouraging and working with him on designing sound gadgets.

Brian affectionately called David 'the upstart', a charming rogue. He was a philanderer and as a consequence, though not intentionally, he upset Delia. He'd bring women back to their flat, and she'd have to cope with the rush of emotions that his 'perfor-mances' triggered. Seeing your partner screwing someone else and being so seemingly blasé about your feelings can be crushingly heartbreaking. But it was uncool to show any resistance or disap-proval or be upset. Experimenting with sex was part of the deal of the alternative way of living and loving. With the availability of the contraceptive pill women were free to have sex without fear of getting pregnant. It gave them and men protection from the disruption caused by parental responsibilities. For the women who did get pregnant there was the option of the trauma of abortion or adoption, or they would have the child, which usually meant taking on sole responsibility. The sexual revolution was a win–win for guys. They got to fuck around without thinking anything of it or their live-in partners, or taking into account the jealousies and sadness they left in the wake of their 'carefree' sex games.

Orgies were a regular occurrence. Someone would suggest they all get it on together. Delia was no 'raver', she was a bit too 'golly gosh' for that, but she'd join in. One particular occasion stuck in her mind from when she was composing the soundtrack for Yoko Ono's twenty-minute film *Wrapping Event*, recording the wrapping of the Trafalgar Square lions that just a few years later I was leaping off for a photograph for COUM's commission for the British Council. Yoko was sleeping on Delia's floor, 'when we were having our or . . . oh . . . orgy on the carpet. We had a . . . golly, my goodness!' Sex was never far from David's mind, judg-ing by the tracks on *An Electric Storm*, and he appeared happy to use the project to assist in his conquests. The track 'My Game of Loving' was exactly that for him. It included just about everyone he met during its making. He'd get girls into the Kaleidophon studio with a pick-up line about how great their voice was and how he'd love to record them. The song typifies the 'free love' era with its synthetic and authentic orgy sounds (possibly including the voice of Delia).

The underground bohemian lifestyle was decadent but elitist, chauvinistic and hierarchical, with leaders and followers. There was a class system, from starving hippies through 'weekend hippies' to hipsters with Rolls-Royces like Brian Jones and John Lennon. Countercultures can open your mind to other ways of thinking and being, offering a 'free' approach to life and art, and for Delia this allowed her to express her individuality and rebellious nature. But there was pressure for women to conform to non-conformity, a new kind of 'standard' but with some of the old expectations still firmly in place. Women had to look good, cook and keep house, be a good fuck, amenable to fucking on request and with multiple partners, or face the pressure of being judged a failure. The dress code and home life were different for sure, and there was the advantage of being with like-minded people. But women were still very much in their 'place', with the additional expected role of supporting men in their 'revolutionary' endeavours, as well as being an indispensable part of the creative process on any artistic project. The underlying subjugation was still well and truly intact despite the claims of liberation and revolution – which isn't difficult to understand, considering everyone at that time had core patriarchal values instilled from birth. A tough nut to crack open and replace with the recognition of equality, tolerance of difference and a huge dose of humanity and selflessness.

Delia was caught up in and buying into another 'act' to be free, playing her part in accepting and being involved in the sex games. But I know from personal experience that there's no such thing as 'free love'; there's always a price to be paid, someone who gets hurt. Delia's feelings about sexual 'sins', trust, love and loyalty, conditioned by her upbringing, came into play during her sexual dalliances. As a lapsed Catholic she'd long since abandoned her obedience to religious doctrine about lust, premarital sex or contraception. Her conscience seemed clear as far as sex went. But it was fatiguing, having to be mindful of the new expectations of women at the same time as being excited about doing what had previously been off limits. And the casual sex and other supposed liberations for women didn't always fit comfortably with feminism. The feminist paper *Spare Rib* considered (but never pursued) a rich Arab sheik as a benefactor to help set it up. It would have been the first time that he would have indulged in such behaviour without sexual favours being provided. Which I find highly hypocritical, considering the writers for *Spare Rib* gave me such a hard time about my sex magazine art project in the *Prostitution* exhibition. Apparently, prostitution could be naively sidestepped as anti-feminist, depending on the 'cause'. Delia was aware of the Women's Movement – she went on the first demonstration with her friend Angela Rodaway in March 1971 – but she never fully subscribed to it.

It's hard to figure out when Delia got any sleep, as she was working in the daytime at the BBC and throughout the night on *An Electric Storm*, let alone the disturbance of David's 'associates' coming and going. Brian was doing his own thing outside of Kaleidophon. He had lovers and day-to-day dramas of his own to deal with, as well as supplying essential special sounds for the songs Delia and David were writing. Somehow, as Kaleidophon and the band White Noise they managed to compose and produce music for their own album and theatre and arts events, and two sound effects albums that came about through the singer-songwriter Anthony Newley, with whom Delia had co-written a song. David was building up the studio further and working hard on putting together his own sixteen-track tape recorder. But it was taking so long and causing such a marked decrease in the time they had to collectively use the studio productively that Delia and Brian got fed up waiting. They decided to split the band up.

Delia left David too. She had invested a lot both personally and creatively but cut her losses. She took away little of the collective studio equipment, much as I did when I left TG. I just wanted to get away from a toxic situation. At the time of departure, the priorities are basic and don't necessarily include even totting up what's a 'fair' share-out between you all. The Kaleidophon studio continued functioning at David's place without Delia and Brian, who were still with the BBC but had plans for leaving and starting up a studio of their own. It would be the opportunity for Delia to further express herself through her independent musical compositions.

13

My first task for the 'Delia' soundtrack was to provide Caroline with an audio backdrop she could use while developing the film. She had given me a breakdown of the scenes and script to work from. Caroline was incredibly generous and trusting in my ability and she understood that my creative process involved allowing time for the sounds and music to take form. I was sat in my office contemplating when and exactly how I would begin approaching the music for the soundtrack when an invitation arrived for me and Chris to perform as Carter Tutti at the 2018 SPILL Festival in Ipswich. We could do anything we wished as long as it fitted the theme of 'Time' – the timing of things, past, present or future, whether it be personal choices and events or people who had made a lasting and significant impression or held a presence in your life. Far from being a distraction, the 'timing' of such an open invitation couldn't have been more auspicious, with Delia having just become a presence in my life and making such an impression on both me and Chris. We immediately accepted and set about exploring the notion of music being a temporal art form, a universal language, and how we could present sound and visuals that were immersive, bordering on the ritualistic. We decided on using the principle of sidereal time, a measurement based on the rotation of the earth in relation to the 'fixed' stars, a concept we'd explored on our 1984 album *Elemental Seven*. We wanted to place both audio and imagery a step outside this world, to represent the continuum of life forms that exist independently of man-made time rules.

The venue was the Grand Hall of the Corn Exchange in Ipswich, a huge space with bare brick walls and a high vaulted ceiling. We named our piece *Inter-versal*. It was one sidereal hour in duration, fifty-six minutes and four seconds, and presented in the round, with us on a central raised platform, a quadrophonic PA system and projections synchronised to our improvised performance – using natural and otherworldly sounds we'd collated, playing off each other, the ambience and responses from the audience. The music crossed over from strong tribal-cum-industrial rhythms suggestive of shifting tectonic plates to more gentle celestial tones, panning particular sounds around the room. The audience were swathed in projections that moved slowly, covering the walls, ceiling and floor of the hall, engulfing the entire space in the time-lapsed growth of fungi and of microscopic organisms from earth and water – all subject to their internal circadian rhythm clock, said to underpin all life on earth. The foundation of the cycle of life, cell renewal and the rhythms of existence.

During my preparations collecting sounds for *Inter-versal* I had set aside any that were more typical of ones Delia would have made, keeping them in a separate folder as reference for when I began working full-time on the film soundtrack. Our paths were beginning to align. The music was making itself heard.

The *Inter-versal* performance had also sparked the idea of making my second solo album, *TUTTI*. I took the recording of the soundtrack I'd performed live for *Harmonic COUMaction* in Hull and reworked sections to create an album that made its own statement, separate from how the music had worked with the visuals of the film. That process of disconnection brought a whole new experience to the sounds, releasing them from their role relating to the images of my life, evoking different emotions. In some ways the music became more powerful and gave licence for everyone to form their own imaginary images. Separating the music from the film to make a stand-alone album wasn't easy. I wanted it to be right. Some of the sounds, like those that went with images of melting walls, didn't earn their place without the visuals. I wanted to create some space.

My work on *TUTTI* was comparable to what I was about to embark on for the 'Delia' film. *TUTTI* was composed from manipulated sound recordings from my life, as I was about to do with Delia's 'recordings', which I regarded as largely informed by her life and charged with her*self*. Working on a film about Delia at a time when my own life was to be the subject of a film based on *Art Sex Music* was a complex situation to get my head around. Here I was, about to represent Delia's music in my own right, working like she had from a script, but one that was about her, while I was collaborating on a film script about myself and dealing with the concept of a stranger being cast to represent me, who would also be attempting to relate to my time and my struggles just as I was with Delia – and Margery. These interconnections were simultaneously bewildering and exciting. It was as if hidden forces were at work, presenting and bringing together the essential elements as I needed them and at a mutually beneficial time.

For months I'd been accumulating and setting aside equipment in readiness for working on the film music, when quite by chance, after desiring it for many years, I managed to acquire an original BBC Nagra reel-to-reel portable tape recorder complete with a BBC stamped metal plate. It seemed beyond serendipitous that another, even more coveted piece of equipment, a Synthi A (a suit-case version of the EMS VCS3 synthesiser that Delia used), turned up at the same time. Together with other objects, instruments and software versions of the banks of oscillators Delia used, this went as near as damn it to being able to mirror her workflow and some of the hardware she had at her disposal. I had designated space in my studio at home for all the equipment I'd use specifically for 'Delia'. I needed that separation so I could avoid falling into my own ways of working and to maintain an awareness of Delia's methods.

My and Delia's starting points and processes differ but the aim is the same: breaking new ground to create sounds we've never heard before, each with our own discipline, while embracing the idea of 'music' being the arrangement of diverse sources of sound. For both of us, finding the process of acquiring the sounds for a composition is just as enjoyable as completing it, sometimes more so. Where Delia differed from me was in using an analytical approach as the foundation. Whatever sounds she had in mind when composing, she could utilise her knowledge of diverse theories, mathematics, sound, physics and hands-on techniques, making use of available hardware and objects, to calculate how it would or possibly could sound, and proceed towards that end. A complex process that resulted in beautiful music that often sounded deceptively simple.

Sound is amorphous, slippery like an eel. There are variables, unexpected sonics and harmonies that resist the rigours of mathematical formulas. Delia believed that the physical perception of sound was ultimately more important than musical or mathematical theory but felt it necessary and useful to know the rules. I'm the opposite. I have a freeform approach. I don't want to operate within or learn any of the established rules, so from the start I'm free to go wherever my instinct and the sounds suggest, with nothing looming over me subconsciously suppressing my ideas. I don't read or write music or adhere to formulas, but I have knowledge of different techniques, equipment and software. The possible theoretical reason why things seem right and fall into place so readily is not important to me. That they do, and that it sounds good and evokes the right feelings, is enough. Although I do tend to have bouts of philosophical moments when I'm making music, when I wonder exactly why I'm even doing what I'm doing, or why one sound takes on such importance that it ends up being a barrier to the whole track – I can't get past it. Then I start questioning everything. It's time for a radically different approach: strip the track down, mute the 'problem', use the technique of 'oblique strategies' or simply move on; maybe come back later – maybe years later – maybe never.

I approached the soundtrack in a holistic way – all-encompassing, fully embracing 'Delia' and what she'd come to mean to me after all I'd learnt about her. I needed to tune into her, to 'hear' Delia's voice speak from within her work and to find a sound that spoke to her and to me. I had in my mind what I felt it was and I worked towards that through months of experimenting.

Starting from Caroline's breakdown of sounds for each scene, I set up a whiteboard and made a master list of all the required pieces of audio, then sub-grouped them according to length and how I intended to source them, either by generating them through electronic and acoustic means, or through recordings of objects, or by making use of anything that took my fancy or offered a promise of a potentially interesting noise. I'd made copious notes on how I'd go about composing and finding the right sounds that would reflect Delia's style while staying true to myself and to Delia's ethos of obtaining previously unheard sounds. In some ways it was a trade-off that seemed fair. Using Delia's archive audio files would have meant my music wouldn't be original, and it was against my principles to use someone else's work, particularly knowing Delia's own views on being 'used' and her music being reworked.

I decided to begin from Delia's starting point and work from her original VCS3 synthesiser patch sheets – A4 sheets of paper printed with a graphic of the VCS3's front panel and patch bay, on which she'd drawn her positioning of the knobs and placement of the patch-bay pins that generated the sonics she'd used for various assignments. It was the only way she had of documenting how she'd achieved, and could retrieve, certain sounds. I also referred to her descriptive notes and graphics for music projects as a bridge to create my own sounds redolent of Delia's. Her original thoughts and ideas and my own, melding us together. Some of Delia's VCS3 patch sheets had multiple settings, a different colour denoting each individual sound. I copied some onto my Synthi, knowing that with its idiosyncratic nature there was little chance of me getting the same sound emanating from the same settings. So Delia's formula mutated and became my own.

Delia was very visual when engaging with music, often using pictorial analogies to illustrate sounds she had in mind, lines and curves denoting the direction or arrangement of the various elements that would make up the work. Building up the sound as a picture. Music begins in your head and starts to play, transferring to paper as drawings or musical notation or mathematical formulas that can then be fine-tuned and moulded until they sound 'right'. Whether by analysing waveforms the way Delia did or by zooming in as I do on the screen of my laptop to make microadjustments, sound can be made visible in a process analogous to collaging, with multiple tracks of sounds layered over and mixed under and across each other. There are obvious similarities – the master recording being the musical work, the finished canvas the artwork, the brushes that apply shapes comparable to the instruments and audio sources employed to make sounds, the paint palette akin to the application of filters to music to add the effect of 'colour' and 'temperature'. Using synthetic or acoustic sounds to create an audio 'image'. I find writing is similar to composing music. There's a rhythm to the 'mix' of elements, with initially wonderful sections that hang around as the work develops and finds itself, and then you realise those sections just don't fit any more. What were once lynchpins are now gone, excised from the remix, edited out.

It was exciting getting to know unfamiliar equipment and using it along with the gear I was accustomed to. I hooked the EMS Synthi up to my Space Echo delay pedal and recorded the output pure, treating it through various sound modules and re-recording the newly combined sounds. I was super-lucky to be sent a prototype of an Instruo Lúbadh looping module – the equivalent to having two tape recorders that could loop my sounds back into each other, relooping, loops on loops, and all in real time. It was wonderfully hands-on and very much in miniature compared to Delia's BBC workshop equipment. I also had an array of Eventide effects pedals, my guitar and cornet (of course) and a remodelled eighteen-inch long acrylic ribbon controller. The latter was designed to vary the pitch of a synth by running your finger along the surface, from high at one end to low at the other, but instead I'd attached to it a long length of quarter-inch recording tape containing a recording of Delia's voice. Chris soldered a tape recorder head onto a length of cable that plugged into one of my modules so I could manually run the head along the tape and get peculiar fragments of 'Delia'.

I could also put all these useful sources through my touch keyboard sequencer to create rhythmic patterns, in rather the same way that Delia would recognise one component within a sound that lent itself to another use, extracting that as the basis of an element of a track, transfigured as a rhythm or melody. It was a technique I'd used for many years but through different methods, using samplers, loopers and software. Reducing recorded sounds to fragmentary partials and then reconstructing and shaping them into music is like mining for gold. When I hear an element within a sound that 'speaks' to me I filter out everything else until I find that 'golden nugget'. When I'm playing guitar I use the band-pass filter in my wah-wah pedal to eliminate everything until I get the partial frequency and tone I want for my guitar sound.

There were similarities in my and Delia's working methods. Her repurposing and reusing sounds wasn't unlike my own practice for my music and art actions, using and then reusing objects as a creative continuum – a reference to the time before within a newly inspiring context. Her making and using physical tape loops and me 'cutting and pasting' using software. I also recorded sounds onto tape using the Nagra, cutting, splicing and making tape loops like Delia had. It was unpredictable (which was great) and so laborious and frustratingly fiddly. I was astounded to think that she did it for hours on end, day in, day out, year after year. But that was her only way of creating new sound. Samplers and loop-making software were yet to be invented.

Using the Nagra was like a step back in time. It was heavy and clunky to operate. The switch from play to fast forward was hard to turn, often sending the tape spinning off the reel if I didn't catch it quick enough. The long loops of tape I set up reminded me of way back in the TG days of the 1970s, when I'd walked into the Martello Street studio late one afternoon to be greeted by the sight of Chris stood among metres of recording tape he'd threaded from the stage and across the floor, looped around numerous glass bottles placed wherever the tape could run free without obstruction. Because he lived in a small bedsit at the time he was taking advantage of having space to experiment with tape loops. Quite different to Delia's purpose or mine – his was for making TG rhythms. He found he could get complex layers by using rhythmic tape loops played on two tape machines. Unfortunately, they were different makes that ran at slightly different speeds. There was an inbuilt drift from the limitations of the tech of the time. The two tape machines would push and pull against each other, with the differences between them creating an unpredictable swing to the rhythms he was trying to produce. There's only so much time you can spend countering such problems and Chris eventually scaled things down. He went over to more manageable and practical looping by using modified cassettes and our newly acquired Eventide Harmonizers, which offered their own type of digital looping. Then we got a Roland Space Echo machine that had its own distinct sound and could also be used to make incredibly long loops.

All these techniques were employed in real time to provide those distinctive, shifting, slightly lopsided TG rhythms. That was until we bought drum machines and sequencers and the tape looping was put to another use, for voices and effects, catching and repeating sounds. The drum machines and sequencers had built-in electronic clocks and were rhythmically very tight. The classic Roland TR808 drum machine we used for Chris & Cosey was so accurate that when we took our tapes of 'October (Love Song)' for mastering at Utopia Studios, the engineer mentioned a distinct spirographic pattern on the groove that he'd never seen before. It was apparently due to an interaction between the drum-machine clock and the rotational speed of the cutting-head lathe. Delia was known for being able to identify when certain instruments were played by the pattern of the grooves they made on a record. I wonder what she'd have made of 'October (Love Song)'.

As I worked my way through Caroline's script it became quite natural to think of Delia being alongside me, keeping me on track and within a process that was new to me and crossed over and combined both our practices. I was adopting and adapting Delia's techniques, playing back tape at various speeds and resampling, reworking, sometimes importing audio into software depending on what I sensed was needed. There were conglomerations of the most unlikely sounds that somehow fitted together perfectly to give the effect and evoke the response I sought. I achieved some astonishing results, as well as many of those magic moments Delia spoke of and many musicians relish – previously unknown sounds we revel in finding. Sitting in front of the equipment and zoning into a particular mindset, referring to the script and audio descriptions to project myself into the scene just like Delia had, I understood first-hand how demanding her method of working was. Interpreting what's needed and what sits well in supportive relation to the 'script', yet also wanting the music to expand and enhance it rather than take the role of mundane mandatory sound effects. I was struck by how my world of music was coalescing with Delia's, like an echo across time, with me placed in the same position as she was at the BBC, with a written brief. I had no visuals to work from, just words and what I imagined the images would be, feeling my way into the reconstructed version of her life – her in the Radiophonic Workshop, ghostly going about her work, and me doing a similar thing in my own studio. At times I felt like I was in a parallel world, 'instrumentally' representing Delia's music as part of a project that was re-presenting her life, extracting, deconstructing, manipulating and reconstructing for a new project based on the past but very much located in and relevant to the present day. In many ways I felt like I was inhabiting her spirit during the process. I was there, with Delia, to create music that sat well for us both, to discover the new, to get that rush of excitement when it happened.

I was so engrossed in the music, adding to and expanding the concept of our 'recordings', that I had a better understanding of what lay behind our unorthodox approach to our lifelong love of creating radical 'music', despite the many challenges we faced. I was forensic in my approach, distilling Delia to imbue the essence of her in the sounds I created. I often wondered what she would have made of the whole project. A film about her, an attempt to represent not only her work but the more personal side of her life, intertwined with the numerous sound experiments; the building of sets to recreate pivotal events in her life – a church interior, the war, the attic of tapes, the BBC Radiophonic Workshop, her life outside work, her addiction to alcohol and snuff.

Delia's introduction to snuff was to feature in the film, accompanied by my 'Snuff Chorus' track, a short, quirky ditty with the rhythm and melody made from samples of sniffs, coughs, the sounds of the opening and closing of snuff tins, and sneezes – including those of my three-month-old grandson Emilio, who shared Delia's propensity for sniffles and sneezes. There were numerous scenes featuring her old bicycle, which she regularly rode to and from the BBC studio, with the shopping basket attached securely to the front handlebars full of papers and her supply of alcohol. She had a habit of humming and singing as she cycled along, trying out melodies or going through possible musical arrangements in her head, then externalising the potential resonances of sound by singing at the top of her voice. Her bicycle was the perfect vehicle on which to freewheel with ideas and far better suited for singing her head off than being on a bus or the tube, which would have drawn attention and broken the spell of secluded concentration she needed. On one evening, way past midnight, she left the BBC and got on her bike as usual to ride home to her flat in Clifton Villas, just a few streets away. She'd been working on a song for the *Poets in Prison* event for the City of London Festival and the ideas were still going round and round in her head. She started singing out loud, going through variations of melodies until one emerged. Perfect! At which point she snapped out of her creative dream bubble, looked around and realised she'd been 'miles away', absorbed in the music. In fact she'd cycled all the way through central London and across the river into Vauxhall, a long way from home. She chuckled as she turned her bike around and headed back across the bridge to Maida Vale. The next morning she burst through the studio door, all excited at having broken the back of the tune, laughing as she told Brian and Dick Mills all about her unintended trip to Vauxhall.

My days were totally taken up with working on the soundtrack. I'd discuss any necessary tweaks with Caroline, making sure we were on the same wavelength so that my music would suit the visuals and moods she had in mind for when she started filming. We worked closely, sometimes talking about just a phrase or word in the script that succinctly captured a nuance of the mood that required expressing with sound. One that stood out to me was 'An electronic ceiling of sickening sound' for Scene 23, where Delia yet again had to deal with men in suits behind desks determining her choices and future. I instantly 'heard' that sound in my head from my own feelings of extreme frustration and anger in similar circumstances. I went straight to work on the Synthi, then mixed and treated the resulting dissonance with recordings of smashing cymbals.

I have a very strange mind because I analyse everything, not just music. The pace, the cutting, the editing of film – even when I'm listening to the news I note every inflexion, every comma. There are so many subtleties to the human voice. I suppose in a way I was experimenting in psycho-acoustics.

Delia was only too aware and appreciative of the importance of the human element in giving a work 'feeling'. Performance by its very nature, being human, is prone to 'faults' and nuances because of individual abilities. Everyone brings something of themselves to the process. It was the unexpected which couldn't be accounted for theoretically that made the music so magical. Delia was open to allowing 'accidents', as Brian recalled:

Delia and I used to say there are arbits and omens, and that's how we worked. The arbit was an arbitrary length of tape which you inserted into something, that suddenly made it all work . . . and an omen was something that happened quite by accident: you'd drop a piece of equipment and it made a magic sound, or you'd fall over something or somebody would spill something on something or a joint would suddenly break in a piece of tape and something magic would happen

It was an attitude and approach that played a huge part in the creation of one of the most iconic pieces of music in television history: the *Doctor Who* theme tune.

14

I was so focused on Delia's life and the music that was required from me that I didn't connect straight away with the *Doctor Who* theme tune – the work she's best known for. I suppose it was because it seemed to symbolise everything that was wrong about how she and her work were treated. It was hugely successful and brought Delia and the Radiophonic Workshop a lot of attention. It was also the beginning of what she felt was a place in which to indulge her love of sound, but which turned out to be a huge contributing factor to her undoing.

Delia's first composition for television in 1962 was for a science-fiction view of the future, a docudrama about increased leisure called *Time on Our Hands*. Her use of pure electronics was praised by the BBC's head of drama and probably played a part in her being assigned to work on the *Doctor Who* signature music the following year. The commission was given to the composer Ron Grainer, in accordance with the Musicians' Union stance that substantial BBC TV programme music had to be scored by a composer, not a RW 'assistant'.

Ron gave Delia a score on a single sheet of paper, including outlines for the bass line and melody and some descriptive words – 'swoops', 'sweeps', 'wind cloud', 'wind bubble' – all relating to the visuals he'd seen for the TV programme titles. Then he went away on holiday. She set herself the challenge of using only electronic sounds, to prove to her boss Desmond Briscoe and other cynics that such sounds could be beautiful. With logarithm book in hand and an 'I'll show you' attitude, Delia set about the job of translating Ron's minimal instructions into music firstly by using mathematics, 'translating notes on the page into cycles per second. Then translating the duration of notes into inches of tape at fifteen inches per second.' The distance between the spliced pieces of tape determined the tempo on playback and also acted as her form of notation, effectively using the tape machine as an instrument.

Ron had plans for the bass line to be played by a bass guitar or bassoon. But Delia's imagination was fired up. No instruments. She found alternative sound sources, in one case by plucking a guitar string stretched across a flexible metal jack-bay panel, recording it, then shifting the pitch by vari-speeding the tape until she got the right note, recording it again, then cutting up the tape into hundreds of 'notes', Es, B flats and Bs, and splicing them together in measured lengths to get the timing of the rhythm right. Not at all easy, with the plastic and wooden rulers she had giving different readings. To avoid a robotic feel she introduced some 'imperfections' by adding a little tremolo, shifting the beat very slightly, a tiny tweak that can give a track an imperceptible swing. Adding grace notes, as Chris and I did on our track 'Dancing Ghosts' using our Roland TB-303. It's about 'feel' to create a groove, not a plod like you get from sticking to a grid. Some of the best dancefloor tracks are not strictly 4/4 but have unusual or unpredictable, even indiscernible, shifts in time signature. Chris and I often bring the vocal in on the third instead of the first bar, depending on the 'feel'.

Delia interpreted 'wind cloud' in Ron's notes as white noise, and 'swoop' as sine waves from valve oscillators, which gave a hint of outer space. Assisted by her trusted engineer Dick Mills, she worked tirelessly for weeks creating 'new' futuristic electronic sounds, using the 'Wobbulator' for the clouds, tuning and recording the Jason valve oscillators, which she 'played' by connecting them to a keyboard, one oscillator 'note' to each key, then treating and filtering the various resulting sounds. The process was incredibly tedious. Using quarter-inch tape, cutting inch by painstaking inch, she gradually assembled the different elements of rhythm, melody and accompanying sounds onto three reels of tape, ready for 'bouncing down' onto the mastering tape machine. Delia described using the three Philips tape recorders as a nightmare, but her large hands and long fingers made it a little easier to get them to sync up, and she became expert at it. With the tape recorders in line, she and Dick would stand and count down from three, and on the word 'go!' they pushed 'start' on each machine as near to the same time as possible. But that slightly out-of-sync feature, frustrating as it was at times, was something she came to feel reflected the theme of the programme itself:

That's why I'm so fond of the original version of the *Doctor Who* title music, because of the way it's never quite in sync. It's almost as though there's one dimension of time dragging against another.

Delia achieved what she'd set out to do in creating the otherworldly theme tune. It was purely electronic, with no musicians and no conventional musical instruments, and nothing done in real time, rather like the time-shifting Time Lord himself. That's an element of Delia's work I admire: there was always within her music in some way, no matter how subtle, a pertinent audio reference to the subject matter of the project. It's an approach I adhere to, delving deep, not skimming the surface but incorporating the purpose and reasoning within the sounds. What seems simple has many layers. It was all about detail. Delia wanted the music to evoke an expectation of otherworldliness by using sounds that weren't grounded in reality but lent themselves to the fantastical notion of time travel.

It wouldn't have been fitting to use a recognisable instrument to represent the unknown. Including something familiar to the ear of the listener would defeat the objective and break the spell of the atmosphere she wanted to produce.

> *Doctor Who* was my private delight. It proved them all wrong. It's not the fact that it was done well that's important, it's the fact that it was done at all.

Ron had intended to use an orchestra, with some additional electronic sounds by Delia, but when he heard what she'd done he was so thrilled he dropped that idea completely. He couldn't believe what Delia had achieved. 'Did I really write that?' he asked her. 'Most of it,' Delia replied. Knowing full well the realisation was her work, he immediately offered to share the royalties with her. The BBC refused, saying Delia was a BBC employee on an assistant manager's salary; that was her payment, nothing more, and they didn't permit credit to be given to individuals in the RW for their music or special sound contributions. Ron could perhaps have found a way around it by making sure Delia was registered as co-composer, but that never happened. Consequently the *Doctor Who* theme tune royalties were paid to him. The extent of Delia's input and the extremes she went to showed her determination to create music despite having to work with limited equipment and accept the BBC rules. She knew that official recognition of her endeavours wouldn't always be forthcoming. For Delia it was all about her love of music, the process.

Doctor Who, with Delia's theme tune, was a triumph. It was like nothing else on TV and a game-changer for children's programming, with its exciting and scary out-of-this-world adventures of an eccentric time traveller. I was twelve years old when I watched the first broadcast in November 1963, so not as easily frightened as the many children who remember hiding behind the sofa. I was transfixed with fascination and anticipation of what would happen next, both visually and musically. *Doctor Who* appealed to all the family. Parents and children watched it together on their small black-and-white TV screens in blurry vision. The medium was poor quality but the music was superb, and with the programme going out at prime time on a Saturday evening, it brought electronic music to a huge audience. ITV had nothing that could compete with it. *Doctor Who* was a resounding success that is still with us in updated form today. And the theme tune continues to be lauded. *Pitchfork* rated it as one of the greatest songs of the 1960s, and it stands as a testament to Delia as someone way ahead of her time in her skills as a composer and musician and her formidable expertise in tape splicing.

Doctor Who was only the second TV programme Delia had worked on and its score was the only one she realised for anyone else. After that, all the hundreds of scores she created for television and radio programmes were her own. Meanwhile, as different producers or directors for *Doctor Who* came along they would ask for the theme tune to be adjusted, made more 'sparkly'. Delia found their interference distressing and insulting: 'The music itself was sacred and beautiful as it was and I thought it was very disrespectful to tart it up.' To her, her music was very personal, something she'd poured her heart and soul into. No matter what the brief was, she made sure the music would fit but always wanted to make it special in its own right. It always had to be more than a job, and in approaching it that way she infused her work with herself. 'Delia' was inherent in all the music she created.

Delia was particularly disgusted by an orchestral version of the *Doctor Who* theme by Eric Winstone and his orchestra, released on record in January 1964, just two months after the first episode was broadcast. Winstone's version went against her original intention of eliminating instruments. A month later Decca (ironically) released the official BBC version, credited to Ron Grainer and the Radiophonic Workshop.

This example of tampering with someone else's music raises the question I often ask myself when doing remixes or cover versions: at what point does a piece of music become a new composition in its own right? When someone's track is remixed there can be very little of the original left, and sometimes nothing at all. But because it has served as the starting point and inspiration, the copyright remains with the original composer, no matter how different the remix turns out, even if it has no resemblance to the original track. That's comparable to what Delia faced with the *Doctor Who* theme tune, when she started from Ron Grainer's single-page score and ended up with something he wasn't sure was his. It may be true he 'wrote' it, but she realised it in terms of all the sound and extraordinary interpretations and methods, something no orchestra could have created, no matter how musically qualified they, the composer or conductor were. Plus a remix usually commands a one-off fee, with no further royalties or payments – just as Delia received nothing on top of her BBC salary. It may not have been regarded as a male/female issue, but I wonder, if Ron had been insisting on behalf of a male member of staff, whether he could have been more successful in getting them co-credited. But that doesn't excuse the unforgivable delay in giving Delia her overdue credit. She was finally acknowledged in 2013, fifty years too late, her name given its rightful place in the *Doctor Who* credits – not as composer but as arranger. Maybe there were worries about the cost of any possible claim for back payment, which, considering Delia's substantial contribution to the theme tune, could have earned her a small fortune in addition to due credit. But it wasn't about the money; it was the lack of full recognition for many of her works that really hurt her. And she died without ever receiving it for *Doctor Who* in particular.

Delia did enjoy one moment of glory, when Munich Radio commissioned the RW to do a signature tune for its news programme – a compliment, since Germany had been the source of inspiration for the formation of the workshop. Delia was given the job of composing the theme. And she got a credit when it was first broadcast, as 'a British lady composer' – not mentioned by name but at least recognised as an individual rather than grouped into the RW.

15

As part of the 2017 Frieze Art Fair I was on a panel chaired by Alison Gingeras discussing 'Alt-feminisms' with Penny Slinger, Marilyn Minter and Renate Bertlmann. We were all artists who had experienced censorship and been restricted in pursuit of our art, either shunned by the commercial or 'fine art' worlds, which favoured male artists, or criticised because of the sexual content of our work, our use of our naked bodies, our sexualised performances and, in my case, exploring and taking part in pornography as part of my art practice. Due to my using my body as the site of my art in my sex magazine works I've been accused of being anti-feminist. I've also been hailed as a feminist for asserting my autonomy in forging my path to freedom of expression, claiming my body as my own and my right to choose what to do with it.

Like some of the other artists on the discussion panel, after thirty years my so-called 'scandalous' and 'depraved' works of the past have been acknowledged as 'art' by an 'artist'. My feelings about acceptance, having been ostracised for so long, continue to raise questions as to whether my outsider approach is reconcilable with inclusion in the mainstream. Thankfully attitudes can change, and sometimes for the better, leaving the integrity of my work uncompromised.

With the Frieze discussion in mind, alongside my work on 'Delia' and finding out more about Margery's life, everything seemed to be focusing in on the strength of women in the face of adversity, about freedom and choice.

Directors who came to see me work used to say 'You must be an ardent feminist' – I think I was a post-feminist before feminism was invented! [The interviewer suggests she is 'an individualist'.] . . . 'an independent thinker'. I think that sums me up. I did rebel. I did a lot of things I was told not to do.

What Delia said about herself stayed with me. She wasn't comfortable with being categorised, any more than I am. Like me she saw herself first and foremost as a person, an individualist, an independent thinker, an electronic musician, an artist. Being progressive and challenging boundaries is about defying categorisation, reaching for something new, questioning accepted norms, especially inequality. Our 'recordings' weren't made consciously from a feminist perspective, but it's great if as an unintentional consequence our works and lives offer something positive to the ongoing struggle for equality.

Musical innovation is full of danger to the State . . . for when modes of music change, the fundamental laws of the State always change with them.

With Delia's love of the Greeks she must have been familiar with this quotation from Plato, which is better known in the paraphrase, 'When the mode of the music changes, the walls of the city shake.' Instigating change is disruptive and some find it scary, as had been Delia's experience at the BBC and my own throughout my life making music and art. Of course, some people 'get it', some love it, but creating work that's received predominantly with puzzled looks, curiosity and disdain, even anger, can be wearing – yet oddly it also gives you an incentive to carry on. If what you're doing is weird and so out of step that it provokes such a severe reaction, it must have something special, a newness that is out there to be discussed and taken further. Or, I ask myself, do negative reactions have anything to do with being a woman? Yes, for sure, at times a huge part of the reason behind criticism of my work has been to do with me having the effrontery to assume I, as a woman, have the right to take a place in a 'man's world'. Whether with my music or art I've managed unintentionally to incur the wrath of a lot of people.

Margery and her book have been the subject of analysis in many academic theses, including whether she could be regarded as a proto-feminist, with some criticising her for 'failing' as a feminist – which I find unreasonable considering she risked her life to do what she wanted to do. It was impossible for Margery to understand her actions in feminist terms as the notion of feminism didn't exist then, but by doing things she shouldn't as a woman, seeking and getting access to male areas closed to her, she was raising issues of inequality in a far more fiercely restrictive and dangerously misogynistic society than we live in today.

Me, Delia and Margery had to work with and sometimes subvert the limited freedoms available, the opportunities that were open or closed to us as women, as well as the results of the choices we made in constructively engaging with the means to facilitate our needs. It wasn't deemed appropriate (or tolerated) for women to demand our right to anything established as being the prerogative of men. Delia had come up against gender bias very early in her life and music career, and it continued to dog her throughout her time in the music business. Her single-mindedness is what carried her through some difficult times, even though she was constantly swimming against the tide – a character trait which to her delight was recognised by one of her friends, who sent her a birthday card addressed 'to an independent thinker', depicting a shoal of fish swimming along together, their mouths turned down, and one highlighted as 'Delia' swimming in the opposite direction, smiling.

—ɱ—

The month prior to the Frieze Art Fair I'd had the privilege to take part in a talk with Maria (Masha) Alyokhina of the Russian collective Pussy Riot, as we were promoting our recently published books. We were both sporting bright blue nail varnish, something I noticed because she was picking it off bit by bit throughout the conversation. Having read her book *Riot Days*, a harrowing account of her arrest, trial and imprisonment, I hadn't expected her to be so petite, considering the physical strength needed to get through some of the cruel treatments inflicted on her. I was astounded by her fortitude during her two years of 'corrective' labour in a notorious Russian penal colony in the Ural mountains. Her 'crime' was asserting her belief in freedom, making a political protest about the collusion between the Orthodox Church and Vladimir Putin by performing 'Punk Prayer' (with its lines begging the Virgin Mary to 'banish Putin') in a Moscow cathedral. Masha's political action wasn't acknowledged in her official conviction but dubiously defined as 'hooliganism motivated by religious hatred'. Representing the crime as an anti-religious act conveniently redirected the protest away from politics and Putin. But the world knew the truth. The Pussy Riot story went viral. As Masha toured her book she received threats for her political and artistic stance. Her words in her book speak for so many:

> Freedom does not exist unless you fight for it every day. This is the story about how I made a choice . . . actions break fear . . . To Back Down an Inch Is to Give Up a Mile.

Masha's use of the Church to protest and demand freedom was deployed against her with charges suggesting heresy, much as Margery's very vocal outpourings had been for her. In fifteenth-century England, the Church and politics were also closely linked, and Margery's loud 'performances' in St Margaret's Church didn't adhere to the established rules of either religion or female behaviour. She was out of line and treading a dangerous path forbidden to her – the domain of the all-male clergy. Women of her time were not allowed to preach or speak publicly on religious matters. Public preaching was a capital offence for any lay person. Margery, with her internal discussions with and visions of God, was effectively taking it upon herself to speak directly to him, and her speaking of his teachings in the community was judged as her defiling the word of God. All intercession with God was through man. All requests by women had to be made to and granted or refused by men. Women were the property of men, whether it be their fathers, husbands, brothers, the king or the church. Margery's public wailing was like an utterance of 'free' *self*-expression. Weeping was supposed to be done discreetly, preferably in silence. Speaking in church without permission wasn't tolerated, for anyone, let alone if a woman dared to make her voice heard. I recall breaking that rule as a child with my friend Les, using empty churches as our playgrounds, screaming, laughing, shouting and singing the hit songs of the day from the pulpit, knowing what we did was sacrilegious, but that was part of the mischievous appeal. But those rules of authority and privilege were well and truly drilled home. Even though we never went to church we knew the pulpit was the preserve of appointed male priests, from where they delivered the word of God. Women were yet to be allowed to become priests.

Margery was only too aware of the risks she took in behaving the way she did. To some extent she was protected because of her father's mayoral and judicial positions in the town and was wealthy enough to pay any fines. In some ways she was lucky. Prisons were very different from today, much smaller, with just a few cells where debtors, murderers and other offenders were held awaiting trial or execution – which could take years. Offenders were rarely given custodial sentences like Masha's, hidden away at the mercy of a harsh penal system. Punishment in Margery's time was a very public affair, carried out in front of an audience, a ghoulish entertainment to deter others from stepping out of line. If the shame and humiliation and any physical injuries from being whipped, locked by either your feet or your head and arms in the stocks or pillory, left defenceless and pelted with rotten food, stones and excrement (and opportunistic 'payback' beatings), weren't enough disincentive, the sight of people being hanged and burnt at the stake must have been. Margery would have seen many punishments and public executions. She mentions the punishment of women being placed naked on a crude wooden stretcher, then dragged through the streets to their execution.

The stocks and pillories (mandatory to retain the right to hold a market), bloody whippings, hangings and burnings all took place in Tuesday Market Place. It was Bishop's Lynn's largest public space, so the miscreants and sinners got the biggest possible crowd to mock and taunt them. Punishments and torture could be gender-specific and sexualised. Depending on the offence, men could be castrated, while women could have their breasts torn off using clawed metal tongs, 'suitably' named breast rippers. The ducking stool was designed for women. It was the law that every community had to have one. Lynn's ducking stool was beside Colville Fleet, close to where Margery lived and went about her everyday life. It was left in place as a reminder of what awaited unruly, 'mouthy' women. A heavy wooden chair with restraining straps was attached to one end of a twenty-foot wooden beam, which was laid across a centre post, like a see-saw. The contraption was placed on the edge of a river, pond or open sewer, and with the woman hanging in her chair over the water, a group of men pulling on a rope at the other end raised her up, then repeatedly ducked her beneath the water for however long and as many times as was ordered. Being semi-naked in public added to the indignity for women sentenced to the ducking stool. They were first paraded around town, their modesty stripped away as they were reduced to wearing just their cotton shift, which gave little protection from the elements and when soaked through from being ducked left little to the imagination of the lecherous, voyeuristic men. The wet T-shirt competitions of today serve a similar titillating purpose – without the risk of death by drowning, of course.

Tuesday Market Place will never feel the same to me again. It's always been a happy, bustling social place. With the eight hundred-year-old fair at King's Lynn Mart every February, and organised free music events throughout the year, it offers such different public entertainment to the horrifically cruel and merciless events Margery witnessed there. When Chris's mother visits us from London she always stays at the (supposedly haunted) seventeenth-century Duke's Head Hotel, renamed by our son as 'Grandma's holiday home'. The hotel overlooks the market and was built on the site of the old Griffin Inn. It is said that a maid-servant from the inn was boiled in oil in the Tuesday Market square for poisoning her mistress, and Mary Read, one of the last witches in England to be executed, was burnt alive there. A well-known legend has it that Mary's heart burst out of her chest and landed on the windowsill of 17 Tuesday Market Place, the chambers of the judge who condemned her. It then fell to the ground and rolled into the river, where it sizzled and sank. Marking where her heart splatted against the building is a diamond with a heart in the centre engraved into the brickwork.

Women who were found guilty of being a witch, possessed by the devil, an adulterer, a strumpet, a blasphemer or, most commonly, a 'scold' (an outspoken woman) were harshly punished. Escaping the noose or fire didn't necessarily mean dodging death. Some punishments left people with life-changing debilitating injuries or dying from severe infections. If Margery had been poorer or less articulate, unable to defend herself against some of the accusations she faced, she would likely have found herself in Tuesday Market Place, on the receiving end of severe punishment or even death. By her own account her reputation around town and the hostility of the townsfolk towards her was so bad that at one point her confessor advised her to leave the area, presumably before she met her fate.

16

The personal is such an important influence when creating music. It's from that private space that inspiration and creative ideas emerge as expressions of emotional responses to moments of sadness, joy, fear, love, especially when it comes to music and our favouring of particular sounds, harmonics or melodies.

It may seem strange that I've said how private a person Delia was and then revealed and speculated about aspects of her personal life. But as my work on the soundtrack progressed it grew into something much greater than just the music as it led me through the phases of Delia's life, revealing her emotional and musical moods. It became clear to me that religion and life events had a considerable influence on her work. Her presence was inherent in the music she created.

What happens in the past doesn't stay there, as I know and Margery knew with the burden of her secret sin. The same was true for Delia, especially with regard to her Catholic upbringing and family dynamics, which all had an effect on her musical compositions. For reasons known only to Delia, she carried guilt over her younger sister's death. In 1943, when Delia was six, her four-year-old sister Benita developed acute appendicitis that progressed into agonising peritonitis. It was before the creation of the National Health Service so any visits to doctors and hospitals had to be given due consideration, and this may have delayed a diagnosis that could have prevented her death. Delia must have witnessed her sister's pain and felt helpless. Benita was whisked away and confined in the austere surroundings of the local municipal hospital, a former workhouse. The war was still going on and the hospital was treating casualties, so visiting was discouraged. Delia never saw Benita again. Separation anxiety must have been extreme for her, Benita and their parents. They'd survived so many times huddled together comforting each other during dangerous circumstances in the war, only for Benita to be lost to an arbitrary illness and disappear from Delia's life. She died in hospital on 27 October.

Delia attended Benita's Catholic funeral service, which would have been an overwhelmingly emotional experience for her, her sadness intensified by seeing the tiny coffin being carried to the altar accompanied by the heavenly harmonics of the choirs. I was told that Delia's relationship with her father was never the same afterwards; that he became distant and rather cold towards her, leaving her feeling like she was a poor substitute for her sister. His emotional detachment from Delia likely contributed to her lifelong problems with socialising – not always feeling quite 'right' or 'enough' as herself and sometimes 'over-acting' to compensate as a means of getting through what at times could be an ordeal. I can understand why, having witnessed her parents' grief over the unbearable loss of their child and suffered herself, she made the decision not to have children. The only children she referred to were the musical works she created for other people that she had to part with after all the love she'd poured into and felt for them – another separation.

'Memento Mori' was the first piece of the film music I worked on for Caroline. It was for the attic scene of Delia's hoard of relics – all the boxes of tapes and keepsakes discovered after her death. The script gave the impression of the attic being a very personal and sacred space, which led me to think of basing the music for it on something reverential. Delia's composition *Amor Dei* came to mind and I started reflecting further on the influence religion had on her music. Regular church attendance, communion, all such rituals feeding the importance of a higher (male) power and of an exemplary female to emulate, the Virgin Mary, alongside other female saints. Women to look up to, the drip-feeding of what she should aim to be, the unattainable 'perfect' woman.

There was a scene in the 'Delia' script that included saints' cards. I remembered them well from my second visit to the archive. They were tucked away among Delia's schoolbooks, enclosed in their own special small envelope. Something about them gave me a feeling they had been of particular personal significance to Delia. I handled them with great care as I took them out of the envelope and placed them on the desk in rows. A set of twelve 'Our Lady of the Flowers' picture cards, given to Delia as a child by female relatives, each inscribed on the back with love and saved by Delia as precious mementos. The cards were in pristine condition, not bent or scuffed at the edges, only a few marks from where Delia had handled them. Coloured in gentle pastels and illustrated in the style of a children's book, each card depicted a different Marian symbolic flower, linked to the scenes of the infant Jesus and his mother Mary carrying out her maternal and domestic duties, helped by a young girl angel. It wasn't a big leap for me and possibly Delia to look at the angel as her sister Benita. What could be more comforting for Delia than to think Benita had gone to a heavenly place as an angel at the side of Mary and Christ? After all, that's what some people like to say to children, that the dead have gone to be with the angels. I imagined Delia sitting with the cards, laying them out in front of her, arranging and rearranging, as there seemed to be no set order, and like me 'reading' the scenes, using the visual symbolism and projecting herself into them – seeing Benita as the angel helping Mary, and herself as the second sister angel at Benita's side in another scene, cuddled together singing a lullaby to the sleeping infant Jesus.

My fantasy about what the cards may have meant to Delia didn't seem so far-fetched after I looked deeper into them. Individually and as a group they were connected to her in meaningful ways through the many references to flowers, the Virgin Mary and Benita's namesake, the thirteenth-century St Benita Zita. They were all purposely centred on the image of women as dutiful, virtuous, doting mothers. Mary as a mother had duties of washing, sewing and childcare, all the tasks St Benita would have carried out as a pious household servant. The promised reward for living such an obedient, devoted life would be the keys to heaven – as shown in the card for 'Our Lady's Bunch of Keys', with Jesus first in line and Mary, keys poised, stepping up to unlock the door. On an earthly level, keys were a token of the trust employers placed in their servants, so losing them would be a serious, even life-changing matter. Keys had importance to wives too.

I thought of Margery losing her keys during a psychotic episode and being overjoyed at having them returned to her. There was a cult of St Benita in Lynn; she was very well known to Margery and revered by medieval servants. But in terms of religious significance, losing keys meant the loss of entry to heaven, and people prayed to St Benita to provide protection and guidance if keys went missing. St Benita is still celebrated each year, with flowers representing her miracle of the leftover bread she smuggled from her employer to feed the poor, turning it into flowers when caught red-handed. Delia would have been familiar with the symbolism of the flowers and would have known St Benita as the patron saint of servants, flowers and keys.

The card 'May' seemed the odd one out. It depicted a flower I couldn't easily recognise – possibly a mayflower symbolising spring.

Or it had some other reason for being part of the set. Not being religious and knowing little of Catholicism, I discovered that it's the month when Catholics worldwide celebrate Mary with flowers – and also the month Delia was born. I then found out that for the ancient Greeks the month of May was dedicated to the goddess Artemis, from whom Delia's name derives. In combination the cards' gentle, playful, pretty presentation delivered a strong message of expectation for such a young girl, with hopefully the benefit of some comfort. Delia's faith helped to assuage some of her childhood distress and fears. But her father's was sorely tested. He'd had a work accident that left him with a permanently injured leg, and he remained very bitter about it. Then, when his youngest daughter died, he was left wondering why, when he'd been such a good Catholic all his life, these things had happened to him. And how could an all-powerful God allow the almost complete destruction of Coventry's medieval cathedral? Were they all tests of his faith? From Delia's experience of being raised a Catholic, she knew of the pros and cons of faith. Religion could provide solace, structure and answers to life's problems, but it was also authoritative, intolerant, demanding and repressive, especially for women. She had much to draw on for her musical project on God.

Amor Dei: A Vision of God was composed in 1964 for the second of Barry Bermange's four *Inventions for Radio* and is one of Delia's most loved 'heavenly' works. Bermange had recorded the voices of people who believed in God and those who didn't as they attempted to articulate their thoughts about faith and divinity. The challenge for Delia differed from her usual commissions and from her work for the first programme in the series, *The Dreams*. Bermange instructed her on the kind of music he wanted, and importantly what he didn't want – no electronically derived sounds, only sounds created from voices – going on to describe the music he envisaged as an image: a Gothic altarpiece. When Delia asked exactly what he meant, he asked her for a pencil and paper and carefully drew tiers of elongated panels of the kind usually painted with religious figures, all with pointed tops, giving the impression of rows of triangular sound waves. He wanted to conjure up an image from sound, like a painting featuring believers in God, with non-believers lurking in the background. That resonated with Delia, who often saw sounds as pictures, and the subject held further meaning to her as a (by then) lapsed Catholic.

Her religious upbringing certainly helped inspire her. On the first day of working on the track she selected her sole source material for the score, a library recording of *Rorate Caeli* sung by a boy chorister, John Hahessy. A well-known Christian liturgy very suitable for an altarpiece, Gothic or otherwise. A 'religious sound' of exceptional vocal purity was in perfect harmony with the subject matter. Delia's pages of notes and manuscript scores with logarithmic workings on organising and transforming sounds by mathematical calculations and varying methods of cutting tape show the complexity and catholic approach she took, citing the intensity-scale technique used by Stockhausen of '6 values, 6 db differences between each' and other processes she'd employ:

> Take 'rorate', make detailed analysis (serial, statistic and linguistic), rebuild a fragmented variation – serially organised fragments of voice . . . Find best techniques for cutting fragments: normal cut, switched, scanned, long cut, spaced fade up, etc . . . Very very fast at first in short groups, then in breathtakingly long complex dramatic sections.

She spent weeks extracting syllables, removing consonants, filtering, compiling numerous layers of differing tones, pitches and clusters of sounds and creating sustained chords that her old friend Jonathan Harvey described as having a 'breathing' quality. (He recalled that it had in part inspired his 1966 work *Symphony*.) The rearranged vocal fragments retained their religious feel and seemed to echo the fragmented vocal descriptions of the people and their views. Delia went deep with her analysis in relation to accommodating the four sections of the programme:

Arrange sections so that they jump from point to point in this complexity row, in an enlightening way, but perhaps with more emphasis on the denouncement direction.

She wanted to give voice to the opposing views, and this made me wonder if her idea of placing more emphasis on 'denouncement' was a reference to her lost faith, inserting herself and her view about God into the piece. When the voices are cut up to create a dialogue between the different opinions the music shifts to slightly discordant angelic voices, as if undecided and upset by the conversation. There are more descending bass tones and a suggestion of 'wrongness' and disapproval when the denouncers speak of belief in God as mere superstition, ridiculous, irrelevant to anything imaginable, saying that people are just atoms, that religion is a ritual used to avoid personal responsibility and praying is like talking on the telephone with no one on the other end. Those with absolute faith in God get the last word, asserting that it's natural, that you can't be successful in life without belief in God, that religion offers comfort and structure, with heaven the reward for being good, and that those who sin must be punished. And, quite shockingly for me as a non-believer and 'sinner', that people like me are miserable and unhappy and might as well be dead. A bit harsh and certainly not my experience. For those who believe,

God is everywhere, all-seeing, and religion plays an important role in their lives, influencing what they do and how they live – as it did for Margery. The *Vision of God* programme illustrated how important faith was and also how denouncing God was regarded, that non-belief seemed to be against the general view in Delia's time, but nowhere near as much as it was in Margery's.

17

I'd been reading about Margery's pilgrimage to Jerusalem while I was referencing Delia's favourite and most hauntingly beautiful work, 'Blue Veils and Golden Sands', as inspiration for a part of the film script where Delia is in a heightened state of mind, striding along the BBC corridor en route to the RW studio. I thought of Delia's own life mission as being a pilgrimage of sorts, and her atmospheric music for the inhospitable terrain and extraordinary journeyings of the Tuareg tribe across the Sahara desert brought to mind Margery's less than idyllic crossing of the Judean desert on her long journey to the Holy Land.

'Blue Veils and Golden Sands' was commissioned in 1967 for *The Last Caravans*, a documentary on the Tuareg tribe, as part of the BBC TV series *The World about Us*. Delia used one of her favourite sound sources, the green Coolicon lampshade from which she created and recorded ringing tones, modified in various ways to produce a multitude of very effective frequencies. From a gong-like tone of the lampshade she extracted particular elements, passing them through filters to suggest the whooshing sound used for the camels moving slowly along. She referred back to the tones and frequencies and used them time and again. Delia's voice played a role too as another kind of 'instrument', not in the conventional way, but as a source for the smallest of frequencies, perfectly suited to what she wanted to imbue in her music. She was creating an ambient landscape of otherworldly sound – a mirage and the shimmering heat haze of the desert. Delia sat in front of the film viewing desk, her eyes glued to the screen, and watched the camels moving along, counting their feet to formulate a rhythm. She worked with a metronome, following the tempo of the camels with one hand and marking the beat in sync by tapping her foot, clad in a shiny patent leather slingback kitten heel. The tempo had a swing – maybe one camel had a bit of a limp – but it was most likely intentional, although there was always an imperceptible lag between hearing the metronomic 'click' and marking the time. There was no quantising to give precision to the rhythm then, which for me is a good thing as you get a nice off-beat that adds the subtlest amount of movement. Most people would have accessed the BBC sound effects library for a suitable 'camel hoof' sound, but not Delia. She recorded one note of her own voice as the sound source for the rhythm of their hooves. Another note, a sustained 'aaaah', she then pitched, spliced, filtered and added reverb to, making it sound like an Eastern wind instrument – or, as she called it, a 'castrated oboe' – perfectly evoking the peaceful isolation of the sand dunes.

So the camels rode off into the sunset with my voice in their hooves and a green lampshade on their backs . . .

I wondered, with Delia's love of medieval music, what soundtrack she would have created for Margery and the pilgrim group plodding along on foot and donkey. They wouldn't have been in step like the Tuareg's camels, so there'd be no obvious source of rhythm to work from. I could picture Delia with all her knowledge of medieval instruments and time signatures weaving her magic spell, creating futuristic mutations of the sounds that would have been familiar to Margery.

I looked into what overseas pilgrimage entailed for Margery and was astounded by the scale of the task she'd set herself – even with the advantage of the guidebooks and established pilgrim routes organised by Franciscans, who had worked out the safest roads to the shrines, providing accommodation and even guided tours, like a very early 'package holyday'. Pilgrimages were pretty big business. They not only met the needs of pilgrims but provided income for lay people and the Church, who supplied the travellers with food and other necessities, as well as relics and pardons to help avoid purgatory and speed up their passage to heaven.

Pilgrim badges were very popular, mass-produced and sold in their thousands. Travellers would pin them on their coats to show they were on a holy journey of penance, a souvenir depicting a shape or image specific to each shrine, and keep wearing them afterwards to prove they'd completed the pilgrimage. Not unlike people today buying merchandise from their favourite bands or gigs they've been to. There were even 'bootleg' versions, but anyone who got found out making these was severely punished. There was a saying: 'Go a pilgrim, return a whore.' Some women had to turn to prostitution while away due to lack of money, and less dedicated pilgrims took the opportunity to play the field and generally let their hair down. As far as lust was concerned, Margery didn't have to rely on her own willpower to stay on the straight and narrow. Many churches en route displayed images of enlarged male and female genitalia, perhaps to ward off evil and remind pilgrims that succumbing to lust would lead them in time to hell – or, as others suggest and I believe more, the figurative carvings may be pagan symbols of fertility like Sheela-na-gigs. Alternative pilgrim badges could be bought, erotic ones that, depending on a person's point of view, were either a warning against or a celebration of lust – like a pilgrim figure with a body in the shape of a vulva holding a rosary in one hand and a staff topped with a cock and balls in the other. Others were of couples fucking or human–beast hybrids displaying oversized genitalia with claws, wings and serpent-like ornamentation – or a large vulva being carried aloft by a team of tiny penises. I'd quite happily pin any of those badges to my clothes without the slightest thought of sin or damnation crossing my mind.

Considering how often Margery faced abuse and persecution for daring to be different and refusing to disavow her individuality, it's not surprising that her anecdotes focus more on herself than on the conditions and practicalities of her complicated journeys. Also it wasn't seemly for pilgrims to brag about all the fabulous sight-seeing they did and the great time they had. Their focus should be on contemplation only, the job at hand. Anything else was deemed sinful self-indulgence. But Margery's travel experiences must have exceeded her expectations on every front, good and bad. I was particularly curious to know what it would have been like for her before and during her six weeks or more on board the galley ship from Venice to Jaffa, to get some idea of what could have landed her in the predicaments she found herself in, why she was treated so badly, bullied by the pilgrims she travelled with. Yes, her weeping and praying were a problem for many people, but she didn't seem like a nasty person. Perhaps they just didn't want to be associated with her, in case her sullied reputation rubbed off on them. Before Margery set off for Jerusalem, one of the first things she did was to have the parish priest of Lynn ask for anyone owed money by her or her husband to come forward. She paid them back in full, fulfilling her promise to John by paying off his debts. Settling your affairs was mandatory to get permission to travel – as was making a will, because many pilgrims didn't survive the journey.

Margery cleared things up in readiness for the next phase of her life. Her priest-confessor, Robert Springolde, bade her a safe journey. She said her goodbyes and started the sixty-mile trek to Great Yarmouth, making offerings at Norwich Cathedral and Yarmouth Minster before boarding the ship for the short crossing to Zeeland in the Netherlands. She and her maidservant had joined a small group of mainly male pilgrims, which was normal for safety reasons, and more so for women pilgrims, who were unusual but not totally unheard of. Margery had a priest from the group as her very own spiritual confessor – which I think was convenient for her. She could consult with him about her prayers and what instructions she 'heard' from God. The priest could then give his approval when her penitent actions needed adjustment to suit the conditions of the journey. She'd been fasting, but once she left England she got 'word' in her prayers that she should now cease abstaining and return to eating meat and drinking wine. Fasting wouldn't have been a good idea on such a long journey, she'd need all the nutrition she could get – that is, unless the meat had gone bad. When it did, she abstained again, annoying everyone in her group by being so contrary as well as sanctimonious.

It wasn't long before her crying and droning on about God drove people crazy. They wanted an easy ride to Jerusalem, and Margery was spoiling it for them with her outbursts and reprimands about their lack of piety. Some were making hay while the sun shone, indulging themselves, sinning while they could because no matter what sins they amassed, they'd all be forgiven in Jerusalem. Until then they fully intended to enjoy themselves. They ganged up against Margery, calling her all the insulting names under the sun, going as far as saying they wished she'd just drop dead to put paid

155

to her nagging once and for all. She was thrown out of the group, robbed of her money and told to make her own way to Jerusalem. Her maidservant deserted her, staying with the group and leaving Margery alone and vulnerable. She begged them to let her tag along for safety as far as Constance in Germany. They relented, on condition she stayed absolutely quiet. Then they amused themselves at her expense, cutting her dress to an indecently short length and tying a coarse white apron round her to make her look like a fool for people to sneer at. The humiliation added to her suffering and tested her faith. It was demoralising, being bullied day after day after day and made to sit away from everyone at the end of the dinner table, not daring to say a word in case the tirade of abuse started up again.

When they finally reached Constance, Margery went straight to an English friar and told him everything that had happened to her. The group was staying at the friary before the next leg of their journey, to Bologna in Italy. As they all gathered for dinner Margery obediently took her designated place in silence. Her tormentors began criticising her and told the friar that they'd be leaving her behind. He was disgusted by what they said, spoke up for Margery and took back the money they'd stolen from her – what was left of it. At least she had that to help her.

Margery wasn't going to give up, even though she was now abandoned in a strange country where she didn't speak the language. She set off on her own, with no map, not knowing how or if she'd get there. As she sat by the side of the muddy road, at a loss for what to do or which way to go, a strange old man came along and introduced himself as William Weaver, offering to walk with her as her paid guide. The two of them travelling together were less likely to be attacked. It was a risk she had to take. What else could she do? Wait to be robbed, raped or killed? The possibility of being raped and surviving worried her most. It would undo all the hard work she'd gone through to stay chaste. To her mind, William was a 'godsend'.

As it turned out, the journey wasn't too bad. She met kind, hospitable people along the way and arrived in Bologna ahead of the rotten mob who'd rejected her. They were so impressed, probably expecting her to have got lost or worse, that they invited her back into the group – on condition she chilled out, joined in the mealtime fun and didn't jabber on about the gospels or behave outrageously. She sensibly agreed and they set off together, eventually arriving in Venice. There Margery left the group and went to stay at a convent, where she could weep and pray to her heart's content, making up for lost time and opportunities. There was plenty of time to indulge herself. She and other pilgrims were held up in Venice for thirteen weeks waiting for a suitable ship and good weather. For six of those weeks Margery was gravely ill, probably with one of the many sicknesses that spread among the pilgrims en route. The nuns nursed her. But not one person from her 'Christian' pilgrim group looked after her. She recovered without their help, still ostracised.

I'd call it some kind of a miracle that Margery had got as far as Venice. She was forty years old, had been seriously ill and had to put up with some horrendous treatment from people who should and could have behaved better towards her considering she was possibly pregnant. The voyage from Venice to Jaffa across the Mediterranean Sea was a more frightening test of endurance. There was no means of predicting storms at sea, and travellers faced the prospect of their ship sinking, with the loss of everyone on board. Even if they survived the trip, it was fraught with danger, from food poisoning and seasickness to the diseases and parasites that could be caught from fleas, rats, mice and fellow

157

travellers – including typhus, dysentery and plague. Those who died (unless they were rich) were wrapped in cloth, weighted and unceremoniously dumped overboard. Other hazards came from drunken behaviour, violent arguments, knife fights and the constant threat from pirates who knew the galleys carried valuable cargo and pilgrims – whom they saw as easy prey, their possessions a lucrative booty. It wasn't unusual for pilgrims to be killed. By law each galley had to carry guns and armed men in case of marauders.

The Venetian galleys, used by merchants (or for war when needed), were over fifty metres long, powered by oars and sails, and could carry as many as 350 people. Some were essential crew – captain, oarsmen, a cook and gunners – while the passengers included up to 170 pilgrims, merchants, priests and monks. Margery was familiar with her father's and husband's ships, but the galleys offered a different and rather extraordinary experience that turned out to be worse than the rough journey she'd had so far. It must have been daunting for Margery, even though there was a well-established system in place because of the sheer number of pilgrims sailing from the port. The Venetian authorities tried to ensure reasonable conditions on board, but once out at sea fresh water and food soon went bad, so pilgrims were advised to take their own provisions as well as their own cooking and eating utensils, clothing chest, bedding and mattress. It wasn't a cheap trip; you needed money as well as guts. Margery had both. When a ship finally became available and the weather was favourable, Margery was left to fend for herself as she booked her passage and all she needed for the journey. She bought herself and her disloyal maidservant beds in the 'cabin' of the galley, a huge open space that ran the length of the ship. She boarded the ship with all her belongings and entered the 'cabin' to see the beds lined up side by side, only a foot apart. She shuffled along until she saw her name marked in chalk. Setting the bedding down, she had her trunk of belongings placed in the centre alongside all the others, each one locked to deter thieves. The space was cramped enough with the merchandise, beds and trunks, but once everyone else turned up the cabin quickly got uncomfortably hot and stuffy.

With so many people cooped up together it wasn't a healthy space to spend any time in or even get much sleep, with drunken arguments going on and the rats and mice scurrying over everyone and getting at any accessible food. People's personal hygiene deteriorated and the travellers were constantly woken by the itching of lice and flea bites. There was the stench of ripe body odour, shit, farts, piss and vomit, and the high chance of stepping in and over-turning someone's full chamber pot and having to walk through the filth that covered the floor. It was hardly a comfortable cruise across the sea, but then a pilgrimage is all about penance, self-imposed suffering, so the terrible conditions, although extreme, could be said to have been an appropriate ordeal for Margery.

Noise on board ship was another source of nuisance and a con-tributing factor in conflicts that broke out between passengers. It was constant. Not just people snoring or chattering at all hours of the day and night but the creaking of the wooden boat when it was buffeted by the stormy sea, setting people off praying or cry-ing, scared that the boat would break apart and they'd die. They were helpless, at the mercy of the elements (and God), tossed around on the open black mass of sea, penned in a wooden box that could easily serve as their communal coffin if things went ter-ribly wrong. There was also the blast of trumpets used for various reasons – at daybreak and sunset, twice a day for mealtimes, when everyone would rush to get the best seats, then again at the end of the meal, and when departing or docking at ports for fresh water and food. Live animals were kept on the upper deck, the hooves of horses and donkeys used for transport clacking as they tried to stay steady when the boat rocked. In the pens next to the kitchen pigs, poultry, sheep and cows made themselves heard, also scared by the movement of the boat, then screeching in fear and agony when they were slaughtered by the ship's cook.

The noises were all the more noticeable because there was such a lot of free time to kill. To distract themselves from the perilous sea and relieve the monotony, the passengers below deck would lighten the mood, creating a party atmosphere as best they could with games of catching vermin, dancing, singing sailors' songs, playing lutes, bagpipes, drums and violins, with a lot of lecherous behaviour, swearing and blaspheming thrown into the mix. The very thing Margery couldn't tolerate. I suspect that while Margery found the behaviour of others inconsiderate, they found some of her ways just as irritating. People from diverse social and cultural backgrounds living cheek by jowl with others they'd never met before – and who had differing standards of what was acceptable – meant annoyances were intensified, with quarrels often breaking out, some ending in violence. Even queuing for the communal toilet on the upper deck could cause fights, especially if you had dysentery and had to get to it fast. The galley ship Margery was on was like a medieval version of a TV reality show like *Big Brother* or *I'm a Celebrity . . . Get Me Out of Here!* They illustrate what a powder-keg situation it is to confine people in restrictive spaces under oppressive conditions. It tries people's patience, characters are assessed and judgements made, and things soon start to break down between groups, with individuals becoming scapegoats. Like Margery was.

Being from a busy port with lots of foreign visitors, Margery was used to diversity, but there were no separate spaces she could go to for her contemplation. The ambience of the galley was pandemonium. A claustrophobic environment that showed up those who were different and didn't want to play a part in the goings-on. Margery stood out a mile, not only as one of the few women on board but because of her piety and strange behaviour. Imagine you're having a good time and someone across the room is watching stern-faced, telling you off, praying and weeping loudly enough to be heard above the general boisterousness, disrupting the atmosphere, rebuking everyone for being so outrageously heathen. She was seen as a holier-than-thou, uncompromising spoilsport. So it's maybe not so surprising that Margery was picked on and told to shut the fuck up. Having said that, the abominable bullying from her group had never abated, going beyond verbal abuse to stealing her food and money. Even her priest-confessor stole her bedding. When the galley finally docked at Jaffa, Margery apologised if she'd upset them in any way. A very charitable parting gesture, until she added a masked warning by saying she hoped God could forgive them for what they'd put her through. As if the conditions hadn't been enough to deal with, her fellow pilgrims had added to her suffering – which Margery took as part and parcel of her penance, as God's will.

Franciscan monks ran the hostels in Ramlah, where Margery and many other pilgrims stayed. The final leg of the journey to the Holy Land was made from there by donkey. Margery had given up asking for permission to travel with the group and just tagged along with them, regardless of their catcalling. To see Jerusalem was the highlight of her trip, and when she finally caught sight of it from Mount Joy she was so ecstatic she fell off her donkey and had to be helped back on.

In Jerusalem Margery and other pilgrims were given a guided tour of the most important holy sites by the monks. When you whip people up about how magical things like relics are, then they're going to want to get to them before anyone else. People would rush forward at shrines, pushing and barging others out of the way to make sure they got the best position. Building up people's hopes and expectations can lead to sensory overload, resulting in displays of uninhibited theatrics akin to the euphoria or hysteria some music fans experience at live gigs. When Margery got to Mount Calvary, where Jesus was crucified, she broke down, collapsed on the floor in tears. She had a horrific 'vision' of him with his crown of thorns, hanging on the cross by his 'blissful' hands and 'tender' feet, with blood flowing out from the wounds all over his mutilated body. At the Church of the Holy Sepulchre, the site of Christ's grave, she and the other pilgrims were locked in overnight to contemplate. That really lit the fires of her love of Christ, intensifying it so much she went into a state of rapture, overcome with emotion and writhing on the floor. The people around her were stunned by the jaw-dropping spectacle. Margery looked possessed, arms outstretched, her face contorting in expressions of agonising sadness, roaring at the top of her voice between cries of ecstasy as she mimicked Christ's pain. It was here that Margery claims to have received the 'gift of tears' ordained by God in her 'conversation' with him. That drove her onward.

The route to the River Jordan, where Jesus was baptised, and Mount Quarantine, the site of Christ's temptation by the devil, went across the desert, culminating in a very steep climb. It was a climate and landscape utterly unlike flat, boggy, cold Norfolk or anywhere else Margery had been. The blazing hot sun sapped every bit of energy out of her. She was thirsty but had no water left. Her feet felt like they were on fire. Her leather shoes didn't provide much protection from the scorching sand underfoot. Each step she took was painful and she reached a point where she couldn't carry on. She was dehydrated, starving hungry and physically worn out. There was no offer of help or water from her pilgrim 'friends'. They left her behind, slumped on the ground. She was fortunate, or, as she says, 'blessed by God', that the friars and local people were more 'Christian' towards her, even if she had to pay a passing man to carry her the rest of the way on his back. The indignity of clinging on for dear life up the steep hill was nothing compared to what she'd already put up with. Getting to the holy site was everything, and she'd do it, whatever it took.

Margery spent three weeks in Jerusalem taking in the different phases of Christ's suffering – his crucifixion, death, burial and resurrection – all the time praying, weeping and having mystical visions in which she saw and spoke with him and Mary. Jerusalem was the crowning glory. She was now washed of all sins, having completed the official process of pilgrimage. There were two additional bonuses: her weeping and wearing of white clothes were now legitimised.

Margery hadn't finished travelling the world quite yet. She was going to Rome, the second-holiest place after Jerusalem, obeying God's orders and following in St Bridget's footsteps. She still believed she was under God's protection, he'd 'told' her that, and yet it didn't seem to ease her fear of being sexually assaulted, which was very much a possibility in her precarious situation. On starting her solo trip to Assisi and Rome, Margery came across an old Irish hunchback beggar named Richard. Another 'godsend' like William Weaver, he also acted as her paid guide and protector, despite his concerns about being seen with her. He knew she'd been disowned by her pilgrim group, so he was happy when he could hand her over to the care of two Franciscan friars and a woman they'd met on their way to Assisi. In exchange for Margery praying for them, they provided her with food, drink and lodging. It was an arrangement that suited everyone. Richard could beg by day and all he had to do was check in on Margery at night and first thing in the morning. Assisi was the home of the Franciscans, so when they reached there Margery and Richard needed to find others to accompany them to Rome.

On 1 August 1414 Margery and other pilgrims were at the Church of St Francis for the Lammas Day indulgence. Among them was a lady whom Margery calls Margaret Florentine, who happened to be on her way to Rome to purchase further plenary indulgences. Richard, with his well-honed beggar ways, focused his pleas on the protection of Margery's honour as a holy woman who had just returned from her pilgrimage to Jerusalem. He succeeded in getting Margaret to agree to Margery and him joining their rather splendid entourage. They must have cut quite a picture, with Margery in her long, dowdy, baggy pilgrim smock, hooded cape and broad-brimmed hat, Richard the ragged beggar, and the colourful, lavishly dressed Margaret, other gentlewomen, servants and horses – all in procession, escorted by numerous knights ready to defend them against anyone who dared attack. Margery must have felt safer than ever.

The Pope's plenary indulgence was the main reason for pilgrims to go to Rome. In exchange for confessing all their sins before a priest, they were given full absolution, free from future punishment in purgatory. As well as being cleared of past unholy deeds they were able to attend all manner of devotional activities, religious festivals and spectacular processions. All irresistible opportunities for pilgrims, and for the tourist businesses built around them. The city was brimming with gloriously decorated churches, shrines and relics of apostles, saints and martyrs. There were guidebooks listing the Stations of Rome, the holy places for pilgrims to visit, with gory details about the horrors of torture inflicted on various saints – not forgetting Christ. Pilgrims were spoilt for choice – there was even the enshrined relic of Christ's foreskin on offer for those worshippers so inclined. Margery had got to Rome in late August 1414, a time of political unrest. Pope John XXIII wasn't in residence due to the Papal Schism. He and two other candidates were vying for the papacy, and the Council of Constance was due to start in a few months to finally sort things out. Preparations were already under way for this huge event when Margery passed through Constance on her journey to Jerusalem. Thousands of people were flooding into the city, with over a thousand musicians and 1,500 prostitutes employed to 'entertain' the high-ranking visitors and their retinues. The churches were extra busy with those seeking pardon for succumbing to carnal lust. It's said that hundreds of men died through various overindulgences, some falling into Lake Constance, presumably while drunk – or maybe foul play was involved, with such an abundance of rich pickings up for grabs.

On their arrival in Rome Margery and Richard thanked Margaret for her help and went to the hostel for English pilgrims, the Hospital of St Thomas of Canterbury. Who should be there when she walked through the door but her old band of bullies. Yet again they were taken aback and confused at how she'd made it there alive with just a beggar for company. Some of them thought it was nothing short of miraculous, but others suspected there was some devilry at work. None of them would have dreamed that she'd actually travelled under the protection of an esteemed lady – let alone guarded by knights.

And than sche went and ordeynd hir white clothys and was clad al in white liche as sche was comawndyd for to do yerys beforn in hir sowle be revelacyon, and now it was fulfilt in effect. [And then she went and arranged white clothes for herself and was clothed in white, as she had been commanded to do years before by revelation in her soul, and now it had been achieved.]

Rome was where Margery put into action all the things God had commanded her to do. Encouraged by the friars, she wasted no time in buying and wearing white clothes. On 9 November, St Lateran's Day, at Santi Apostoli Church, she entered into a 'mystical marriage' with the Godhead in a ritual she must have had in mind years before back in England, where she'd had a ring made in preparation, engraved with the words *Jhesus est amor meus* ('Jesus is my love'). She'd carried it with her, tied to the strings of the purse that she hung round her neck and hid beneath her clothes for safe keeping. There was nothing ethereal about the vows of the 'wedding ceremony', they were very traditional – the same as she'd taken when marrying John. But the congregation and witnesses were celestial, made up of Christ, the Holy Ghost, the Virgin Mary, the Apostles, angels and saints, including two of her favourites, St Katharine and St Margaret. Her senses were super-heightened in her 'spiritual' state. She experienced intense physical sensations of sweet smells, heard melodic sounds that drowned out everything else and saw bright white, delicate, fire-fly-like organisms flying all around her. The apparitional ceremony had lit the fire of love in her. Mystical marriage signified the highest union with God – and Margery was aiming high.

Dowtyr, I wil han the weddyd to my Godhede, for I schal schewyn the my prevyteys and my cownselys, for thu schalt wonyn wyth me wythowtyn ende. [Daughter, I will have you married to my Godhead, because I will show you my secrets and my schemes, for you shall dwell with me without end.]

In theory she would be privy to and speak authoritatively about God's intentions and 'live' with him forever. She didn't need an intermediary, she had established a direct private line to God – in her own mind.

Everything seemed to be falling into place for Margery. She must have felt closer to her complete self than ever before, especially as by staying at St Thomas of Canterbury Hospital she was able to take regular confession in English and respond to her urges to enact her 'gift of tears' without fear, criticism or inhibition. Her violent sobbing and ululations weren't a problem for the friars, and neither was her white clothing. They accepted her demonstrative displays of piety as a sign that she had been blessed by God.

Her old pilgrim pals, including the priest who stole her bedding on the galley, were still hostile towards her and soon picked up where they'd left off. They stalked her, turning up at the shrines she went to, heckling and denouncing her as a fraud. They badmouthed her to the friars at the hospital, with the priest being especially proactive in spreading vicious rumours of her being a heretic. He warned the friars that by sheltering her they were condoning her ungodly, improper actions, which was highly inadvisable in light of the ongoing efforts to get rid of heretics – a matter high on the agenda for the hundreds of high-ranking religious figures sitting on the upcoming Council of Constance. Margery was summarily thrown out onto the street. She was distraught, not only at being homeless in winter but at no longer having an English-speaking confessor.

Her faithful friend Richard found a highly regarded German priest called Wenslawe who was willing to vouch for Margery's sincerity and take her confession. Although he didn't speak English, Margery got by. Growing up in cosmopolitan Lynn, she had been used to communicating with her father's German-speaking business associates. The malicious priest took exception to Wenslawe helping Margery and his approval of her wearing white. Things got so heated between the two priests that Wenslawe told her to go back to her black clothing. She agreed, drawing further taunts in the street as to what had happened to her God-given white outfit. As an added precaution, he also gave Margery a job to do as a public show of contrition. For six weeks she became a servant, nursing and tending to the needs of a sick old pauper woman, fetching and carrying for her, living in squalor, sleeping on the filthy floor with no bedding, becoming riddled with body lice, her skin in a terrible mess from being bitten all over.

Then, in an act of total role reversal, Margery gave all her money away, putting herself in the dire position of having to beg and rely on the hospitality of friends. Being banished from the hospital had provided the opportunity for her to further align herself with St Bridget's life of charity and poverty – having already followed her in her marriage to Christ. The efforts by her enemies, the priest and the band of rogue pilgrims, to defame Margery had turned out to have the reverse effect – they'd led to her doing penance, which in turn brought her respect. One day Margaret Florentine saw her begging for food on the street. She was shocked by Margery's predicament, gave her food, wine and money and invited her to dinner every Sunday. That led to her meeting Margaret's high-ranking friends, dining with them on weekdays and being made godmother to one of their children. The friars' fears of offending the gentlewomen and men of Rome won Margery a place back at the hostel. Her humble good work and piety had at last gained her a favourable reputation in Rome, enough to have people ask her to pray for them and for an English priest to offer to accompany her and pay for her to travel back to England.

Margery had stayed in Rome longer than anywhere else she'd been on pilgrimage and she'd accumulated numerous indulgences that covered her for all manner of sins. Among the many sites she'd visited she'd made a point of seeking out those associated with St Bridget. She heard a sermon about Bridget's visions and life in the room where she had died in 1373. She called in on the saint's old maidservant to hear first-hand what Bridget was like, and was surprised to hear that she was meek, kind, polite, unpretentious and very cheerful – rather 'normal' really, compared to Margery herself and to what she'd expected of a saint.

It meant so much to Margery to finally see what she'd heard so much about. To be in the actual places where Christ and other saints had lived gave a physical dimension to her spirituality. A highlight and golden opportunity, given her focus on Christ's suffering, was that she got to experience the dramatic Passion Plays of his agonies on the cross, his burial and resurrection. She must have really felt in her element and indulged herself in unrestrained physical and vocal empathy as she took part in extravagant Easter processions, ceremonies and prayers. It's strange for me to think that someone's pain and poverty can be a cause for celebration on a scale that includes the wearing of the finest vestments, golden crosses, chalices and other extravagant, expensive 'holy' objects. Such excess seems totally at odds with religious teachings, a criticism levelled at the Catholic Church by many – including Margery. I can understand the beautiful painted altarpieces, the ringing of church bells and the glorious angelic voices of choirboys singing from church bell towers. I see those as jubilant gestures, expressions of love and respect. I'm sure Margery set aside her disapproval to bask blissfully in the fetishistic splendour.

Soon after Easter 1415, Margery said a tearful farewell to the friends she'd made in Rome and to her confessor, Wenslawe, whose belief in her had never wavered. On her return journey to England, she had to take a route that avoided France, where Henry V was preparing for another invasion as part of what's now known as the Hundred Years War. One of the knights who travelled with and fought alongside the king at that time was one of my paternal grandmother's ancestors, Sir John Pilkington. I have a mental image of a map showing Margery heading home to England and in the opposite direction one of my lineage making his way on horseback in full armour, en route to fight in the Battle of Agincourt. Margery and Sir John, two dedicated crusaders who could both lay claim to victories of a kind.

On reaching Middelburg in the Netherlands, Margery chose to wait until violent thunderstorms had passed before setting sail for home. Her unkind fellow pilgrims and the pesky priest, who had left Rome before her, took the first available ship, but she refused to travel with them and ended up hanging around for nearly a week, having to make do with a small boat that didn't look all that seaworthy. It was rickety and unlikely to hold up against rough seas, but as usual she said a few prayers for reassurance. Not long after setting off a storm broke out; rain was pelting down and the boat was tossed about by strong gales and huge waves. Margery prayed throughout the two days it took to reach Norwich, where Margery alighted and *fel down on hir knes kyssyng the grownde* – kissing terra firma in relief. She was penniless and exhausted but she'd survived.

Over the next few days in Norwich she visited friends including her old vicar Richard of Caister, who was pleased to see her again. That wasn't the case with the Dominican anchorite she'd once been so close to, who had heard all kinds of gossip about her, including that she'd conceived and given birth while she was away. Maybe the rumour grew from her having been pregnant when she left for Jerusalem. She doesn't provide a full explanation, just says that she brought the child home. But in his eyes Margery had lost her way, was no longer chaste, and he'd have no more to do with her. He would not give his permission for her to wear white: it was forbidden by God. Margery disagreed: she was following God's orders. Undeterred, she went in search of a priest who was more obliging, finding one who not only agreed to her wearing white clothing but paid for it to be made for her. On Trinity Sunday she received communion dressed head to toe in white, gown, hood, kirtle and cloak.

How people dressed was a big issue. Sumptuary laws dictated the wearing of specific items of clothing according to status, making everyone's social position immediately identifiable. Margery had defied the rules when she was younger by wearing fabrics and accessories strictly forbidden to her as a merchant's wife. She dressed to impress in extravagantly colourful clothes, displaying her wealth and social aspirations. She even had gold piping sewn onto her headdress – a feature the clergy cited as the 'gold'-standard sign for the sin of vanity. To her that was another example of the hypocrisy of churchmen who had such opulent vestments. Her disobedient streak was still intact. Wearing white was in total contrast to her earlier display, but she was still breaking secular and church laws. Her dress code smacked of her impersonating someone she wasn't, much as someone today might pretend to be a police officer or vicar by donning a uniform or dog collar.

Margery's husband met her in Norwich and took her back to Lynn. The physical effort of pilgrimage had taken its toll on her and she became so ill she was given the last rites. It made me think of all the touring I do for gigs and how exhausting long-distance travelling is. How when you finally get home and relax the exhaustion hits you and you get sick and collapse into bed. At least I get to be driven and flown from place to place, unlike Margery. She finally emerged from her sick bed, feeling 'saved' and fit enough to think seriously about another pilgrimage, this time to Santiago de Compostela in Spain. But when she went into town it soon became obvious that her unholy pilgrim compatriots had been spreading all kinds of scandalous stories about her and how she couldn't be trusted. Adorning herself in chaste white led to her being mocked and maligned as a hypocrite. She was sworn at, spat at, had water thrown over her in the street, and was shunned by many of her friends and clergy. It wasn't the joyous homecoming she'd anticipated. Margery was taken aback. Having returned from the Holy Land, she'd expected to be shown respect. More than that, she was now 'married' to the Godhead and had received the 'gift of tears' in Jerusalem's Holy Sepulchre. She felt assured of her holiness. But her 'gift' went down like a ton of bricks with the locals. They thought her howling like a dog was unseemly for a so-called holy woman; they said she must be mad, drunk, delusional, ill, evil or cursed. She writhed about so much on the floor, some people thought she must be possessed by the devil, as no other saints gifted with tears had conducted themselves that way. Her thrashing about was so violent that she was bruised black and blue. And as far as her 'visions' were concerned, they simply didn't believe her.

Margery carried on with her crying. Her tears were 'divine', legitimised by God, not just your regular penitent sobbing. There was nothing predictable about the bouts of weeping: they could come on at any time – once fourteen times in a day. Maybe that was a reference to the number fourteen's religious symbolism of salvation and deliverance, the fourteen generations leading up to the arrival of Jesus – or a sobbing session for each of her children, her own 'generations'. The number was also linked to certain saints she admired and took care to mention in her book. Around the time of the Black Death a group of fourteen saints had emerged known as the Holy Helpers, whom people prayed to as intercessors in times of disease and illness, including St Katharine, St Margaret and St Barbara. Interestingly, in numerology the number fourteen is associated with expressing personal freedom, self-determination and independence. A cap that fits Margery for sure, even if she may not have been aware of it. There was method in Margery's 'madness'. It was well thought out, calculated even.

As the volume of Margery's wailing escalated, she was banished to a small chapel within St Margaret's and visitors to the church were warned not to get annoyed or embarrassed by her acting so strangely. There was a new and intolerant friar in Lynn who thought she was either suffering from some sickness or a fraud, and he barred her from his sermons for years. Not only that, he wanted her out of the private chapel, well away from him. He thought she was contaminated. No doubt her face turning purple from screaming, dripping with sweat, and her screeches of 'I'm dying!' didn't help convince him that she was a good person to have any-where in the church, even if she did have the written permission of the Archbishop of Canterbury. But orders were orders. Margery was entitled to communion, and so eventually she was allowed back in the public part of St Margaret's – but never anywhere near the friar. She'd irritated him so much he criticised her when he preached, and if anyone complained about it on her behalf, he told them that they were evil like her. Yet despite the disapproval of locals, Church elders, anchorites, monks and her own confessor, Margery wasn't quite alone. Her husband John stood by her and there were some who believed in her and gave her money to pray for them, as well as one priest who took a risk and continued to read the Bible and other religious and spiritual works to her. Margery wasn't going to stop doing what she wanted.

There are so many elements that feed into making music and art. The inspiration doesn't come from nowhere, it comes from the realities of life and emotions, as well as mood, the environment and the subconscious. And then there are things that arrive like perfectly timed gifts, as if from the ether. As I was writing this section of the book, I broke off to talk with Caroline about an extra sound element for the 'Delia' film, 'a tone', she said. It was to thread throughout the film like ectoplasm, three elements together, and to have a subtle presence, 'something like the solfeggio frequency', otherwise known as the healing frequency. Unknown to Caroline, a note to myself to check out these frequencies had sat on my studio desk since the beginning of the year. Our discussion seemed to be the kind of happenstance that would have made Delia's heart flutter with joy, especially as it was her birthday, and because these particular frequencies were directly linked to some of my own experiments with vocal tones.

Back in 2003 I'd explored Mongolian overtone chanting, attending a 'healing voice' workshop, primarily to learn the technique for my music and art projects. At ten o'clock on a sunny but fresh June morning I arrived at a huge house in London. I registered with about thirty-five other people, after which we were directed to a large airy room with a Bukhara rug in the middle and a small table set with a lit candle. We all sat around the edge of the rug, waiting in awkward silence. A guy to my right had been twitching nervously and suddenly said, 'I'll be the one to break the silence.' No one seemed bothered, but he obviously was and prattled on about how he lived in Deptford and wasn't used to the prices of Hampstead. Everyone just shuffled and muttered, then the room returned to silence until our instructor entered. She was a large barefoot woman with hippy hair and a long flowing skirt. She lit some more candles and sat on a director's chair draped in tribal print fabric. She didn't speak for a while but bent her head as if meditating and absorbing the vibe in the room, which had many of us feeling a little perplexed and uncomfortable. Then she got up and went round each of us in turn, burning sage to cleanse us of all the negativity we'd brought with us. The sage stank to high heaven and I just waited for the feather-fanning she did to disperse it, thinking that she probably packed a fair punch, going by the way she waved that huge feather. Returning to her chair, she finally spoke, asking us to introduce ourselves in turn by sounding a hand bell, taking a deep breath, saying our name on the exhalation, taking another breath, then saying what had brought us there – and stating any issues we might want to address while we were there. Oh hell, I thought. That's permission to offload. Maybe I was in the wrong workshop.

I was willing to suspend my cynicism, but it was proving difficult within the first hour. I'd paid to learn the technique of overtone chanting, which is said to heal from within, so I knew it was a healing voice workshop, but it was threatening to turn into a therapy session. I hadn't really thought about what kind of people would be there but I soon found out. Some people grabbed the opportunity to unburden themselves, and I was sat willing them to ring the fucking bell and let the next person introduce themselves. It came to my turn. I sounded the bell, said, 'Cosey,' and that I was there to learn the technique of overtone chanting so I could use it for my work. Some people were there because they were asthmatic and thought the breathing exercises would help them, but some of the stories were sad. One woman said that she'd lost her singing voice after her son had attempted suicide and swiftly passed on the bell to the next woman. A tiny voice sounded and everyone leaned towards it to try and hear. Ah, a 'low talker', I thought . . . or maybe not. She clutched a huge rose quartz crystal in her hand. Our instructor asked her to say two words that would explain why she couldn't say her name or speak out loud in public. 'Anthropology and fine art!' she shouted. She explained that she'd never made choices in her life and now she had to choose anthropology at Oxford when she wanted to do art. Then she buried her face in a cushion and hid from us all. Up next was a guy in shorts with an eighties surfer hairdo who told us all how he'd been diagnosed with cancer and given five weeks to live, but he'd done a strict cleansing diet and was now completely cured. A miracle – but he still needed the 'healing voice'. Things really turned cringeworthy when a Canadian therapist uttered her name and burst out crying. 'I'm sorry, I was just so touched by the stories.' She set three others off sobbing – a psychic faith healer, a meditation teacher and an uptight schoolteacher.

Introductions over with, I expected to get on with things, but our instructor took a deep breath, then exhaled her name, to show she was 'one of us', I assumed. After that she said nothing, just stared into the eyes of the therapist. I thought it was embarrassingly clichéd and couldn't bear to watch so I closed my eyes. The meditation teacher suddenly broke the silence to tell us all that she woke up full of joy and love for her children, adding, 'But I don't get this, I have a hard time taking what is being said as real. Maybe it's me . . .' Our instructor just nodded. Then an opera singer spoke up about her scepticism. The atmosphere got more tense, until it was broken by a very nice girl who said she had done some chanting previously that had made her cat run away and she hadn't seen him since. Everyone laughed. Then a woman started weeping, then wailing. Some people closed their eyes as if in meditative sympathy, at which point the woman let rip with the most ear-piercing scream, sobbing her heart out. Our instructor charged towards her, thundering across the wooden floor barefoot, throwing her arms around her, vigorously rubbing her back and chest, inducing more heart-wrenching sobbing, until it gradually subsided.

We finally got down to the overtone chanting and were given a demonstration of the technique. It was incredible and very, very loud. Sounds spun round the room like horns and jaws harps, in addition to a bass tone. I was stunned and impressed. Our instructor started by explaining the use of vowel sounds and, rather confusingly, how to achieve the overtones – you must remember to forget what you're doing, which is difficult because you forget to remember to forget, and when you do, you've forgotten that you were supposed to remember to forget. What? But I understood. It was basically using the principles of meditation. Then came the technique of using our bodies like a musical wind instrument, breathing in deep and chanting as we exhaled all the air. In and out like bellows. We sat cross-legged on the floor for some considerable time chanting vowels. The harmonics were fantastic and very calming. We were shown the key to overtone chanting and the basics of using the tongue to manipulate the sounds to create different tones. And I did it. I felt such a sense of elation hearing both low and high tones. The harmonics from thirty-five people chanting together were powerful enough, but then when the ultra-high notes emerged they swirled around the room, seemingly hovering in the air, sounding like someone rubbing the rim of a crystal wine glass with their wet finger. It was an amazing experience. I wanted to do more tongue technique, but all hope was dashed when we were instructed to walk slowly around the room greeting and blessing one another while chanting '*Om Mani Padme Hum*'. In our instructor's wisdom, and as she said, 'to make it more fun', she'd set the chant to a tune like something you'd hear on a Disney ride. A lot of the group seemed to love it and were like happy clappers, swaying from side to side and chanting faster and faster, smiling inanely as if they'd been 'saved'. But a whole day of chanting had left me feeling at peace. I had the best night's sleep in years and I now knew how to produce those elusive overtones. Whatever else the workshop offered up, it was worth it for that moment of being bathed in those ethereal, hovering tones.

At least the loud wailing at the voice workshop was in a sympathetic context, unlike Margery's, which was seen as inappropriate and disruptive in church, taking the focus away from God and putting it on herself. Her screaming like a banshee really pissed a lot of people off. Some said it was just an act, all staged, that she was an attention-seeker. Going by Margery's descriptions of her public wailings, they were impossible for anyone present to ignore. They looked and sounded like she was having seizures, with her gasping, grimacing and thrashing about on the floor. She gave a very dramatic public display of seeking mercy. She couldn't help herself – even though she was wary of displaying her tears in public so frequently, she couldn't suppress them. They and her vocal outpourings would have had a consoling, healing effect on her, releasing endorphins and relieving her of the painful angst she felt.

After reading about Margery externalising her pain in penance through her voice I was reminded of my own vocal explorations, not only into the beautiful sounds that were possible but into the power of the voice to express the full range of emotions. The frequencies and tones that can be generated through chanting, singing or wailing are widely accepted to have healing qualities, to give a sense of wellbeing, as I'd discovered from the overtone chanting workshop. Not knowing about that, Margery wouldn't have realised just why she felt better for doing it. She thought it was all attributable to God. She also wouldn't have known about the 'stories' tears could tell, that their chemical structure varies depending on the reason for them. Artists and photographers like Rose-Lynn Fisher in her book *The Topography of Tears* have explored the theory and captured the beauty of teardrops using optical microscopes and microscopy cameras. How beautiful to think that Margery's story was encapsulated within each of her teardrops.

The effect of frequencies and tones was of great interest to Delia. She'd studied the human voice at school, learning all about how the nuances of the structure of the mouth made it possible for it to be used like an instrument, to shape sound. But she also had a very practical fascination with the effect of externally sourced frequencies.

While in London Delia had rented places close by the BBC's Maida Vale studios, within a short walk or bicycle ride. When she moved further away to Camden Town with David she'd often take the canal boat from Camden Lock. The boatman was a firm admirer and would announce to his other passengers that he was making an unscheduled stop to drop Delia off for work at the BBC. Before meeting David she'd lived alone. Her home had been hers. The place she had above the flower shop was a private space where she'd escape to at lunchtimes to play her precious spinet, a small harpsichord.

I got so addicted to the sound of the spinet and the way the high frequencies fill your mind, that I'd walk home at lunchtime and just play Bach and Bach and Bach. It was only a small room but you couldn't hear the telephone ring while playing the spinet because it totally absorbs the whole spectrum of the sound. Also it doesn't pass through walls or floors so nobody else can hear it.

Playing the spinet so manically was an outpouring that generated frequencies to displace the chaos in Delia's head and push the stress away. A way to clear her mind and soothe her emotions, to be uncontactable, to isolate herself and detach herself from the world and all who called on her. To re-energise herself. A kind of self-administered audio therapy – practising psychoacoustics for the benefit of her own health.

19

I've got an open attitude to sound . . . I was there in the Blitz and it's come to me relatively recently that my love for abstract sounds [came from] the air-raid sirens: that's a sound you hear and you don't know the source of as a young child . . . then the sound of the 'all clear' – that was electronic music.

Knowing how hugely effective tones and frequencies are, and how important the sounds of wartime sirens had been for Delia, I wanted the music I created for the scene of the Coventry Blitz to be a soundscape that captured the atmosphere. As far as possible from what I'd learnt about Delia's life – and from my childhood memories of playing in the ruins of bombed houses in Hull, when I'd imagine what had happened to the people who lived there I tried to put myself in Delia's place as a child in the war. She had many experiences of hearing war sirens, but the worst must have been on the night of 14 November 1940, when Coventry was all but razed to the ground.

That night people were going about their lives as usual. The adrenaline surge of fear must have been huge when the siren 'Air Raid Message Red' sounded unexpectedly at 7 p.m. Within minutes of it fading away and people having scrambled to safety in the shelters, the ominous low drone of the first group of a total of 450 German bomber planes and the thunderous roar of their engines was heard overhead, swiftly followed by the first of a staggering thirty thousand incendiary bombs being dropped to light the target areas for the next wave of planes. The medieval cathedral was hit within the hour, ending up burning out of control, as did over 240 other fires after the water mains were destroyed. Delia's family, like many others, had their own Morrison Table Shelter cage installed in their home. Her mother, father, Delia and ten-month-old Benita were huddled together, both girls too young to really understand what was happening but knowing all too well the feelings of utter terror generated by the noise of explosions, shattering glass, falling bricks and the hissing from burst water and gas pipes. All intensified by the screams of fear, pain and anguish of adults and children. As the attack continued the noise would have filled her head, painfully and terrifyingly loud, accompanied by the sound of her mother counting the seconds between the bombs. It became a lasting memory for Delia, wondering why her devout Catholic mother chose to count rather than pray.

The raid continued for eleven hours as the Luftwaffe flew across Coventry systematically from east to west and north to south, bent on wiping out the city, dropping 1,200 high-explosive bombs, 1,600 oil bombs and fifty land mines. All in all, five hundred tons of high explosive were dropped on Coventry. Finally at 6 a.m. the all-clear sirens signalled its end, sounding 'Raiders Passed' with a continuous two-minute tone followed by an eerie silence. People knew they could resurface safely from their shelters. None had expected what greeted them when they emerged that morning. The ordeal of the night's air raid was exacerbated by the traumatic sights of death and destruction. Their city was in ruins. It had been a freezing cold moonlit night when they'd scurried for refuge, but now there was no frosty nip in the air, only warmth from the still raging fires. And no sunlight, just the air dark and thick with ash and smoke, and the stench of burning flesh and burning oil. There were great craters in the roads, buildings still ablaze, bodies laid out, covered over and left to be removed after more than 1,200 living casualties had been tended to. Ambulances and fire engines were rushing back and forth with their bells ringing out, resounding in chaotic chorus. The sense of emergency was palpable as weeping and screaming people dug desperately in search of their loved ones buried under the debris.

Hitler had succeeded in his quest to create terror and devastation by bombing Coventry, destroying the factories and infrastructure of the medieval city as his revenge for the British attack on Munich, the home of the Nazi party, on 8 November. He'd also inspired a new verb for German propaganda that described total destruction – *coventrieren*, 'to Coventrate'. The effect on such a small city was immense. Ten days later a trench-like grave was dug for the first 172 of the 568 people who had been killed that night. Union flags were draped across it at intervals. A procession of mourners passed along, laying their wreaths close to where their loved ones were buried three deep. Nearly half the population of Coventry moved out, either because they felt so unsafe or simply because their homes and the amenities of Coventry had been so severely damaged.

Delia's family were among those who relocated. She, her mother and sister went to live in Preston with relatives, while her father stayed in the family home in Coventry, applying his skills as a sheet-metal worker to aircraft in aid of the war effort. Some of the eyewitness accounts are heartbreaking and harrowing, while also conveying the wartime bulldog spirit and humour that helped people survive the brutality of war. Life went on – it had to. Children went to school, and some of the factories producing war materials survived the raid sufficiently to operate as normal. Coventry was down but not out. But it was a very dark time, not only because of the bombing but also literally, because the mandatory blackouts meant no street lights, no light at all in the evenings. Windows had to be covered to eliminate any light that could give the German bombers a target. Soot was dropped on the canal to prevent the surface of the water from shining in moonlight. Life was lived around defence against the Germans and the effects of the air raids. Until the utilities could be repaired people had to use stirrup pumps for water because mains water was unsafe to drink, and mobile canteens were set up on the street.

The connections between the 1940 raid on Coventry and Delia's work are curious but somehow make sense in strange ways. Hitler had specifically chosen the date of 14 November because the full moon would provide good visibility. The campaign was named 'Operation Moonlight Sonata' after Beethoven's 'Moonlight' Sonata No. 14. Beethoven was one of Delia's favourite composers, his piano sonatas among those she liked the most. I thought about Delia sat at her piano innocently and lovingly playing the sonata, as I had in my piano lessons, both of us completely ignorant of its historical role in one of the most frightening moments of her life – and one that impacted directly on the music she went on to make. Beethoven was used by the BBC in a kind of counterpunch of resistance in the Second World War. They took the first three notes of his Fifth Symphony for their ident for European broadcasts, cleverly translating them into Morse code as three dots and a dash, which stood for the letter 'V' – for 'Victory', or possibly a two-fingered 'fuck off' salute. Delia's fascination with Morse code made me wonder what she would have thought of this dig at the Germans. I think she would have found it amusing. She applied Morse code to some of the subjects of her compositions, translating related information through various methods to connect the coded language to the subject matter and transform it into musical sounds.

Converting material related to the work into audio is something I do. Not using Morse code (as far as I can recall) but other 'languages', in different ways and for different reasons to Delia. For my 2012 piece *Bioschismic* I took the sounds of the chemotherapy treatment of my friend Xeni Jardin and images of the physical effect it had on her and processed them to create music that was fully expressive and rooted in her experience. The process is invisible and sometimes sounds end up buried, becoming subliminal but essential as an added element that gives a feeling of completeness to a piece, a layer that is inaudible to the ear but enhances and influences without affecting the overall sound. Hildur Guðnadóttir's Emmy and Grammy Award-winning soundtrack to the HBO series *Chernobyl* is an excellent example of the depth of connection that can be achieved through the use of the subject matter itself as audio source material. Almost all the sounds she used in her composition were sampled from the site of the Chernobyl nuclear power plant. It's this kind of open-mindedness about what constitutes music and what it can provide informationally, emotionally and physically, over and above what is heard, that is fundamental to my own musical output.

It would have been great to have been there when Delia first used the Radiophonic Workshop oscillators. Being reintroduced in such a different environment to the sound of those wartime sirens must have triggered some memories she may have felt were best forgotten, but which had a lasting positive effect in how they informed her attitude to music. The air-raid sirens of the Second World War were mechanical machines, so although they sounded like the tones made by an oscillator they were not electronic. Because a lot of the machines were hand-cranked the person operating them acted as the modulator of the sound, much like the user of the Wobbulator or the bank of oscillators Delia used in the workshop. Certain frequencies like those generated by the siren machines are audible for miles. When Chris and I first moved to Norfolk in the 1980s we experienced the sound of the local wartime siren that was still in operation to warn of floods. It was three miles from us in the next village but the sound was incredibly loud and disconcerting, stopping us in our tracks fearing flood waters, until our neighbour told us it was the annual test. (The sirens were later taken out of use, replaced by phone calls and texts, as we found out one evening while sat watching TV. All the phones in the house rang at once and text notifications pinged – the only thing missing was someone hammering on the door. The chorus of disparate calls was disorienting and it was difficult to identify where each different ring tone was coming from. We rushed around the house answering our mobiles and the five landline extensions. It was effective but in a different way to the frequencies of the sirens.)

The use of frequencies for signalling and creating emotional responses goes back thousands of years. The bullroarer, a long, thin, usually fish-shaped blade of wood, flint or other material that's whirled lasso-like on a cord above the head, was and still is used across continents. It emits a low frequency and an ominous siren-like buzz that can be modulated by varying the length of cord, the size and shape of the blade or the speed it's swung. In TG we used frequencies both audible and inaudible to induce particular effects and atmospheres. The track 'Hamburger Lady', with its unsettling, creepy rising and falling drone, and similarly the introduction for TG's live ICA gig signalled a warning, a sense of trepidation, that something was about to happen. The same sense of impending danger was generated by the wartime air-raid warning siren, in contrast to the relief of the continuous tone of the 'All Clear'. It just goes to show how a siren 'call' functions on an infrasonic level. Those 'buried' sounds I mentioned. What you hear affects you, but also those low frequencies you can't hear are at work evoking brain responses just like those generated by overtone chanting, or the strange feelings you get when a thunderstorm is brewing and the atmosphere seems to shrink. The euphoria, melancholy, angst or anticipation I've felt in the studio or at gigs is attributable to the complex interplay of the audible and inaudible musical elements as much as it is to the environment.

Delia's piece *Music of Spheres* undeniably shows the influence the wartime sirens had on her work. In 1970 she was set the challenge by the director John Glenister to realise music for a programme about the sixteenth-century astronomer Johannes Kepler, as part of a biographical TV series. It had to represent his theory of the Harmony of the Spheres, a celestial scale of music based on the harmonic relationship of the motion of the planets, using mathematical calculations. His linking of geometry to music seemed a good match with Delia, but Kepler had discarded the Pythagorean scale that was Delia's key companion when composing. His stepping away from an established scale, as well as referring to harmonies as earthly and celestial, not necessarily music per se, meant she could be free to structure her music as she wished. Her *Music of Spheres* doesn't appear to have any overtly mathematical structure, which seems out of place with Delia's disciplinarian ways and may be why she opted for something free of those constraints, a number of tones in harmony with each other, like Kepler's theory suggested. The only sounds she used were the noises we associate with sirens. Four or more tones at different frequencies, low to high, their intermodulation affecting each other. A choir akin to Kepler's celestial choir, both based on motion. How and why the sirens reappeared after so long as part of her interpretation of Kepler's concept probably didn't enter her mind. It was just the sound that seemed to fit so well, those psychoacoustics at work again.

What also interested me about Johannes Kepler, but in relation to Margery, was that he was writing his book *Harmonices Mundi* (1619) during the European witch-craze period. He had to ensure that his theory came across as godly, not based solely on man's numerical calculations – a workaround to avoid being seen as a heretic. But he got embroiled with the zealous witch hunters when charges were brought against his sixty-eight-year-old mother, a herbalist – an easy target, as anyone who mixed potions, especially an old woman, could be denounced as a witch and thrown in prison on trumped-up charges. Kepler acted as her defence for the trial, which lasted six years, with her imprisoned and chained to the floor for more than a year before he managed to get her released. Kepler's success was down to his disproving the accusations against his mother by careful dissection of their inconsistencies. It was a tactic that also proved useful for Margery in battling accusations of heresy, due in the main to her outpourings of reverberant emotional tones that were deemed irreverent and offensive.

20

I could relate to so many of Margery's struggles as a woman, but it was something about Delia that opened up a way into Margery's world and helped me understand her more. Delia found it advantageous to know the rules so she could work with and against them. That struck a chord with me about both Margery's actions and the writing of her book. Margery wrote that she '*was governd aftyr the rewelys of the Chirch*'. She had to know the Church's rules inside out because everything she did in her life was viewed through the lens of religion and judged accordingly. She was an expert on orthodox religion. She'd had it drummed into her from birth, had learnt the Bible from having it read to her and through sermons she attended, and was always very aware that the Church would be watching for any unorthodox or deviant behaviour. Adversity is the mother of invention, you do and use what you can to make your life bearable and hopefully fulfilling. Some, like Margery, take it that much further, to the very edge. That's what made her so visible. She broke with convention but made very good use of the rules of the Church to defend herself, as her escape route out of a life that she no longer felt was for her.

One thing that stands out about Margery's tales of her many struggles with the Church and secular authorities is that when she was repeatedly accused of heresy her defence was impeccable. She was indomitable – which really infuriated the men who accused her, that a woman could get the better of them. She was thought of as inferior to them and as such she shouldn't have been able to outsmart them. Whatever tricks they tried to outmanoeuvre her failed, and in some cases she ended up winning their support and respect.

During the prolonged persecution she faced in Bishop's Lynn Margery had managed to retain the support of some influential clerics and wealthy, important lay people who believed in her visions and were only too happy to help her out of some of the tight spots she got into. They were there for her when she needed money to fulfil her vow to go on pilgrimage to Santiago de Compostela. She visited them to tell them about her plans, fully aware they knew she was flat broke. As it was usual for people to pay pilgrims to say prayers on their behalf, saving them the trouble of travelling, her friends were more than likely to help her finance her trip. She secured a substantial amount of money, enough to buy an expensive, warm fur cloak and to reimburse Richard the hunchback the money she'd borrowed from him in Rome. She was able to repay him when she met him on her arrival in Bristol, where she was to sail from. She also ran into an old friend, Thomas Marshall, who was going to Santiago too. He paid for her passage in full and escorted her. After being held up in Bristol for six weeks because all the ships had been ordered to Southampton for yet another English invasion of France, they made the journey to Santiago, staying just two weeks. It was long enough for Margery to visit the shrine of St James, thereby chalking up the third and last of the three most important pilgrimage sites.

After she and Thomas returned, Margery made a brief stop on her way home to Lynn to see the relic of Christ's blood at the Cistercian abbey in Gloucestershire. Then she headed for Leicester. That's where she met with real trouble. While Margery had been away in the Holy Land in 1414, the Suppression of Heresy Act had been passed, enabling secular authorities to burn heretics – notably by the Leicester Parliament, at the Grey Friars' priory. Margery had entered the lion's den. Leicester was a hotbed of Lollard activity that was seen as a threat to both the Crown and the Church with its numerous criticisms of exploitative practices, hypocrisy and corruption. Lollards wanted religious reform, which included notions of equality – they wanted the Bible and other religious works translated from Latin into the vernacular to make them available to all, not just the clergy. They disapproved of many things, including the Eucharist, the idea that salvation could be attained through confession – and pilgrimages. All things that Margery religiously adhered to. Unfortunately for Margery, anything that gave a hint of being a Lollard was jumped on and reported to the mayor – such as her unorthodox acts of devotion, which now included wearing white. Margery went to church to say her daily prayers and, as was usual for her, things started getting lively, with her sobbing and writhing about 'hideously', as she described it, shocking the people in the church and drawing some unwelcome attention. One man in particular grabbed her by the arm when she went to leave, demanding to know what her screaming was all about. She refused to answer, shrugged him off and went with Thomas to their hostel, had dinner and thought no more about what had happened. They were more focused on how to sort out the next part of her journey back to Lynn because Thomas wasn't going that far. When he was sat writing to her husband, telling him to come and collect Margery to take her safely home, the door suddenly burst open. The innkeeper charged at Margery, snatching her purse, shouting at her that she was under arrest by order of the Mayor of Leicester. She was bundled out of the inn.

Margery stood in front of the mayor, not understanding why she was there but having a fairly good idea it had something to do with her altercation in the church. The mayor was grumpy and aggressive as he began to interrogate her. What was her name? Where was she from? And who was her father? She politely replied, *'I am of Lynne in Norfolke, a good mannys dowtyr of the same Lynne, whech hath ben meyr fyve tymes of that worshepful burwgh and aldyrman also many yerys, and I have a good man, also a burgeys of the seyd town, Lynne, to myn husbond.'*

Her answer seemed clear and above board. She was from good, respectable stock. The mayor wasn't impressed by her answer and thought she was boasting by mentioning her father's mayoral position and her burgess husband. He likened Margery's answer to that of St Katharine, one of her favourite saints, during her trial, but he was certain Margery was no saint. *'Seynt Kateryn telde what kynred sche cam of and yet ar ye not lyche, for thu art a fals strumpet, a fals loller, and a fals deceyver of the pepyl, and therfor I schal have the in preson.'* To be called a prostitute, a liar and a Lollard was insulting and serious enough, but his reference to St Katharine brought Margery up sharp. She knew that despite Katharine's expertise in debate, her trial over her faith had ended very badly. She'd been stripped naked, whipped, tortured and thrown in prison for weeks without food or drink. Fear kicked in – this cross-examination could be a precursor to her being tried for heresy and burnt at the stake.

The mayor had already made his mind up about putting Margery in prison, fully intending to have her put to death. She knew severe public punishments had recently been meted out to women charged with the same offence she was accused of. The mayor didn't have the authority to pass sentence but he knew a man of higher authority who did. She realised she needed to assert her innocence articulately and quickly. She answered the mayor in the first person, no longer as 'this creature' but as a lay woman from Norfolk, sticking to God's will like a leech as her defence. She was fighting for her life. She kept her nerve, calmly answering that if imprisonment was what God wanted, then she was fine with that, just as the mayor (if a true believer and not a heretic himself) should be obedient to God's wishes too. '*I am as ready, ser, to gon to preson for Goddys lofe, as ye arn ready to gon to chirche.*'

She had a perfectly good answer for every question the mayor threw at her and was beginning to get the others in court on her side. He was seething. He wanted her to beg for her life, goading her and trying to get her to crack, but she responded to his interrogation and insults with unusual intelligence for what he saw as a simple woman pilgrim . . . which in itself made him think she must be in league with the devil. He was losing, sick of her impudence and being made to look a fool. He shouted for the jailer to take her out of his sight and lock her up in the only space he had for her in jail – a room full of men. That sent another adrenaline rush of fear through Margery, with thoughts of the certain and horrendous prospect of being gang-raped. '*I prey yow, ser, put me not among men, that I may kepyn my chastité and my bond of wedlak to myn husbond, as I am bowndyn to do.*' From what the jailer had seen and heard of Margery, she'd come across as honest and innocent, in contrast to the mayor's vindictive performance. He didn't think she should suffer in jail and offered to lock her in a room in his own house until the trial. The mayor agreed. Then out of spite towards Margery he imprisoned her two pilgrim friends, Thomas and a man she knew from the nearby village of Wisbech.

Some days later Margery was summoned by the Steward of Leicester. His opening question to her was spoken in Latin – a test Margery immediately recognised. Although it was acceptable to know a few Latin words from hearing them at Catholic masses (that 'abstract' language Delia spoke of), it was a forbidden language for lay people like Margery. He and a group of priests and clergy waited for her answer. She came back at him with the only life-saving reply, asking him to speak in English: '*Spekyth Englysch, yf yow lyketh, for I undyrstonde not what ye sey.*' The steward's first tactic hadn't worked. He fired questions about the Bible at her to try and trip her up, but she replied word-perfectly and intelligently. Frustrated at her not falling into his traps, he grabbed her by the arm and dragged her into his chamber, grunting in her ear in graphic obscene detail about what he was going to do to her, before, during and after he raped her. So far Margery had got the better of him, so the next best thing was for him to get the better of her in another way, by violating her – unless, of course, she confessed to heresy. She had no one to help her and screamed and pleaded for him to stop. It was rape or prison, the choice was hers. She chose prison, all the time struggling as he mauled her, desperately shouting at him that her spiritual communications were sacred words from the Holy Ghost himself. That scared the hell out of him, deflating his urge for sex. He sent her packing back to the jailer.

Margery's troubles weren't over. The mayor was like a dog with a bone. She was taken for yet another interrogation, this time to All Saints' Church to face the Abbot of Leicester. She was stood in front of a group of Leicester's most powerful men – the abbot, the vexed mayor, the abbey canons, the Dean of Leicester and so many lay people that they had to stand on chairs to get a good view of her. She was the talk of the town, a curiosity. The abbot sat at the high altar and challenged her to convince him that she wasn't a Lollard heretic by swearing she believed in the Eucharist. She answered this satisfactorily and every question that followed, much to the increasing annoyance of the agitated mayor. The issue of Margery wearing white clothes was another offence she had to answer to, and the mayor was keen to bring it up, thinking he'd succeed in getting her declared guilty on that charge. I've got to give credit to Margery, she didn't hold back, even in the dire position she was in. The fearless lengths she went to in order to maintain her right to *self*-expression are frighteningly and staggeringly impressive. She told the mayor he didn't deserve to hold office, treating her the way he did without any proof for his allegations, that his daring to question the word of God was against God's teachings and punishable. It should be him on trial, not her.

The main problem the mayor had with Margery was that she was a bad influence on women and she'd encourage them to leave their husbands and follow her – literally or by example. He did have a valid point about her wearing white, as I mentioned before. Clothes were an outward, immediate sign of identity and status. White was a symbol of virginity, purity and holiness. By wearing it Margery was doing what we would refer to today as 'virtue signalling'. She was convinced she was entitled to dress that way, having done years of penance and stayed celibate, and especially because of her visions of God not only calling her his bride, his maiden, but instructing her to wear white: '*And, dowtyr, I sey to the I wyl that thu were clothys of whyte and non other colowr.*' The reason behind her white clothes was nothing to do with the likes of the mayor or laymen in the audience, it was an ecclesiastical matter. The court was emptied except for the abbot and clergy, and Margery knelt in front of them and explained her justification for wearing white. It was simply God's will – and that was incontrovertible – so they should take up their disapproval with God, not her.

Margery was dismissed, cleared of all charges. The mayor still had his doubts and wouldn't let her leave his district until she got a letter from the Bishop of Lincoln relieving him of all responsibility for Margery's actions . . . or what might happen to her. A veiled threat. After all he'd put her through, she was then asked to wish him well. Knowing how compromised she was, that she wasn't free to go until she did as he asked, and needing to keep up appearances as a charitable holy woman, she cried as she bowed down to him to ask his forgiveness if she'd hurt his feelings or caused trouble for him. It was passive-aggressive and cruel, making her supplicate before him just so he could get some satisfaction by seeing her brought down. He made an exaggerated show of accepting her apologies, not meaning a word of it. He had further plans for Margery that she would find out about later.

Margery knew there was every need to think ahead and be on guard against whatever else she might have to deal with. She was in a state of collapse from the stress of the trials and took shelter in an abbey, where she was looked after until she felt well enough to travel to Lincoln. She'd secured a letter from the Abbot of Leicester certifying her orthodoxy, which guaranteed that the Bishop of Lincoln would supply the letter requested by the mayor. She set off for Lincoln but didn't get far. She realised she'd left her purse behind, and a precious walking stick she'd brought back from her pilgrimage to Jerusalem, but she dared not go back. She'd hired a reliable man called Patrick, along with a horse strong enough for both of them to ride on. He rode back as fast as he could to get her things, while she waited in an old blind woman's cottage, out of harm's way. A prudent move, because Patrick was arrested, only just escaping being imprisoned by the mayor and having Margery's purse confiscated into the bargain.

More positively, the Bishop of Lincoln, who had already overseen her vow of chastity, was on her side. He was only too happy to write the letter to the Mayor of Leicester ordering him to let Margery travel where and when she wanted. The mayor's vendetta had kept her from moving around freely for three weeks, being batted from pillar to post, from one man to another to get their permission. At last she could heave a sigh of relief and go on her way without any life-threatening interruptions. Or so she thought.

Margery visited the shrine of St William in York Minster to give prayers of thanks for her escape from death at the hands of the zealous mayor. Her reputation had preceded her. Some of her friends were worried about being seen with her, including an anchoress she had trusted. Fortunately, there were lay people who had no problem with her and let her stay with them for a few weeks. But the rumours, suspicions and slander worsened. Clerics would come up to her during her prayers, condemning and criticising her, telling her to get her ridiculous sham display over with quick and leave. Swearing at her got them a lecture for blaspheming. She argued and defended herself every time, even when one grabbed her by the neck of her white gown, saying she had no right to wear it. All the time her visions of Christ reassured her that the more tribulations she suffered on his behalf, the more it proved her love for him. She put up with them all 'for the love of God!' as we say when exasperated by one thing after another going wrong. Some of the clergy made it abundantly clear they wanted Margery gone. They'd had enough of her weeping at communion and being disruptive. After prayers one day a priest asked her why she was still hanging around when she'd said she would only be there for two weeks. She told him she'd changed her mind and wasn't going yet – which wasn't the answer he wanted to hear, and he ordered her to go to the York Minster Chapter House to explain herself.

If Margery had learnt anything from all that had happened in Leicester, she knew that the more people you had on your side when brought before a court of any kind, the better your chances. There was a huge crowd, including many of her lay supporters and a few friendly clerics she'd managed to get to come along. She had to squeeze her way through all the people to where a priest sat waiting for her. The whole atmosphere was intimidating. He asked her why she was in the town. She said she was there on pilgrimage like all the other pilgrims. There was nothing wrong with that, so why pick on her? Her impudence didn't go down well. The priest asked her if she had her husband's permission to be out and about. Yes, she said, she had John's verbal (but not written) permission. He examined her on the Articles of Faith. She passed with flying colours and fully expected to be set free. But the priest wanted her to be interrogated by Henry Bowet, the Archbishop of York, at Cawood and said that until then she'd be put in prison. Her lay friends protested and saved her from jail, promising to look after her and take her to the archbishop themselves.

It was a ten-mile walk to Cawood for Margery and her chaperones. As she waited in the chapel for the archbishop, his servants swore at her, saying she should burn like all heretics. Margery stood her ground, telling them they'd burn in hell for cursing her. They scuttled off when the archbishop and his clerics turned up. The archbishop was more officious than holy. He got straight to the point. The issue of her white clothes again. Why are you going about in white? Are you a virgin? Admitting she was not a virgin but a married woman got her shackled and declared a heretic. She was left standing in chains and so petrified she had to put her hands inside her clothes so no one could see them trembling. The possibility of being martyred got too much for her and she broke down, falling to her knees. The archbishop wasn't at all sympathetic, only irritated, and made her testify to her belief in the Articles of Faith – which she did. He didn't know what to do with her. He didn't trust her and he didn't want her around. She was wicked and might corrupt people into behaving like her. Either out of bravery or desperation at thinking she had nothing to lose,

Margery said she'd heard rumours that he was so wicked he was doomed to go to hell if he didn't change his ways. She refused to be told when she could leave the city. She'd leave when she was good and ready.

Taking the high ground over a man of his status was a pretty feisty thing to do, especially when she went even further by saying she had every intention of continuing to speak about God. There was a battle of words between her and the archbishop, each quoting from the Bible to prove their points. The archbishop argued that no woman should preach, and Margery countered with a passage that suggests a woman, being God's 'creature', can. After all, she said, she wasn't going to use the pulpit – that was a man's 'place' but she wasn't going to be stopped from talking about God, even if it was a punishable offence for any lay person, man or woman. She was quite pleased with herself, using '*hir not lettryd witte and wisdom to answeryn so many lernyd men*'. So she should have been. The Church and king were both so powerful. She could have done as she was told, shut up and put up and behaved herself, stuck to the rules for women, carrying out her duties in the right places and not straying outside. But she didn't. She had the courage of her conviction; so safe was she in the extensive knowledge she'd accrued as a faithful Catholic that she wouldn't hesitate to reprimand mayors, priests, bishops or archbishops when they got 'the word of God' wrong, misappropriated it or behaved hypocritically. They should have known better than her, and she'd warn them that if their actions and the language they used to condemn her didn't adhere strictly to the teachings of the Church, then they were the ones open to being perceived as wicked heretics.

After her trial Margery was marched out of York and walked forty miles from there to Bridlington, staying with her confessor William Sleightholme and other friends, who gave her money to get home. She said her farewells and with her escort walked the twenty-five miles to Hull for the crossing to Lynn. She was feeling weary but pretty positive considering all she'd gone through, expecting the last leg of her journey to be uneventful.

—⁂—

When I was living in the oldest area of the town centre of Hull I witnessed the drunkenness every weekend, the fights, the street sex, the vomit in the gutter and the inevitable arrival of the police to cart the worst of the louts away to the lockup overnight. It was a very different landscape back in 1417, when Margery arrived in that same area of Hull. And yet she was greeted with the kind of reception I experienced when I was regularly heckled in the street and harassed by the police for being 'different' because of my demeanour, style of clothing and what were judged to be outrageous public theatrics. We were both targeted and taken off the streets, with threats to put us away where we couldn't cause trouble with our unwelcome and radical ideas, then run out of town. The people of Hull weren't happy to have Margery there. She was surrounded by crowds of local men and women jostling and insulting her, threatening to beat her up and shouting for her to be put in prison. Margery was terrified. The situation was on the verge of getting out of hand when a kind stranger stepped up, pulled her away from the mob and took her to his house for safety. She sat with his family, relieved she had a place to sleep and food to eat. But the peace didn't last long. The baying mob turned up outside the house, screaming for Margery to be thrown out, threatening the man and his family for helping her. He hadn't expected his kindness to Margery to end up with him and his family in fear for their lives. There was no alternative but to make it clear to

Margery and his angry neighbours that she'd be gone from his home and Hull first thing in the morning.

Margery was taken at dawn to Hessle foreshore so she could catch a boat back to Lynn, a relatively short trip across the River Humber. But she had no idea that word was out about her being in Hull. Two friars and two of the Duke of Bedford's men were lying in wait, sent by the duke specifically to arrest her. The duke was the brother of King Henry V and had taken enthusiastically to his assigned role to hunt down, persecute and wipe out heretics. He'd been successful in having the Lollard leader Sir John Oldcastle burnt at the stake, taking pleasure in watching the execution. He was determined to root out and dispose of troublesome women like Margery. His relentless pursuit bordered on obsession when he later focused his attention on Joan of Arc. He commanded the English armies in France and Joan was his enemy – and worse, a woman who dressed and acted like a man and spoke her mind, all amounting to her being an abomination in the eyes of God. She was a constant thorn in his side, and he revelled in her eventually being burnt at the stake in 1431.

The duke had offered a huge bounty of up to £100 for the capture of Margery Kempe, the 'greatest Lollard' in the country. She was outnumbered and had no chance of running away. If she did, she'd be deemed a fugitive from the law and could be decapitated or hanged. She surrendered and had to stand by as her travelling companion was put in prison for nothing other than guilt by association.

The duke's men took Margery to Beverley for interrogation by the Archbishop of York on suspicion, yet again, that she was a Lollard heretic. Their route took them back through Hessle, where Margery's reception was just as hostile as it had been in Hull, the villagers' loud chants of 'Burn the heretic!' sending shudders down her spine. There was a little relief from persecution. Some of the people in Beverley liked her. She was a likeable person as well as holy, a good conversationalist and a fantastic subject for gossip. A crowd of local women went to the house where she was staying to have a look at her for themselves and see what all the fuss was about. They shouted for her to come outside and get what was due to her, but she'd been locked in her room, so all she could do was open the window to try and calm things down by giving them an impromptu storytelling performance. They were fascinated, totally taken with her. She'd won over her would-be attackers, as well as one of her captors during the walk to Beverley.

Margery didn't know what was waiting for her this time. Accusations of Lollardy were a certainty, but then another charge was thrown into the mix. A spokesman for the irksome Duke of Bedford informed the archbishop that Margery had visited Lady Westmoreland and spoken to her daughter, Lady Greystoke, advising her to leave her husband. A flood of lies followed. Margery handled them all well by simply pointing out that the supposed events had taken place in the period of her pilgrimage to Jerusalem – where all her sins had been forgiven. So not only had she been out of the country, all that she was accused of wouldn't have counted anyway.

Margery tangled with some powerful men. The Duke of Bedford, as acting Lieutenant of England while the king was away, had a lot of authority, influence and forces at his disposal to carry out his orders. But so far, Margery had managed to see him and others off. She had people on her side, ecclesiastical and secular, who helped her out of some very dangerous situations. The judgement went in her favour. She was acquitted and escorted safely back to the River Humber, free to go.

News, good or bad, didn't travel fast in the fifteenth century. It took days for letters to arrive, so no one across the Humber had heard of Margery's acquittal. As soon as she stepped off the boat, after being greeted by Robert Springolde, she was again arrested for Lollardy. As chance would have it, someone who'd seen her trial in Beverley spoke up for her and she was freed. That made her think that one letter of acquittal certifying her orthodoxy might not be enough to stop her being arrested again, so she went to London with her husband and got written permission from the new Archbishop of Canterbury, Henry Chichele, for her to have access to confession and communion as often as she desired. She needed it as a double indemnity alongside the Archbishop of York's letter.

It's exhausting to think how much Margery had to put up with just to go from one place to another. All the time she was on the road she had to get permission from men to continue to go about the country, constantly being interrogated to prove she had the right to be out in the world. She was like a ping pong ball batted from one male authority to another, not only to be certified as orthodox, a decent person, but to have it in writing. Documents of validation were life-saving and life-changing for her. They not only gave her freedom to live her celibate life in peace, they also gave her the right to be 'free', to be herself on the limited terms she'd managed to achieve through incredible tests of endurance. Her life depended on the written approval of men. Her being incessantly hounded and brought to book gives some idea of how much importance was placed on people, especially women, being compliant and not upsetting the balance of things. How she dealt with and coped with all that shows she was resourceful and intelligent. It's plain to see, from how she organised her travels and survived so many charges of heresy, that she was driven, strong and unstoppable in reaching her goal. 'Putting on an act to break free' comes back to mind. For Margery, being artful was key to her achieving a degree of autonomy, but at huge risk and cost. She wasn't a madwoman nor totally out of control. She was in control, as much as she could possibly be with what knowledge was available to her and her careful use of the rules.

1970 had been a tough year for Delia and she was finding it increasingly difficult to cope with the pressures and workload at the BBC as well as her personal issues. In answer to the RW's many pleas for new equipment Desmond Briscoe had a curious answer to justify his refusal – that if an idea was that good, then you would always find a way to make it happen, regardless of the lack of resources. To some degree I can agree with him, having struggled to realise my ideas with little or no money at times as well as dealing with technological limitations. Yet his reason for underinvestment didn't seem to apply when in 1969 he had purchased two analogue voltage-controlled VCS3 synthesisers at £300 each, then in 1971 an EMS Synthi 100 (aka Delaware) which on its own came at the hefty price of £5,400. This new 'member' of the Radiophonic Workshop had unexpected repercussions.

The acquisition of the EMS gear came through Delia and Brian's connection to Peter Zinovieff. Electronic music was moving on in terms of technology providing new equipment for the synthesis of sounds, and that became problematic for Delia. The giant EMS Synthi 100 was the equivalent of three VCS3s, incorporating oscillators, filters and a digital sequencer. It differed subtly in sound from the VCS3 Delia was used to but its sheer size, with two sixty-by-sixty patch-bay grids as opposed to the single twenty-by-twenty grid on the VCS3, was intimidating. It offered endless possibilities, almost too many to contemplate. Whereas the VCS3 was portable and could be carried under one arm, the Synthi 100 was the size and weight of two wardrobes, which meant widening the door to Room 10 to get it in. Not only that, there was no instruction manual, so Brian spent three days and nights putting one together before they could even start to use it. To Delia it appeared unwieldy, unintuitive and unstable, and it was prone to malfunctioning because of static build-up caused by the front panels not being earthed. But the main bone of contention for her was that it appeared to offer an immediacy to producing readily accessible and adaptable sounds that were quirky, and could seemingly do a lot of the work for the 'assistants' instantaneously. In Delia's mind, it reduced the workshop to a sound-generating factory rather than a creative, explorative workspace. It offered a faster turnaround for commissions, which meant increased income for the BBC but went against everything she stood for. It no longer provided time for her usual way of analysing a sound she had in her mind and then experimenting to create that particular new music.

On 19 May 1971 the Institute of Electronic Engineers would celebrate its centenary with a gala at the Royal Festival Hall, and the RW was to present a multimedia programme of 'Ingenious Electric Entertainment'. It was also the thirteenth anniversary of the RW. The queen and the Duke of Edinburgh would be attending, and the Synthi 100 was to be shown to them after the performance. Desmond Briscoe had said in an internal memo that since the event was a social one it would be best to focus on and promote the more popular RW works, with nothing too technical, especially as there would be ladies present. How shockingly condescending to the ladies, especially as the evening would feature so many solo and collaborative works by Delia. It raises the question of whether he acknowledged how exceptional a 'lady' Delia was, or whether it was just down to assumptions about women and class, that lady socialites would be indifferent to the artistic and technical skills of Delia and other women like her. Desmond certainly valued her work, but sexism runs deep, often revealing itself buried within what some may think are quite innocuous remarks.

Delia's skills and musical talents were a great asset to the BBC and by this time she had also worked extensively outside the Corporation, increasing her public profile and reputation for innovation among the avant-garde, underground and more popular musicians she'd worked with. Considering all those factors it's not really surprising that Delia was handed the prestigious commission to create the only new work for the showcase event, which she titled *IEE 100*. Additionally it was decided that she would also be 'performing' a demonstration of the new Delaware synthesiser on stage. Delia ensconced herself in the studio and set about deciding how to represent a century of electronic achievement with sound. Her mind was firing off in all directions. She hurried, scribbling down ideas – a possible tune and counter-melody, or 'End *Doctor Who* slow and bloopy'. She wanted the music to be 'Enjoyable, spectacular, beautiful, amusing, meaningful. Episodic, with unifying tune &/or rhythm', with a 'Fanfare (Morse pattern)', listing in her notes groupings of 'String and sealing wax, Early radio Hums and rhythms, Computers . . . wireless whistles . . .'; 'Countdown to lift off – Apollo 11 Neil Armstrong Eagle ld'; 'Apollo & blast off – swoopy . . . Early Sputnik & Early bird, Russian countdown'.

She began by interpreting 'IEE 100' in different ways, using Morse code, adding full stops between the letters to create a more appealing sound, then converting the letters and numbers into musical notes, with 'B' in place of 'I', 'E' as it was and 'C' for 100 (the Latin number). The next task was to source sounds that were linked to or suggestive of the progress of electronics, radio, early satellite communication ('early bird via synthi'), the moon and outer space. Such a vast array of objectives was a huge challenge and Delia struggled to get the work up to her standard, to create something good enough for her to present . . . and, of course, to keep it entertaining and lightweight. Such flippancy was counter to her nature and her complicated interpretative approach. She worked day and night for weeks, with Brian for company and moral support, helping her source the voices of Thomas Edison, William Gladstone and Neil Armstrong from the sound library, along with other pieces she'd been working on.

Brian was getting worried. He sensed Delia's waning interest and angst. Her moods were erratic and her drinking accelerated. As a safeguard he instructed an assistant to make a copy of the tape she'd been working on. Lucky he did, because on the morning of the performance Delia turned up at the Festival Hall in floods of tears, saying she'd destroyed the tape. After being up for two nights in a row she hadn't been able to complete the piece in the way she'd wanted. When Brian told Delia not to worry because he had a backup, she was furious that he was going to present what she considered to be a substandard work of hers without her permission. How dare he, how could he do that to her? Despite her being so angry and upset, she was still expected to play her part in the evening's proceedings and fulfil her duty to the BBC and the RW.

Much to Delia's relief it had been decided that the Synthi 100 couldn't be removed from where it had been installed and that it was too unreliable to use live for fear it might produce either nothing at all or offensive noises that could be an outright embarrassment for the RW in front of the royal party. So EMS loaned another Synthi 100 and six VCS3 synthesisers, which were lined up on chairs, spotlit but silent throughout the evening. I understand their predicament but I've always embraced the unpredictable in a live situation. In the days of TG our equipment was always breaking down and misbehaving because it was either home-made by Chris or modified to our needs and therefore precarious. Setting up and leaving it all switched on while it was working helped, as any movement could result in something burning out or that dry solder joint finally giving up the ghost. I must admit that when things did go wrong it was fun to deal with the challenge and was guaranteed to make almost every gig more interesting than any of us or the audience had expected. I guess that making a 'professional' impression wasn't our aim as much as it was for the RW. They had a lot riding on such a rare public appearance, the kind of obligations that I haven't needed to consider.

I found the content of the IEE show revealing of what must have felt to Delia like a subtle amplification of her 'otherness', accompanying her like a whisper in the background as she was put on public display as a lone female among so many males. The evening began with Desmond Briscoe making a grand entrance onto the stage, stepping into the spotlight, speaking about the work of the Radiophonic Workshop, then narrating the programme throughout. There was a huge high-specification PA system, a central screen for film clips and associated images, and silver foil panels to project disco-type lights, slides and lasers onto. It was a spectacle fit for a queen. Keeping within BBC regulations on named credits, Briscoe used the collective terms 'we' and 'our' in relation to the workshop. Many of Delia's works were presented as some of the most exceptional works 'they'd' created. Delia was not mentioned in relation to the *Doctor Who* theme, only 'our old friend [Ron Grainer] who, of course, wrote the *Doctor Who* Signature Tune, which is entirely electronic'.

Even more surprising is that Desmond had praised Delia's abstract incidental-music solo work *The Delian Mode* (so aptly titled because it was so very 'Delia') as 'without parallel' to anything else by the workshop. But, again, her name wasn't mentioned in connection with this, or the work she had done for his *Inventions for Radio*, when Desmond played *The Dreams* or her other works. The emotional effect on Delia of having so much of her work applauded yet not being mentioned as the creator, and even having others credited for it, must have been dreadful. Only at the very end of the evening did Delia's name ring out across the auditorium as her new work *IEE 100* was played. Her presence and what I'd like to think represented her anger at her predicament was felt by all when the great thunderous sound she'd made for Neil Armstrong's rocket launch shook the building. Brian Hodgson can't remember if Delia was there for any of the show or if she got the 'honour' of being presented to the queen. But a compensation of sorts was her getting the only namecheck for her composition in the *IEE News* report of the show.

Compounding Delia's discomfort over the new arrival and her ongoing situation, Desmond Briscoe had introduced the Delaware as being the saviour of the workshop, enabling a faster turnaround on commissions. It saved time – something that Delia was struggling with, as well as her status. Under what category did Briscoe place her in his description of the amazing Delaware? Composer would be most appropriate, seeing as she had programmed it to produce *IEE 100*.

This device together with a multi-track tape machine is a complete electronic music studio capable of realising the most complex music, with maximum precision, in minimum of time, that is of course with the right composer to programme it!

Delia had actually looked forward to using synthesisers, having worked with her own VCS3, taking it to the workshop prior to the

BBC buying theirs. Although it was unstable due to being sensitive to fluctuations in temperature that made the sound change after spending ages getting it as she wanted, she thought such a machine could potentially help speed up the work. But she was disappointed at how inflexible the VCS3s were and wanted to get into the workings to see what could be done to make the sounds more human, 'warmer' to the ear. The idea that the Delaware could possibly replace that process and those who preferred working that way was anathema to her. It really wasn't the 'be all and end all' it appeared to be. The engineers were also unfamiliar with the new technology – it wasn't the same as getting inside the old junk equipment – and the Synthi 100 kept breaking down. And as far as its capabilities were concerned, it was a sound generator, not a processor, so there was still the need for recordings of external sounds and voices, as well as whatever audio the Synthi 100 produced. So Delia used it to generate sounds much as she had with a single VCS3, recording the audio output onto tape, then applying her favoured techniques to ensure she continued to create original music and not always the same kind of sound anyone who owned a Synthi 100 could produce.

The arrival of the Synthi 100 was what split the workshop into two: those who were happy to embrace a 'hands off' approach using the new technology, and those like Delia who preferred the original 'hands on' ways. She liked getting inside to work with the 'mechanics', and that wasn't an option for her with the Synthi 100. What Briscoe saw as a solution to the RW's increasing workload, Delia regarded as a problem that further added to her struggles.

22

In spring 1972 Delia was yet again in the workshop in the dead of night, feeling the strain of working on the thirteen-episode series *Tutankhamun's Egypt*. She'd found herself trying to finish the music as the programmes were being dubbed, and was ferried back and forth by taxi to deliver tapes to Broadcasting House in time for transmission. She'd spent a lot of time planning all the programmes and was on track, when without notice she was faced with demands for last-minute changes. The sequence of programmes had been altered, destroying her perfect progression of sounds that flowed from one to the next. It meant she had to start over again. She found that crushingly stressful and dis-respectful of all the time and work she'd put into the project. She was so upset by it, everything that she'd held down for so long surfaced. She couldn't cope with the level of pressure placed on her, the time constraints, the interference of the committees of men who couldn't accept anything unusual. She felt whatever she did was going to be criticised or turned down as unsuitable, 'too sophisticated', 'too lascivious', and yet outside the BBC people loved what she did.

The bureaucracy of the BBC was creatively stifling, with no time for her to expand on ideas or start again if things weren't working out. Her love of the process was why she had trouble with deadlines. Her indulgence in the exploration of sound could go on forever, so much so that reaching the goal also brought to a conclusion the part she found the most rewarding. Making that final commitment, that 'last' tweak, would put her in a quandary of having to let go and leave behind the possibility of something even more wonderful. She found it exasperating and one time said to Brian Hodgson, 'I think I must have reverse adrenaline. As the deadline gets closer most people speed up – I just get slower.' I've felt that feeling of frustration in not being able to finish a project, but for a different reason that has nothing to do with deadlines. What's known as Project Fulfilment Fatigue Syndrome. Working on something for so long, knowing you must bring it to its end but just can't. It feels like you're getting nowhere, treading water. Nothing can compare to the exhilarating feeling when making music is going well, when it's seemingly creating itself. It's as if an indefinable force is at work and you want to hold on to it as long as you can. But it's not always like that and dealing with those times can be tough.

Delia's obsession with perfection would have increased her frustration at the pressures she had to deal with. Seeking perfection can be fruitless. Imperfection is inevitable. As Delia discovered, you can fine-tune forever, but the piece can end up unfinished to the point of dissatisfaction, as she had found out with *IEE 100*. She never had the luxury of setting aside tracks that are resistant. Their potential is clear yet that missing five per cent, the golden key to completeness, is frustratingly elusive. And just as important is knowing when to stop. It's good to break off. Just stepping outside the studio can make you hear the sounds quite differently. Like the bass becoming more obvious, raising the question that maybe it's too dominant. Other elements sit further back and the arrangement takes on a different 'mix' that can sometimes totally change the direction and arrangement. That's happened so many times to me over the years. Being too close and 'inside' the music is not always constructive; you can't hear where it's leading or what direction it should take. I never force it. It's important to give your ears a rest. When you've been listening to one element too long to get it sounding as you want within the track, you no longer hear the other elements in their own right – what they may offer in terms of a possible melody or sequence. You can come back the next day and wonder what the fuck you were doing. Or suddenly you hear a tone emanating from the harmonics built up from particular sounds beating off each other, suggesting a totally new mood – at which point I mute a load of tracks and work on the potential of the fresh idea. A positive out of what seemed a negative stalemate situation. Nothing goes to waste.

Delia's scribbled notes look like mind maps of her responses to the sounds she was creating, recognising as she went along those that were more suited to other projects she had planned – something I do and did for the 'Delia' film soundtrack, earmarking certain sounds for different projects, jumping from one thing to another, being led by the sound itself. Having an awareness (as did Delia) that the process of creating is where the priceless discoveries are made, I had set aside possible 'Delia' sounds while in the middle of recording for other unrelated work. During the hours spent teasing out and capturing 'gems' for other uses I was also alert to unexpected sounds that might never occur again but could suit 'Delia'.

The workshop had become what Delia called 'a creative treadmill'. It was a victim of its own success, and so, as it turned out, was Delia. The triumph of *Doctor Who* had been a double-edged sword: it elevated the profile of the RW, bringing more commissions and a lot of attention from the public and other musicians, all wanting a piece of Delia and what she could offer them to further their own artistic ambitions. She couldn't keep up with demand. The workload escalated and all the 'assistants' were feeling the pressure. They were stretched to their limits, with some having to take sick leave, including Delia. Working night and day for so long had taken its toll physically, mentally and creatively. She needed to refocus, to find her 'place'. The largest word among a page of Delia's RW notes around that time is 'DOCTORS!!' written in pink ink and boldly outlined. Another box with the note 'pressures of today cause drama screaming' may have been a description for a job at hand but could just as easily be indicative of how bad she was feeling. Events in Delia's private life, her ill health, problems with alcohol, the changes happening with electronic music moving away from her preferred techniques, alongside the ever-increasing pressures of BBC deadlines and her outside work, had built to a climax. She was physically exhausted, at the end of her tether after having had to battle to preserve her personal and artistic sensibilities for so long. She refused to compromise her integrity any longer.

In May 1972 Delia told the BBC she wanted to leave. She was given time off because of her health problems, in the hope she'd come back refreshed, ready to carry on. The break didn't change her mind and in 1973, after thirteen years at the BBC and having composed over two hundred works, Delia left. She packed boxes with reels and reels of tape and masses of papers from her RW room and took off with them all. They were never unpacked again but moved around with her.

Delia's decision to leave the BBC was a damning indictment of the accumulated effect of her expending so much of her physical and emotional energy on delivering works on time as well as countering the negative aspects of the job. It was an act of defiance rather than defeat. She was refusing to sacrifice herself, awakened to the necessary shift in priorities. Some years later, in the same way, I recognised when the time was right for me to break free from TG. Like Delia, I was disillusioned that what was once excitingly challenging had become daunting and unsustainable on all levels, personal and eventually artistic.

> Something serious happened around '72, '73, '74. The world had gone out of tune with itself and the BBC went out of tune with itself.
>
> I still haven't worked out why I left – self-preservation I think.

Delia's words on why she left the BBC have been quoted time and again. They've always screamed so much more to me than that it was just a bad time for her. When she says the BBC had gone out of tune it's assumed quite rightly that she couldn't cope with being there any more, but when she says the world had gone out of tune I take it to mean everything in her world was in utter disharmony – as much as the world around her. Music was her world. It makes sense that she would explain her feelings in musical terms. That nothing struck the right chord for her any more, there was no melody. All was chaos. She felt lost, out of place in a world that itself was confused and messed up. The halcyon psychedelic party days were all but over. It had started off with such hope and was so much fun, then the crackdown changed everything. Things got serious. There were drug raids and trials, the Indica scene and Arts Lab were no more, the happening cool music venues had either been closed down or taken over by 'businessmen', and the middle- and upper-class hippies had matured, opted back in, some becoming entrepreneurs. The counterculture was in the throes of change and the economy was in big trouble. There were strikes by miners, dustmen, nurses and gravediggers, rubbish piled up in the streets, violent protests, IRA bombings and high unemployment. It had gone from peace and love to politics and violence.

The swinging, permissive, loved-up sixties had given way to the 'anything goes', decadent but dark, harsh times of the seventies.

Sounds grim, but for me it was an amazing time. I seemed to thrive on the turmoil around the prospect of change. The struggles and darkness fuelled and inspired so many great things. New scenes were emerging and a different kind of civil rights activism that was angry, uncompromising, in your face. The right to freedom of speech was expressed in many ways across culture and society. By 1976 punk had arrived and along with it home-made fanzines that fed the hunger for new music, which included my and TG's industrial music. Although TG's intentions and methods were different, we were allied to some of the core punk movers and shakers. We all had the same mindset as far as being 'free' and expressing our discontent was concerned. We went about it in different ways but always reinforcing the need for anarchistic behaviour because of the dire state of the country.

Now that she had finally broken away from the BBC, Brian expected Delia to join him as they had previously agreed, but she was unsure about fully committing to or investing in setting up the Electrophon studio, so Brian took the plunge without her, financing the studio by cashing in his pension and setting it up with his friend John Lewis. When Delia visited the studio once it was up and running in Covent Garden, he tried to make sense of why she seemed so reluctant and unenthusiastic. He wondered if it was to do with her always having been the girl who succeeded, the star, the one to go to for guaranteed competence and perfection, which had left her quietly carrying a lot of responsibility on her shoulders for a very long time. Or maybe it was the strain of pulling against that, her nonconformity, her feeling out of place despite being able to play her part so well. All he knew for certain was that she was struggling, and it was uncomfortable for him to watch her flounder. The Delia he knew was disappearing. Her depressions had worsened and she was withdrawn. It became obvious to Brian that the reason lay in her personal life. Her affair with David had ended long ago. She'd taught him everything he knew about electronic music and had he not met her he wouldn't have gone in the musical direction he did. He owed all that to Delia and had so much to thank her for. But relationships don't last on 'obligation' and gratitude alone. Now she had a new boyfriend, who Brian realised wasn't good for her.

Delia was fascinated by oddball people. One of her boyfriends camped in a tent in the garden where she lived. She'd 'inherited' another from Brian after he'd picked the guy up when trolling Hyde Park one night but quickly distanced himself, finding him really peculiar. Delia took him over. Brian had been right. The guy believed he was a saint and lived in the alcove halfway up the stairs leading to Delia's flat. She never thought of dispelling his fantasy and indulged him for as long as he needed the space. Her latest lover was another very strange guy whom she'd taken under her wing. She had moved in with him to a flat in Powis Square in Notting Hill, the centre of London's alternative radical fringe. It was a cosmopolitan ghetto, a late-night place that attracted all classes and types of people, from musicians, hippies and drug dealers to government ministers. An eclectic mix of social misfits, artists of all persuasions and anti-establishment political activists. Delia's new boyfriend was heavily into politics and regularly attended Socialist Workers Party committee meetings, driving Delia with her tape machine to record the proceedings. Reels and reels of the stuff were later found in her boxes of tapes and discarded as being irrelevant to her work. It wasn't 'Delia' to sit around listening to committees endlessly discussing rules and talking of taking action . . . followed by little or no action but plenty more meetings. It was totally out of character for her to spend hours in a passive and uncreative role on something so boring – a waste of good tape and her time. Combined with the dynamics of the relationship, the environment she lived in wasn't too healthy.

I remember my stay with the art theatre crowd at Colville Terrace in Notting Hill, just around the corner from where Delia was living at the same time. It's odd to think we were so close but never bumped into each other. I guess it was because we moved in different circles, mine among those who were demanding rights to do with sex, sexuality and equality, and hers centred on the political interests of her partner. If 'it's grim up North', where I hail from, Notting Hill seemed worse to me. Portobello Road and Westbourne Grove buzzed with life, and the flamboyant appearances of the Gay Liberation Street Theatre and smiley chanting groups of Hare Krishna disciples gave the impression of it being a joyful place to live. But the surrounding streets were mainly derelict, with lots of run-down properties rented cheap or squatted, left over from the Peter Rachman slum scandal days. The antithesis of what Delia had been used to. Even Camden Town, where she had lived with David, wasn't as bad as Notting Hill. Her world had gone from mood-enhancing bright colours and mainly working and socialising with artists to the muted shades of the bleak landscape and serious subject matter she was engaging with in support of her boyfriend. They weren't of great importance to her. The shift she went through was like the difference between the psychedelic richness and fantasy of the film *Performance* and the black-and-white gritty reality of the sub-underground of the film *Duffer*. Both were filmed in Notting Hill around the same time, *Performance* in Powis Square in 1970. Delia created the sound effects for *Duffer* in 1971. All the music she made was electronic, using the Doppler effect so well on the audio for passing traffic you'd be hard pushed to distinguish the synthetic sounds from the real thing.

Notting Hill Gate was depressing, dirty and dangerous, with political graffiti everywhere, much like Hackney, where I lived. You never knew what was going on behind closed doors or when it would spill out onto the street – or even end up released as a film. Like the black-and-white sadomasochistic film *After Cease to Exist* that Chris, Sleazy and I made in 1977 using the same Bolex 16 mm camera used for *Duffer*. Some people find *After Cease to Exist* weird and hard to watch, but *Duffer* is the strangest film I've ever seen – so bizarre that I can never decide whether I like it or not, while constantly revisiting it in my head. I'm still trying to make sense of the story of a middle-aged man carrying out his sadomasochistic fantasies on an obliging bisexual teenage boy who then in further compliance gets pregnant and gives birth to a baby that's a doll. All the while he's going back and forth to a motherly, plump, soft-fleshed, satin-and-lace prostitute for respite, comfort and tender sex. I wonder what Delia thought about it. Maybe she had a better handle on it than me as she probably knew the director, Joseph Despins, who was also the editor on BBC programmes like *Horizon* and *The World about Us* which she worked on.

Brian disapproved of and loathed Delia's socialist lover intensely and was concerned for her. He found it hard to know what she saw in him, with him being so heavily into politics, not good-looking, and small. Delia towered above him. Brian described the time when Delia was with this troublesome lover as 'the dark ages'. He was like a 'black hole', the kind of person who sucked all the energy out of a room. The opposite of Delia, who lit up a room with her presence. He wasn't someone you'd want around you if you were a sensitive, creative person like Delia. Much to the annoyance of Brian, on the occasions she went to work at

Electrophon her lover would go with her. He'd drive her to the studio and she'd arrive dishevelled, pulling at her hair in frustration at not being able to connect with and contribute to the music. The whole time he'd sit in the corner of the room, a sinister, malevolent shadow exuding negativity and impatience until Delia gave up in exasperation and fled the studio with him. He didn't seem to care much about her distress. Her failure to get into recording music could perhaps have been avoided had he encouraged or supported her. She'd managed to help in the production of a few radio commercials and works for theatre but was in no fit state to contribute much on the Electrophon commission for the film soundtrack of *The Legend of Hell House*. Her archived notes and music sheets show she did as much as she was able, and you can clearly hear her sounds and influence. Nevertheless, Brian completed the project, crediting her as co-composer. Quite the opposite of what she'd been used to.

It's hardly surprising that Delia's latest lover wasn't welcome at Electrophon. He was disliked for what he was and because his involvement with Delia seemed to have cost her dearly. Her clean-cut, elegant dress sense had already changed when she met and lived with David but had now deteriorated into a grungy, granny-ish hippy look consisting of a minimal wardrobe of a few kaftans and trousers, and her crowning glory of red hair scraped back and covered with a byzantine-patterned scarf. She was dressed head to toe in shades of cinnamon and brown, accessorised by the matching brown residue of snuff and its pungent, invasive aroma. Seeing her sniff prompted her hip friends to ask her where she got the 'stuff' from, and she'd laughingly reply that it wasn't cocaine, not 'stuff', but snuff. She'd become a physical manifestation of her mental and emotional state and was in a relationship that seemed to be destroying her. Her boyfriend was sucking the life out of her, he was vampiric. Living with him and being caught up in his work meant she had little relief from him.

When I was told about this relationship it rang a very familiar bell – my own experience of being with someone who had honed all the necessary skills to draw in people he wanted to use for his own personal and 'creative' purposes. That you were only an incidental in their plans, a mere facilitator but made to feel special, 'loved' as a ploy to ensure your compliance. I don't know the details of what happened to Delia, whether there was anything similar to the abuse I suffered. But what went on was enough to push her over the edge. From what I've learnt of Delia, I think I was more able to cope with the situation than she was for the simple reason that I never reached the depths of despair that she did. Or maybe it was also because of our different circumstances and the timing. I'd met Chris, who was genuine, and we were in love, whereas Delia was suffering from physical and mental exhaustion, addicted to alcohol and snuff, possibly bipolar, and had no regular income after leaving her job at the BBC. Whatever the differences, the effect of being deceived by someone you are led to believe cares about you is the same. You're consumed by feelings of being used, betrayed and disillusioned, your emotions in turmoil, knowing you have to find a way out. We both did.

Delia's attraction to strange men had been her undoing. She unravelled completely. She'd reached the most important crossroads in her life and, as time would prove, she took the right decision for her*self*. Despite all the bad things her lover had brought to her life, the one good thing to come of the relationship was that he turned out to be the straw that broke the camel's back, forcing her to break free of all the accumulated negativity that overshadowed the many good times she'd enjoyed in London. It was her coping mechanisms that had begun to falter because of the pressures of not only her music projects but her personal relationships. The alternative path has its upsides and downsides and can be difficult to navigate. So far it had proved to be a pathway to heartbreak and dispossession for Delia. She needed space and sleep. She 'ran away', as far north as she could after answering a newspaper ad for a job in Cumbria as a radio operator for Laing, who were laying a gas pipeline. She got the job and moved to the border of Northumberland and Cumbria. Delia had found a way to extricate herself from the destructive relationship and left London wrecked and broken, exhausted, empty and disillusioned. Not her*self* at all.

In the summer of 1973, when Delia left London, I'd arrived having moved from Hull – well, I was hounded out of the town, deemed to be an unwanted, disruptive degenerate because of my lifestyle and activities as an artist. Unlike Delia I wasn't out of tune with the early seventies, I was very much in tune, if not with the people in Hull. Delia may have been burnt out, but I was on fire. I was ready and willing to connect with new technological developments in music. I'd been introduced to electroacoustic music after taking part in multimedia art and electronic music festivals and soon hooked up with the London avant-garde fringe, a quite different crowd from those Delia knew. I'm sad to say we never met. We both continued on our own paths but veered off in different directions, becoming part of groups that were indirectly connected but geographically miles apart. I was unaware of Delia's work. Had there been the internet or mobile phones it might have been easier to make contact through our mutual friends, but technology had not yet provided us with that luxury.

Rather than questioning the source of our problems, people ask why Delia stayed so long at the BBC with all its stresses and why I stayed so long in an abusive relationship. The personal issues and character traits of other people that manifested in their shameful behaviour towards us were secondary, a downside that was at times depressing, heartbreaking and shockingly unacceptable, but we dealt with it pragmatically, always ensuring we protected our *self*. The negatives were outweighed by the advantages, until the drawbacks became too detrimental in terms of having to expend too much precious energy on undeserving people and concerns. We had something far greater and more powerful – self-will. There's a moment when the survival instinct kicks in. The bottom line for me, as it was for Delia, was *self*-preservation.

23

'Recordings' are bubbles of our history, locked in time and our psyche. They are precious, so when they are appropriated or exploited, our copyright breached, it feels like a personal violation.

My most enduring, fulfilling and true collaboration has been my work with my partner Chris. I've also worked on many separate collaborative projects with and without him, the vast majority of which have been amazing. But on a few occasions the use of the collective term 'we' or 'our' has been a bone of contention for me, as it was for Delia with the RW, mainly because there's always one self-promoting person who takes on being the public voice for the group, whether they contributed a small amount or nothing at all to the collective work. Consequently the actual composers are banished to the shadows, and the works and ideas of others in the group can go largely unnoticed. A further drawback is when the one voice speaks for itself as 'we', which can be very problematic when speaking about the group as a whole. It effectively places words in the mouths of the other people, as if 'we've' all said them. That one person's opinions, of which some can be highly offensive, are then wrongly ascribed to all members. Some people within a group prefer to be in the background, but that doesn't mean they don't want to be acknowledged for their contribution or that they're content for their voice to be silenced.

One of the biggest issues that arises from collaborative projects is when the name of the actual writer doesn't get registered and copyright is assigned to someone else. Then credit is not given where it is due, and conversely credit is given undeservedly – as happened to Delia on numerous occasions and to myself when my work has been unjustly attributed to a person who had an arrogant sense of self-entitlement. It's what I regard as appropriation, whether unintentional or, in my case for sure, blatant and by stealth. A strategy made all the easier as a result of the other collective members being so amiable and trusting in the spirit of collaboration above all else – that being 'seen' and 'heard' to 'do' is not as important as 'doing'. I dare say the use of 'we' for the Radiophonic Workshop was for well-intentioned practical reasons. Nevertheless, it serves to legitimise the taking of credit for works the collective as a whole may have had no hand in and the denial of credit to the person who did. Delia wasn't the only RW composer this happened to.

Desmond Briscoe's attitude to giving individuals official credit wasn't always consistent. There were many requests and occasions when he could have given members of the RW their individual due but he seemed happy to stick to the rules, even when asked from within the BBC, for example when the head of drama and sound asked for Delia in particular to be credited for her work on *The Tower* – for good reason, as her music was acknowledged as important to the success of the play. Similarly, when the lighting and costumes departments were lobbying for credit for their contribution to *The Naked Sun*, Desmond chose not to join the throng on behalf of Delia's music. Yet he was happy to put his name down for some collaborations, omitting his co-contributors. Maddalena Fagandini had similar experiences to Delia in not being credited for her work with Desmond, who described her as 'a lady of considerable talent and spirit' and took credit for their 1960 collaboration on the RW's twenty-first-anniversary compilation album. What seems worse to me is what happened to Maddalena's

Time Beat composition when it was 'co-opted' by the Beatles' producer George Martin, who added his own music to hers and released it as a single. The credits listed the BBC Radiophonics Workshop and 'Ray Cathode' (George Martin's pseudonym) – not a whisper of the original inspirational female composer.

An important part of working collaboratively is the spirit of generosity. Delia was modest about her achievements and always very generous in sharing her knowledge of electronic music and techniques. She found that others weren't so inclined but were happy to take advantage of her enthusiasm, to appropriate the secrets behind her techniques. She felt exploited by some high-profile musicians who came to her because of her skills and ideas. It didn't faze her to meet famous people; she was the same with them when showing them around the RW as she was with students. When your generosity is exploited, as Delia's was on occasions, it leaves you feeling used. Competition and ego weren't the driving forces for Delia or myself. It was and still is for me about sharing the excitement of discovery, the joy it brings. It's all about the music, not kudos or money. As Delia said, 'People that are just interested in self-promotion and money are not my thing.'

TG works were considered and promoted collectively as 'All tracks written and performed by Throbbing Gristle', listing all four of our names. As part of the democratic ethos all our collective improvised output was essentially TG. The admin of assigning rights and filling in the PRS and MCPS forms for royalties and that side of 'business' wasn't a priority all four of us shared, nor was looking to the future to safeguard our work. Looking back, I should have been more vigilant. Years later during the second incarnation of TG, when we were recording a new studio album (*Part Two: The Endless Not*), the crediting of our works became a problem and a source of unnecessary antagonism. A collective

'TG' credit as before was fine but demands for additional individual credits that highlighted and benefited only one person were both blatantly misleading and a self-serving ploy that went against the spirit of collaboration. It indicated their having created the music on certain tracks when they'd done little (or nothing), as well as providing unwarranted visibility to one person, and gave the wrong impression entirely about who and what TG represented. When the ego of one member becomes their prime concern there is no longer a collective. After months of 'discussions' and what amounted to blackmail tactics it was agreed that in order for the album to be released the works would not be credited solely to the TG collective but would include some individually ascribed contributions. Such manipulative appropriation goes way beyond registering copyright ownership and listing names on album artwork. The interpersonal conflicts it causes have consequences, the ramifications of which led to the end of TG for good.

There's a fine line between appropriation and exploitation, as Delia knew, and she didn't like it at all but had become resigned to her work being used without credit or notification. She had tried to prevent misuse of her work. Delia, Brian and David had signed an agreement for the music they created for the *Coloured Wall* exhibition in 1968, saying that all rights were retained by Kaleidophon and the music was not permitted to be used for any other purpose.

It often happens that my music is used without my knowledge. I heard some of my music on the radio last year but I didn't get a credit. Sometimes when people use my music they change its name. For example, a few years ago I heard my music on *The Hitch Hiker's Guide to the Galaxy*. I wrote to the producer, who said, 'Yeah, it's called "Dreaming".' I've never done anything called that.

They had picked out a piece which I wrote for a programme about the Aztec and Mayan civilisations. They put a new title on it and used it behind Peter Jones's voice. Such is life!

I'm not so easy-going. I fight against such rip-offs. TG has been the victim countless times and some bootleggers adopt the same tactic applied to the theft of Delia's music – of renaming tracks to get around payment and bootleg charges. It's not about the money (although it's very helpful), it's about protecting the integrity of the music, recognition of authorship, individual 'rights' and retaining ownership of those creative moments, what went into the making of the music, working under difficult circumstances. That's why appropriation feels like such a betrayal, because technique and ability aside, it's so personal. Music is tied in with the identity of the composer.

Many times Chris and I have been asked for the 'secret' to our particular sound production. People have been unashamedly blatant in asking us outright for melodies or rhythms to use for their own tracks, basically wanting a short cut to where we had got to after years of work developing techniques. We actually have a book called 'Studio Secrets' that started out as notes on what we found worked best for certain rhythm patterns and progressions, vocal effects and the overall 'magic dust' for the final mix. No access has ever been granted to our little book. We suffered more from the attempted extortion of information on our techniques and processes pre-internet. Now there are forums where people can discuss how they think we get our sound, which is interesting to read and it's nice to know that what we do inspires others. But there are times when people sample elements from our works, sometimes complete melodies or rhythms, which is when the advantages of the internet come in. Infringements are quickly spotted by dedicated fans, outraged on our behalf, who inform us whenever this happens. Then begins the long haul of addressing the problem through official channels. An unwelcome and unnecessary distraction that could be avoided if people just created their own work and didn't plagiarise someone else's. Some may disagree with me but I'm a firm believer in the value of finding your own ways and means to express yourself. It gives the work intrinsic, idiosyncratic beauty and power. And in that way we communicate our individual understanding of life experiences in preference to repeating those of others.

To have people come to you only when they want something, to talk at length and then to have your ideas appear later ascribed to them, leaves you feeling deceived and utterly disrespected. Even more so when the perpetrator then claims that what they did to you was out of respect or expresses disbelief at your complaint with 'What does it matter anyway?' Well, the obvious answer is that it does matter or they wouldn't have done it – and without you they could not have come up with or realised the idea themselves. In some instances the fine line between appropriation and exploitation is crossed and it becomes misappropriation. I had an instance recently that went a step too far, usurping my identity by 'appropriating' one of my renowned 1970s works, the sex magazine project. I was told by a close friend that a guy had published the photos in a series of books and was selling them at a princely price based solely on my reputation as an artist. When I confronted the perpetrator he claimed it was done as an act of respect for my work. I closed it down with the assistance of a very kind and honourable lawyer. However, I met with resistance from the owner of a London bookstore who refused to cease selling the books and return them. He didn't see what my problem was (again the 'What does it matter?' defence) and showed no empathy for my situation. Couldn't care less. I guess it was just 'business' – and of course that did 'matter'. The perpetrator, however, understood my outrage and eventually had the grace to relent and apologise. But to this day I'm still looking into illicit appropriations of other works . . . because money matters more to some people and to them the author of the work is just a commodity for exploitation.

Only a few of the people I've collaborated with over the years have taken credit for the whole work and felt entitled to diminish my own contribution, treating it as being of insignificance and 'using' my name, listing it (if at all) subordinate to theirs. One collaboration involved my generating vocal material to use as the sole source for sonic manipulations with which to compose the music for an album. I went into the project fully expecting an exciting venture together, exploring the most intimate of human emotions through my vocalisations, which related to my own very personal experiences, the expression of feminine and masculine and the differences between us. When the project was completed and the issue of a publisher for the work was discussed, an unanticipated problem arose. I had assumed everything was shared equally, as with other collaborative projects I'd worked on. But he had a different viewpoint and demanded the majority share of the publishing because in his opinion he, not I, was the 'composer', and I was regarded as a mere 'source', as if I'd been hired (unpaid) to supply material. Rightly or wrongly, I felt that as a woman I was regarded as lesser than him. I felt insulted but mostly angry at having to deal with such an attitude, which made me feel robbed of my agency, 'used', much as Delia had been. I'd fallen foul again in putting my trust in someone. Maybe I should have known better, having written the song 'Trust' years ago: 'We fall, we rise, we fall and rise to trust again.' The lyrics were about a past relationship and trust in general, how we have to retain faith in people no matter what, but there are some whose priority is self-interest and who will betray and manipulate those of an altruistic nature.

It occurred to me when I thought back to Delia's collaborations at the RW how similar it was to her not receiving any credit for the work she did on *Inventions for Radio*, particularly with her piece *Amor Dei*, when Barry Bermange credited himself with all the sound. His odd rationale, much like my collaborator's, was that he had taken control of Delia's music when he mixed it with the voices he'd recorded. Therefore, to his thinking, the sum of the parts was his alone. Delia's archived notes on *Amor Dei* suggest otherwise. I can't for the life of me understand why anyone would think that someone else's work is their own. That attitude takes a particular kind of mindset and character trait that I thankfully don't have. In some ways what has been worse for me over the years is when I've heard my own words emanate from the mouths of others, my ideas and personal expressions of how I feel about the making of my music and art. I've actually sat speechless during a group interview as I listened to someone next to me replying to a question and uttering verbatim what I'd previously said to them in private. I was left wondering what to say when I was asked the same question.

There was appreciation for Delia's work. Once she was praised by a BBC executive as 'little short of brilliant'. He couldn't quite manage 'brilliant' – just a little less than. Praise had a tendency to be internal within the musical circles in which Delia worked and moved socially. As somewhat of a musicians' musician she was sought out by many people – musicians, playwrights, poets and artists – who wanted to consult with her on different aspects of music and get information on her techniques. In the case of Pink Floyd, she ended up taking them to Peter Zinovieff's studio and paying for the privilege by covering the cost of their taxi fare.

In spite of her brilliance and reputation for successfully tackling what to others seemed impossible musical tasks, she wasn't at all pretentious or elitist. Her interests were wide-ranging, her enthusiasm infectious. She just wanted to work with musicians, be they avant-garde or commercial. She'd gladly give her ear to anything, at least once, and was only too happy to pass on the things she'd discovered. She loved jazz, Stockhausen, Bach and other classical and contemporary composers, the Kinks and the Rolling Stones. She had a soft spot for Brian Jones and had him come to see her at the RW, where he sat in front of the oscillators in his frilly white cuffs – and much to Delia's amusement he tried to play them like an instrument. He left quite an impression on her. She wept when she heard the news of his death on 3 July 1969.

Those collaborative moments with artists meant a lot to Delia. Back in 1970 Desmond Briscoe had put her in temporary charge of the RW while he took extended leave. She felt a sense of freedom from his watchful eye and took advantage of the space and time it provided to spread her wings and extend her explorations into more adventurous opportunities independent of the BBC. A highlight of Desmond's absence was the opportunity of a free studio and the chance to enter into collaborations. One that impressed her was with the jazz-oriented experimental band Soft Machine on two *Study Session* programmes for Radio 3. Delia enjoyed the experience so much she recommended their music to someone who had written expressing admiration of her own work and asking if she could suggest other similar music with unusual time signatures. She'd been experimenting with phrase lengths, moving away from using eight and twelve bars to eleven and thirteen, so the unconventional rhythms of Soft Machine's drummer Robert Wyatt immediately struck the right note with her – a meeting of nonconformists. It was the same non-standard approach to rhythm that was so memorable about my and Chris's collaboration with Robert on *Unmasked* in the 1980s. The rhythm we used kept changing throughout but upheld its swing, something Robert immediately picked up on and which became a point of discussion between us.

I was absolutely thrilled to learn that Delia had worked with Robert. I dare say his short time with her had some influence on opening his mind to the kind of music we were making in TG, because it wasn't long after his RW visit that he first got in touch with me. Delia instilled in him a positive attitude to experimenting with his own work: 'Ms Derbyshire was, crucially, one of the life-enhancing people who helped me clear the way for what I have been attempting ever since, simply by demonstrating her unfettered ideas.' He remembers Delia was the only woman in the small studio, and that she was keen to show the band how the mass of equipment worked and what it could offer them. The regimented feel in the workshop didn't escape his attention either because it felt so at odds with Delia's personal approach to music, what he described as 'her almost childlike enthusiasm for possibilities . . . and her "out there" vision'.

In her letter recommending Soft Machine she modestly suggested her own album *An Electric Storm* at the very end, almost like an apologetic afterthought, outlining her involvement as collaborating in the composition and electronic realisation of the album. Interestingly there was no mention of her lover David Vorhaus, with whom she'd worked so closely on it, yet she heaped praise on the jazz drummer Paul Lytton. I'd be tempted to read something into that omission, especially as her relationship with David was coming to an end or had already ended. Or she could have been sticking to the subject of rhythm, because she goes on to refer to the *Time Beat* rhythm track, taking the opportunity to put the record straight, confirming that Ray Cathode is a fictitious person and the rhythm was done by the RW (a real person – a woman, Maddalena Fagandini). Feeding the reality of its origins to the outside world. A gesture notable for coming at a time when she was feeling passed over for promotions to positions that were rightly suited to her, while at the same time being good enough to act on behalf of Desmond while he was away. Her signing off the letter as 'Organiser, Radiophonic Workshop (Acting)' may have been officially correct but has other connotations considering her continuing disappointment at her skills and achievements going unrecognised (unlike those of her male colleagues) and never being enough to advance her position. It's a point Robert touched on when we talked about his time with Delia: 'Perhaps a man with her ideas would have been more confidently assertive, but it was her far-sighted ideas themselves that made her exceptional. D.D.'s ideas were simply way ahead of the curve . . . she was like a visitor from the future, coming back to offer us a hand . . . !'

In view of Delia's experiences of collaborating with people, the whole issue of collaboration was a significant and important part of my work on the film with Caroline. We both felt a weight of responsibility to Delia, working together to represent her, in a different way from the many male representations and exploitations of her work.

24

I'd set myself a deadline of mid-November 2019 for delivering the 'Delia' soundtrack material to Caroline, to allow for any adjustments prior to the December shoot. As her work on the production increased we'd catch up on any points she needed me to address in the intervals of her incredibly busy schedule. 'Delia' had taken over my studio for the best part of a year. Its appearance was rather reminiscent of her descriptions of her own cluttered space, with an accumulation of papers, notebooks and instruments so that Chris and I had to squeeze past tables and benches heaving with the various configurations of equipment I'd used for recording. The soundtrack whiteboard was a veritable rainbow as each group of requested sounds was ticked off in a different colour on completion. There were field recordings that depended on accessibility to various locations and the vagaries of the weather, so some had yet to be done.

As I continued to work my way through Caroline's script I found myself once again going back to engage with the influence of the sounds of Delia's childhood on her music. Scene 18 called for the deafening percussive sound of 'clogs on cobbles', a known source of inspiration for Delia from when she went to live in Preston after the Coventry Blitz. She stayed with her aunt Annie, uncle John and cousin Edith in Inkerman Street. Uncle John worked at a nearby cotton mill as a tape sizer, a well-paid, skilled job. Each morning he, like all the mill workers, would put on wooden clogs and set off to work at six o'clock. Delia remembered the throngs of mill workers walking past her house and the deafening clatter of their metal-shod clogs on the cobblestone street. The percussive abstract sound of the footfall of life made a lasting impression on her. It was a thunderous cacophony with so many feet setting different paces, but intermittently they'd fall into step – enough to suggest a rhythm. Delia may or may not have known about the other rhythms that emanated from the clogs once work began. The clogs had metal toe caps as well as 'horseshoe' soles and the workers had developed a way of keeping in time with the different functions of the machines, creating specific syncopated rhythms by tapping their feet. 'Dance' movements that beat out an industrial music rhythm. It was as much for their amusement as for safety and efficiency. The mills were so noisy no one could be easily heard. Rhythm was key when operating the machines: it signalled the timing of the various functions, a way of knowing when shuttles and parts of machinery were shooting in different directions, essential to keep hands out of harm's way.

I knew first-hand all about the abrasive sound of metal hitting cobblestones from when I lived down a cobbled street in the old part of Hull and the market traders would trundle their metal-wheeled carts along outside my bedroom window in the very early hours of the morning. It wasn't a rhythmic experience for me so much as an unpleasant scraping and ominous rumbling sound. Come to think of it, maybe that had an influence on my own music too.

Armed with a piece of metal and my hand-held Zoom recorder I went into King's Lynn to the place I felt would be perfect for the recording of 'clogs on cobbles' – Devil's Alley. A narrow cobbled passageway off Nelson Street once known as Miller's Alley, it led directly to the quay and was used by medieval merchants, like Margery's father and husband. Its name was changed after, as legend has it, a priest saw the devil disembark from a ship to search for souls. The priest banished him using religious incantations and holy water. The devil was so enraged he stamped his foot in fury, leaving his hoof print in one of the cobbles.

I walked down the alley away from the noise of passing traffic. It was quiet. I had it all to myself and began beating the cobbles with my metal percussion stick, trying to recreate the footfall of a clog, which I could later overlay to get the effect of marching mill workers. Just as I was finishing I heard a familiar sound and turned to see a guy coming towards me pushing an old medieval-style wooden cart. I kept the recorder running until the sound faded away as he turned the corner. It was like a flashback in time, a brief 'vision' of the alley in the fifteenth century.

Devil's Alley is just fifty yards from St Margaret's Church and I took the opportunity to go inside. I'd been there on numerous occasions before I knew about Margery and its huge importance to her as her precious space. I recorded the ambient sound as I sat on the pews in the place where she had prayed. I wanted to use it as a subliminal audio 'presence' of Margery. The Parish Register of St Margaret's listed my family names: Chinnery, Newby and Pilkington . . . and also Maull, the family name of my dearest friend and 'brother' Les. His family's roots were in King's Lynn. The Maulls lived in Margery's parish of St Margaret's, in an area known as one of the poorest and roughest, where men and women alike were hard as nails.

Not far from where they lived is Paradise Lane, a cut-through Chris and I always use to get to one of the only music shops in King's Lynn. I often wondered what was behind the name, assuming it may have been some religious 'paradise' – but no. Medieval street names were descriptive of what occupations and businesses went on there. There were red light districts, places to have casual or illicit sex away from the thoroughfare and out of the sight of prying and judgemental eyes. Paradise Road, across from where Margery lived, linked to Paradise Parade, leading directly into Paradise Lane, which everyone knew offered the promise of 'forbidden' heavenly delights. Other provincial towns like Norwich and Cambridge had more direct names for their streets of sex. There could be no mistaking what took place down Gropecunt Lane.

—⚏—

Sex played a big role in both my own and Margery's process of breaking away from being stereotypical compliant women. We transgressed in totally opposite ways. Margery opted out from having sex and repressing her sexuality. I embraced and explored mine in my lifestyle and art, infiltrating the male-dominated sex industry, taking myself into very different male spaces to Margery and receiving vitriolic public criticism for daring to make my own choice about how to express myself and how to use my body. Like Margery I found myself subjected to character assassination, but twentieth-century style, through an onslaught of abuse in the daily press, TV and radio, being doorstepped by journalists, and hearing questions asked in the Houses of Parliament about my outrageous behaviour. They were aimed at my being a woman and (woman) artist. To my critics I didn't know my place. I definitely do. My place is where I decide it is. Their reaction to my work epitomised the problems 'other' people face when they make their presence known by taking their rightful position in situations where they are judged as misplaced and unwelcome. I know first-hand how Margery would have felt being the target for such narrow-minded, misogynistic intolerance and hatred. Whatever that early unconfessed sin was, it stayed with Margery all her life. I see it as a positive thing – that sin played a huge part in determining her destiny. It set her on a path she might never otherwise have taken, into new and sometimes forbidden places for a woman. A course that dominated her life with celibacy and travelling on pilgrimages, the key factors of her process to find her*self*.

The whole idea of celibacy goes against everything I understand and hold dear about human nature. The need for physical contact, skin on skin, sexual union and being held close and loved is so strong, there's no wonder Margery had such a hard time denying herself the most fundamental instincts. She described her cravings for sex as the devil tempting her to succumb to her lustful urges. By successfully resisting she showed that she (not the devil) was in control of her body. That's not how I or Delia would describe our sexual desires. We both indulged ourselves as we fancied and when we chose to, if any appealing opportunities arose, and considering my work in the sex industry, Delia seems to have been more sexually active than I was. And she wasn't shy about it. In one interview she suggested they put at the end that she'd been 'having it off' in the Derbyshire Dales on the way back from a convention.

Prior to Margery's vow of chastity in marriage she was propositioned for sex by a man in church on St Margaret's Eve. She found the idea so arousing and distracting she became deaf to the sounds of evensong and was left speechless – stopped in her tracks, unable to say the Lord's Prayer. It was only sex with her husband that repulsed her, not other men. She couldn't get the lustful thoughts out of her mind. That night she lay in bed with her husband, fretting about 'falling' into temptation. She finally succumbed, and the next day went looking for the man to have sex. When she found him, the spontaneous lustful moment had passed and he'd lost interest (or she'd hurt his pride). He looked Margery up and down and more or less told her that he wouldn't touch her with a bargepole – but that if he did desire her again he wouldn't bother to ask her, he'd take her by force.

This is a great anecdote to illustrate Margery's saintly aspirations of temperance and commitment – she is tempted by an offer of sex, resists, is tested again and succumbs to lust, only to be rejected. Margery's appetite for sex was what she considered her downfall. She had to be seen (and read) to renounce it as sinful. Her visions of God were sometimes replaced by devilish hallucinations of men, including priests, waving their cocks at her, offering her sex with them all, one after the other – and in public. Such a full-on sexual fantasy appealed to her – or was it just to show how strong she was in managing to reject such an irresistible offer of an orgy?

It's a terrible and difficult thing to have to deny yourself such pleasures, especially when your sex drive is so strong. It requires immense willpower not to give in and indulge yourself, knowing how wonderful it can be. Margery couldn't fully trust herself around men or trust them, and she fought to control herself and her fantasies at the same time as fearing being raped.

> . . . sche was evyr aferd to a be ravischyd er defilyd. Sche durst trustyn on no man; whedir sche had cawse er non, sche was evyr aferd.
> [. . . she was always afraid of being raped or dishonoured. She dared trust no man; whether or not she had reason, she was always afraid.]

Her rationale was that her lasciviousness was God testing her resolve to stay on the straight and narrow. She had to work out a way to reconcile her Catholic faith with her sexual desires, eventually finding the solution by directing them at someone safe and orthodox when she began her 'affair' with Christ, sacrificing her physical sexual self for her individual kind of sainthood. There were many times she 'heard' Christ speak of lying with her as his lover, his bride. Some have said she was still submitting to male control in the form of Christ and the Church. But there were very few options open to a woman in medieval England who hated her assigned role and needed or wanted to escape. Many women stayed put, making the best of a bad situation, more comfortable in their discomfort than the idea of the unknown and the prospect of public scandal and condemnation. But that wasn't for Margery. She wanted out. And how she did it was her choice to make.

Margery's constant references to resisting her lust were part of her piety and saintliness, but it still bothered me why she seemed so obsessed by celibacy, repeatedly documenting the temptations she overcame. I understood the relevance to her religion but there were other factors involved that for me made more sense. The praying, the meditation, the fasting, the weeping, the pilgrimages to shrines were all 'remedies' for sin, not just as penance for being ungodly, but as treatments for diseases and illnesses which were viewed as punishments for sinning.

At the time physical and emotional health was largely under-stood in terms of Hippocrates' theory of the four humours of the body – black bile, yellow bile, phlegm and blood. Each had its own temperament (choleric, melancholic, phlegmatic and san-guine) and its associated season and element. Any imbalance caused health problems, so it was sometimes necessary to dis-charge bodily fluids to keep everything in check. Women's (and men's) bodies were thought to need regular (but not excessive) sexual intercourse, to expel their 'seed' and remain 'balanced'. If not, the 'seed' would build up to dangerous, possibly fatal levels. This meant sex could not only be sinful in itself, it could also carry serious health risks. Too much or too little was bad for you. No sex was even worse, so celibacy had more than a few drawbacks for Margery. Believing she was damned if she did have sex and damned if she didn't, she would get down on her knees to pray and weep as much as possible in the hope it would redress her humours. Weeping was seen as helpful to chastity, a way to quell lust. All body fluids were thought to be derived from blood, so crying was like releasing 'seed' to prevent it building up in the womb – thereby rendering sex, including masturbation, unnecessary and conquering lust. Weeping was like a form of bloodletting. In the 1984 Chris & Cosey song 'Raining Tears of Blood' the theme and lyrics are about dealing with and expressing feelings of inner and outer torment, finding your place in the world and being persecuted for it:

> An ache in my heart I cannot conceal.
> I'm raining tears of blood
> for the torment in my soul
> And as the tears fall away again, my dove flies free.

Religion aside, both Margery's and my reasons for baring our souls through our actions and 'recordings' are all about the human condition. In my lyrics the dove is symbolic and relevant to both our situations – new beginnings, freedom, truth, peace, love and, for Margery, the divine. Coincidentally the title of the album the track is from is *Love & Lust*. Both emotions for me coexist, each enhancing the other, but sadly it was the opposite for Margery. But she did have one bonus: foreign travel, especially pilgrimage, was believed to be another 'cure' for lust and a womb overloaded with 'seed' from lack of sex. It could cool things down.

The sin of masturbation, as seen by the Church, could lead to being ordered to fast as penance for months or even years, like

Margery abstaining from meat for long periods from as early as 1409. And it posed another paradox for Margery, because it was also recommended as a sin-free treatment by male physicians to women (including nuns) who weren't expelling their 'seed' often enough. They could either masturbate themselves (only if officially prescribed) or go to a physician or midwife who would sexually stimulate them by inserting one or two oiled fingers into the vagina and then set about getting an in/out rhythm going until a satisfactory show of fluid was achieved. I doubt they'd recognise the fluid as being from the resulting natural lubricating vaginal juices or orgasmic squirting. It would be nice to think some of the women had the pleasure of reaching orgasm. The image the procedure conjures up is quite something to try and get my head around. It's sex work but in a completely different context. All I kept thinking was that the physicians and midwives must have been in great demand. But as with sex, masturbation was to be done in moderation – unlike a thirteenth-century monk who inadvertently acted as an example of what could happen if you went hell-for-leather at it. He was said to have lost his sight from wanking over seventy times before attending morning prayers and died from a withered brain. The origins of the old wives' tale that masturbating too much can make you go blind would appear to go back a long way.

Margery's need for physical contact seemed desperate enough for her to request permission to kiss lepers on the lips. Not a request many (other than aspiring saints) would make, but Margery did as part of her offering to help them. Looking after lepers was part of her pious remit. I don't know where kissing would come into it other than an aching for human touch. As a married woman she was forbidden to kiss men but she was allowed to kiss women. The leper hospital nearest to Margery was in Gaywood and dedicated to St Mary Magdalene. Her local Franciscan monks nursed those afflicted with leprosy, and so had her paragon of virtue, Marie of Oignies. Leprosy was linked to the vice of lechery and seen as the result of sexual sins, including adultery and sodomy. Maybe Margery felt some affinity with them, being on her lecherous guilt trip, or possibly because of her partly estranged eldest son John. She'd wanted him to be a monk, but he much preferred a life of debauchery while working for a merchant in Gdańsk. He ignored her nagging about his immoral behaviour – until he contracted a nasty, ugly skin disease, probably a sexually transmitted infection. He and Margery put it down as punishment for his rampant sexual appetite. His face was covered in spots and boils and he looked like a leper. He was shunned, got the sack from his job and went crawling back to his mother, begging her to pray for him, saying he would mend his ways. Margery's prayers worked wonders. The disease went away – and so did John, back to Gdańsk.

25

After all the gruelling journeys Margery had been on, walking, being rolled about at sea and bumped around on donkeys and in hard wooden carts, it's hardly surprising that she developed back trouble and other long-term physical problems. For eight years, from 1418 to 1426, she suffered from one illness after another, nearly dying from dysentery, then long bouts of severe headaches that made her feel so disoriented she thought she was going mad, and periods of excruciating pain down her right side. Every time she seemed to be getting better she'd have another setback. That put a stop to her wanderings, but not her prayers. They were still numerous and noisy and still caused her trouble.

She'd been living separately from her husband as part of a public show of her celibacy. Then her circumstances changed suddenly. John fell down the stairs and landed on his head with such a clatter his neighbours went to see what was going on. They found him lying in a heap, with his head curled under him. When they rolled him over, his head was covered in blood and so badly bruised and broken they thought he wouldn't survive. Margery was sent for and her neighbours blamed her for what had happened. If she'd lived with her husband as a good wife should, he would have been fine, and if he died it would be her fault and she should hang for neglecting her duty to him. His deep wounds were stitched and swathed in bandages, almost covering his entire head. Margery took John to her home, nursed him and became his full-time carer. His accident had left him incapacitated and incontinent, and he most probably suffered from senile dementia – Margery says he *'turnyd childisch agen and lakkyd reson'*. Both had lived longer than the average person of their time. John was in his sixties and she was in her mid-fifties, infirm herself and very poor, existing on the alms she received as charity or payments to say prayers for people. She begrudged the extra cost of food and heating, and the energy she expended on the constant washing and cleaning of him and his clothes after he repeatedly messed himself. The years she cared for him were hard work. It was exhausting but she consoled herself by thinking of it as punishment for having lusted after John when she was young. That didn't lessen the resentment she felt towards him. Having to care for him was a major hindrance to her contemplations.

It had been years since Margery had seen her eldest son John after his last visit to Lynn, pox-ridden and needing her forgiveness and help. By way of attempting a reconciliation, he sent word to her that he was a changed man, now married with a daughter. He returned to Lynn to visit Margery and his father. His dowdy clothes and humble demeanour were a clear indication of his new way of life and he planned to make a pilgrimage to Rome. Margery desperately wanted to see his wife and her granddaughter before she died. She and her son discussed what would be the best way for the family to make the journey to England. It was decided that all three would come by sea, but violent storms changed their original plans, and John and his wife left their daughter in the safe hands of friends before travelling. They arrived in Lynn on a Saturday, and the next day her son John became ill. He was dead within a month. Later the same year, *c.*1432, Margery's husband John also died. Both deaths got only a cursory mention in her book, Margery saying that they had *'passyd to the mercy of owr Lord . . . the way which every man must gon'*. No expression of sadness, just the inevitability and acceptance of death and of going to a better place. Leaving her free of those restrictive obligations.

Margery's daughter-in-law stayed with her for eighteen months before deciding to go back to her home in Gdańsk (formerly Danzig – now in Poland, but at that time held by the Prussian Teutonic Knights). Helping to make the necessary arrangements reawakened Margery's appetite for travel. A plan started to form in her mind. Going to Germany could give her the opportunity for one more pilgrimage, this time to Aachen (known as 'the new Jerusalem'). Her confessor had instructed her not to go abroad again: she was too old and frail, and it was unsafe because of the difficulties English travellers were experiencing due to trade disputes with the Hanseatic League. He would allow Margery to go with her daughter-in-law to Ipswich, where her ship was due to set sail, but then she must return to Lynn.

Taking advantage of their time on the road, the two women visited the shrine at Walsingham. Margery stopped to pray in a small church and (rather conveniently) received 'word' from God that she should go to Germany. Much to her daughter-in-law's disapproval and in defiance of her confessor, on arrival at Ipswich she bought herself a ticket for the crossing. The first day was plain sailing, then the weather changed. Severe storms with strong winds and rough seas blew the ship off course and they ended up in Norway. Margery had narrowly escaped being drowned, her greatest fear. After a day's rest she and her daughter-in-law continued on to Gdańsk, where her son had lived and her father had traded, and presumably where Margery's granddaughter was, though there's no mention of her. Margery stayed there six weeks before going on what would be her last and most hazardous pilgrimage, to the shrines at Wilsnack and Aachen. The timing couldn't have been worse. The Teutonic Order were at war with the invading heretic Hussites (seen as aligned to English Lollards). The safest route for her and her hired companion to avoid the fighting was by sea to Stralsund, then on foot the rest of the way to Wilsnack. The prospect of another perilous sea crossing was far from appealing but necessary. Then, just as her confessor had warned, she came up against anti-English hostility, having to get permission to travel from the Catholic Teutonic Knights because '*sche was an Englisch woman*'. Once again her father's mercantile connections came to her rescue. A Lynn merchant who was in Gdańsk on business argued her case successfully, and she took the ship and landed in Stralsund.

The journey by foot to Wilsnack was still high-risk, with skirmishes going on as well as the usual threat of robbery – and her companion John wasn't much protection. He was young and fit, and she was a sixty-year-old, partially lame woman. He tried to leave her behind more than a few times. Her crying from pain grated on him as much as her prayers, and she hampered his progress by walking so slowly because of her bad foot. She was a liability to his own safety. So he tried to get rid of her by walking fast, knowing she'd more than likely find it physically impossible to keep up with him. It must have been agony for her but she managed to hobble along, pleading with him to slow down and wait for her. When they reached a hostel she collapsed, ill and worn out, with only a bare scattering of straw to lie on. The people at the inn took pity on her, blamed her state on John's ill treatment and provided a wagon for her to go the last miles to the Holy Blood Shrine to view drops of Christ's blood and then onward for the nearly four-hundred-mile journey to Aachen. There was no way she could have managed or survived the journey on foot.

When she and John reached the River Rhine they met more pilgrims. John knew some of the merchants and a monk who was with them, whom Margery took an instant dislike to. The men agreed to join together in one big group, Margery being the only woman. They crossed the river and moved on in their wagons, stopping at a friary for food and drink. It was the time of Corpus Christi, and Margery got to view the friary's sacrament, which triggered her sobbing – and the by now familiar scolding and subsequent abandonment. They threw her out of the group. John gave her back her money and, knowing the dangers she'd face, left her to make her own way to Aachen. To add to her worries, when she managed to find an inn, local priests came along and made fun of her, offering to show her around – '*proferyng to ledyn hir abowtyn yf sche wolde*' – which she read as a sexual innuendo and threat: '*Sche had mech drede for hir chastité*.' She felt utterly miserable and vulnerable and paid the landlady to arrange for two maidservants to sleep in her room as protection against being raped by the errant priests. She was in a desperate situation. On the road to Aachen, the only thing that saved her was coming across a group of beggars who were happy for her to join them. They were filthy and lice-ridden but kind to her – even sharing their fleas and lice. They'd sit at a quiet spot and strip naked, pinching off the bugs and picking at their scabs, with Margery alongside keeping her bug-ridden clothes on and squirming in disgust. It was something she had to put up with until she could find someone else to travel with.

Margery couldn't have timed her arrival in Aachen better. It was probably her last chance to view four great relics held in the shrine of the Virgin Mary, which were only shown every seven years. A heady list of important religious items – the Virgin Mary's smock, Christ's swaddling clothes and two grisly relics: Christ's loincloth from his crucifixion and the bloody cloth from John the Baptist's decapitation. Having made it there after all the agonies she'd gone through and in defiance of her confessor, Margery had managed to complete the checklist of St Bridget's pilgrimages. She stayed in Aachen for ten days, viewing more relics on St Margaret's Day before setting off for Calais to catch a ship back to England.

Finding a group to travel with was almost impossible. She was refused by monks and pilgrims as well as a wealthy widow. They either refused outright or said yes and then sneaked off without her. No one really wanted her with them. She was too old and slow and would prevent them catching their ship on time. There was an 'every man for himself' attitude, giving an overall impression of an old, feeble, raggedy, pious woman being treated abominably by unkind Christians who showed her no compassion. Margery had to take whatever offer there was, switching from one group to another as she failed to keep up with their pace or got cast aside as a nuisance. A good monk accompanied her for the last few days it took to get to Calais. Both of them only just made it across sand dunes, up steep hills and through valleys. There were only a few places they could rest and get food and drink. It's a wonder she made it to Calais. She'd travelled over a thousand miles from Gdańsk, she was worn out, bone tired, dejected and weak after staying on the floors of outhouses, being repeatedly let down by people reneging on their promises. For the three days she waited for the ship she was taken in by strangers who took pity on her and washed her and gave her clean clothes and food. Only a very few good-natured people had shown her kindness and respect, and they seem to have had no idea about her reputation. Those who knew about it dissociated themselves from her on board ship. Back in England, she was left stranded.

With what little money she had left she hired a man to take her on horseback to Canterbury and London, where she had friends who could loan her some cash, knowing through her connections that repayment was guaranteed. Far from being a picture of health or wealth, she was dressed in dark sackcloth with a kerchief over her face so she wouldn't be recognised. It wasn't a very successful disguise. Some people figured out who she was and mocked her as a hypocrite, a woman who professed to be humble and holy but would only eat the best meat – '*A, thu fals flesch, thu schalt no good mete etyn.*' She ignored them. The sneering surfaced again as she sat having dinner at a friend's house. The tipsy guests, not knowing who she was, started poking fun at 'the hypocrite from Lynn'. Listening to their gossip and insults was unbearable. She revealed she was 'Mar. Kempe of Lynne', telling them to keep silent on things they knew nothing about. What they'd said was all lies and – charitable as ever – she hoped God would forgive them.

Margery's last pilgrimage had been a long, hazardous and traumatic experience, with so much cold-heartedness towards her from so many people. When she returned to Lynn her confessor was furious with her for disobeying him, swanning off to Germany when he'd strictly forbidden her to travel abroad. After much begging and persuasion he forgave her. No longer being physically or financially able to go on long journeys, she settled down in Lynn. She was not locking herself away like an anchoress, though. She refused to be 'contained' and stayed out there in the world. Her pastoral duties were important to her and she was always among people, helping them when they were sick or dying, praying for them and giving guidance and support. It was a holy way of life and receiving alms was a respectable way to earn a living.

Her book was also a priority. It's impossible to know her exact reason for writing it, but the most likely motivation was that by leaving an account of her spiritual revelations and how she had overcome so much suffering, like the saints she admired, she too would be perceived as a holy woman. She wanted it finished before she died but not to be read until after her death. There's no evidence to put an exact date on when she began to write the first part but it's believed to have been in or around 1432. The second part is dated April 1438 – around the same time she paid for her membership of the Guild of the Holy Trinity in Lynn, a gesture that suggests she knew she may not have had much longer to live. It was a prestigious guild that controlled Lynn's business matters, but membership had other benefits. Members could be guaranteed a high church funeral service with requiem mass and the guild's own priests to say an abundance of prayers on her behalf. There were few women enrolled in the guild, so Margery's acceptance may not be down just to having paid for the privilege. Despite all her past troubles, she may have re-established her status. Her name appears in the guild records as having paid for her membership on 22 May 1439 and is the only clue to when she was possibly still alive. Her actual date of death is unknown, as is her place of burial.

26

As had become my nightly routine I was reading another book on Margery, but this one had something extra. It told the story behind the chance discovery of her book in 1934 – due to, of all things, a game of ping-pong at the Derbyshire country mansion of the Butler-Bowdons. The ping-pong ball got trodden on and a search for a new one in the cupboards revealed a shambolic stack of old leather-bound books, among which was Margery's *Book* – the only known surviving manuscript. No one knew that at the time. The books were seen as 'clutter' and there was mention of putting the whole lot on a bonfire the next day. By sheer luck 'Margery' was once more saved from the pyre. Two guests at the house worked at the Victoria and Albert Museum. When they saw Margery's *Book* they thought it might be of significant historical value and took it to London to be assessed by experts. After intense inspection its identity was confirmed. In 1980 it was sold at auction and bought by the British Library.

It got me thinking about Delia. Not just because of her surname, Derbyshire, but because Delia's schoolbooks and some childhood relics had been found in a similar way, stuffed up her bedroom chimney in the old Coventry family home, 104 Cedars Avenue, when a new buyer was carrying out renovations in 2011. How they got there is anyone's guess, but I imagine it was Delia who stashed them away for safe keeping for some reason. But I'm thankful she did and that someone had unwittingly put Margery's book in what proved to be a safe place too. Two voices that had been silent for so long, fortuitously revealed to disclose so much about each of them.

I timed my second visit to the John Rylands Library, where Delia's childhood treasures were held, to coincide with a talk I was doing with Jon Savage for Design Manchester 2019. My first visit to the library had been solely in relation to my composing the soundtrack, to examine her archived music files. I booked myself into the same hotel I had stayed in before with Caroline. I'd gone there straight from rehearsing in my studio for the 'Delia' film so was in Delian mode and eager to see and read her schoolbooks.

The archive folders I'd requested were delivered to me as I sat again at one of the long desks in the reading room. I leafed through them, hoping to get a sense of young Delia, her formative years, her aspirations. I got to thinking about her childhood, how we'd both gone to all-girls schools, made our own clothes, learnt to play the piano and been taught within an institutional education system that primed us to be 'good girls' and potential wives, mothers and housewives. It would be easy for me to assume from Delia's cultivated voice and 'posh' demeanour that she was like the wholesome, studious girls I was at school with, whom I called 'all sensible shoes and woollen mittens'. Nothing like me and my friends, who tried our best to integrate something fashionable into our uniforms by way of pointy-toed, non-sensible shoes and received detentions for daring to express ourselves by wearing creative alternatives to the strict regulation uniform. I couldn't quite imagine Delia joining in with other girls like I had when we'd share intimate details about each other's sexual development. I was a late developer in the pubic hair department, with just one solitary hair to my name – which grew to quite some length, then fell out. I was back to square one – hairless except for my armpits, which seemed to be getting bushier by the day. We'd compare armpit hair growth (I was OK there), pubes (zilch), boobs and the size of our Venus mounds. We'd take it in turn to lie on our backs across a desk, with our knees hanging over the edge, which was the best position to see how high our Venus mounds protruded. Some girls were really well developed, most more than me. Somehow that didn't seem like it would have been very 'Delia'.

Sifting through Delia's exercise books it became apparent that her struggles to study the subjects that most interested her mirrored my own. I'd pushed for and was lucky to be allowed to do both science and art, whereas Delia's overarching desire to study music and the science of sound was sadly denied. Nevertheless, I'd anticipated getting an insight into her attitude to music through her school work, so my heart skipped a beat when I saw a notebook marked 'MUSIC'. I opened it expectantly, only to be shocked to see there was just one page of half-hearted notes of no interest to me or, it seemed, to Delia herself. The rest of the book was totally blank. I thought maybe I'd missed another notebook on music, but there was just the one. However, music was always on Delia's mind. One of her Latin homework assignments was to give an example of how to use the Latin future indicative tense. Perhaps she misunderstood the task because her choice was rather telling and predictive: 'they will hear' – 'the future of audio' – '*audiemus*'. It may have meant something of significance to Delia, but her teacher got the red pen out to write, 'Why?' And those two ominous words 'See me'.

Her English book contained essays she'd written about music: one on how Greek music was regarded as being good for the body and soul and for society; another titled 'My Favourite Hobby' announcing loud and clear how important music was to her. Maybe it was a dig at the school, how they'd done wrong by her, or just to express how proud she was of her achievements.

Interestingly it was Delia's physics books that provided the greatest insight into the origins of her love for sound, clues to her future life in music. Unlike the music book, they were completely full. The pages were bursting with drawings and writings about the physics of sound – the Doppler effect, waveforms, wavelengths, beats, the human voice, resonance, pitch, harmonics, and equations to illustrate velocity. It all appeared prescient, considering her future experimental compositions. Her drawings of waveforms would later come to life as she watched them dancing across the screens of the RW oscilloscopes. She had collated all the information under the overall title of 'SOUND'. The rough notebooks were expanded way beyond what she would have had to present to her physics teacher. The writing had a frenetic energy to it and she'd included notes to herself to check out diagrams and pages in the reference books she'd used. These were her personal research books for her self-assigned, extra-curricular work, after discovering and becoming fascinated by acoustics during some school lessons that had touched on theoretical mechanics in conjunction with mathematics. She wanted to know more, but the school hadn't been helpful. Undeterred, Delia had gone in search of what she needed.

My whole time in Manchester was intense. I'd spent three days working in the Delia archive and then moved on to my duties for the festival. I was in conversation with Jon about my work, which was in line with the 'SMART' theme for Design Manchester – described as a celebration of 'those who take their own path, and make and break the rules alongside the resourceful, the nimble, the canny, the people who can lift or shapeshift an idea and inspire us to move forward (wherever forward may be!)'. Yet another strangely well-suited event for me to be contributing to during my time with Delia and Margery. Among the many things we discussed was my involvement in the Mail Art movement during the 1970s – how it had been a means for me and others to explore and disseminate art and make contact with people around the world. It was a free market open to all. The beginnings are traceable as far back as 1943, to the artist Ray Johnson and the Fluxus movement. It offered freedom of expression as well as liberation from the established rules of the art world.

Mail Art was taking centre stage. The previous day I'd been at the *Curious Things* exhibition at the Special Collections Museum, first giving a talk on Mail Art to a small group of people as part of the show. We sat among the exhibits of handmade artistic mailings from all around the world, displayed in vitrines and on the walls. Being surrounded by so many familiar names and images was like walking into my 1970s world. The sight of them threw me back in time to when I was heavily involved in the movement, participating in constant exchanges, with every day taken up with scooping up the daily pile of Mail Art that dropped into the postbox at the Martello Street studio and then sitting at my desk collaging and writing replies for most of the day, into the early evening. I read aloud a section from *Art Sex Music* about how and why Mail Art had started, and the many wonderful friends and opportunities it had brought into my life. Then an open discussion began about the joy of handwritten letters, personal artworks, the relationship between artists and the politics of art. And from there we moved on to the politics of the day – whether the Labour Party could win the upcoming general election, or was even representative, or could be effective in bringing not just change for the better of all but some hope to the present desperate situation, especially for younger generations. It made me sad to think things had sunk so low that the young people I was speaking with were openly expressing feelings of hopelessness. I wanted to hold each one of them and say everything was going to be all right, when I didn't know if it would be. I admitted that for the first time in my life I felt that the odds were overwhelmingly stacked against 'the good of society', but that defeatism and passivity were not options. Effective action was needed to turn things around. People just had to be willing to get involved. I really wished I could have offered more. I felt I'd let them down, so it was heart-warming when afterwards people came and thanked me for the smidgeon of optimism I'd managed to give.

The journey back to Norfolk was taken up with ruminating on my time in Manchester, hooking up with some amazing new people and old friends. I'd taken the latest script for the *Art Sex Music* film to read on the train back home. I'd gone through it a couple of times and made some notes but wanted to read it again with the ideas and amendments in mind that I'd discussed with Andrew before I left. The themes that had emerged were resilience, strength, self-belief and a refusal to compromise, and all had to be duly represented. The script had undergone massive changes and was sent to the BFI to apply for late-stage development funding. All Andrew and I could do was wait to hear back. My nervousness was replaced by trepidation about something that needed my immediate attention – and my presence. I was home long enough to catch one night's sleep, pick up my equipment cases and drive with Chris for three days' filming at Twickenham Studios. My next live performance was to be in front of a film crew in my 'Cosey studio' on the set of the 'Delia' film.

When I'd met with Caroline and Flo the art director earlier in the year, we'd gone through what was needed for the building of my studio set. In the initial stages of talks there'd been suggestions that I appear in the film. I'm not an actor and didn't see the need, but after many chats about what Caroline wanted the film to convey I agreed. I would appear as myself, seen working in my own studio creating the soundtrack, there to represent the female experimental musicians who came after Delia, with our presence made audible through my music.

The film studio was a massive empty space just waiting to be filled with imaginings – and very, very cold. Those in the know were in thermal underwear, but the wardrobe lady, Jo, had huge quilted coats on hand for those of us without and she kept the dressing rooms well heated. It was mind-blowing being in the studio with the crew. I love watching technicians at work. Their quiet confidence and skill, their tender touch for the minutest camera adjustments is kind of sexy. As a team everyone moved as one, like in a choreographed dance, aware of each other and of the camera movements, trailing cables, etc. I loved it. It was my first 'real' acting job – as opposed to the porn films I'd done in the seventies, which strangely enough had been the reason for my only other visit to Twickenham Studios to shoot *Custer's Thirteen*, which had a very different array of sets and 'script'. This time I was to be filmed improvising music live in the context of the 'Delia' script. Once I started I got carried away, totally preoccupied with my sound manipulations. When I looked up everyone was staring at me, kind of mesmerised. I apologised for getting lost in the moment. To my relief they seemed pleased with what I'd done.

Having had the honour of creating a 'recording' for and within a 'recording' to celebrate the life and work of Delia, I was about to make one in my own right. Two weeks later I was due to perform my autobiographical album *TUTTI* at the London Contemporary Music Festival in London. The venue was Ambika P3, the unique, thumping great underground hangar of the University of Westminster, which had previously been used for testing concrete for the Channel Tunnel. I wasn't feeling on top form. I'd been ill with some virus for a couple of weeks and was worried I might not be well enough to do vocals or get to the gig at all. I took to my bed for three days and rested as much as possible, eventually crawling out to go through my set in the studio. I had an early soundcheck the day of the show, so Chris and I got the direct train to London the day before. We checked into our usual hotel close to the station and, as has become routine when gigging, we closed the curtains, got into bed and turned out the lights, hoping to grab some extra sleep before the day of the show.

Feeling recharged the next morning, I arrived at the venue, soundchecked, video-checked and went for dinner. As I sat in the artist area waiting for my call to the stage, my head felt muggy, any noise seemed amplified, muddled and painful. I needed quiet but there were people coming and going and different animated conversations around me, people talking ten to the dozen. My head felt like it was going to explode. I wanted to scream, 'Shut the fuck up!' It wasn't their fault. I was ill. Someone noticed my flagging body language, and suddenly the room was cleared. I had time to rest my brain, get focused. When my call came I headed for the stage, the adrenaline kicked in, and the second I began to play I was in a different headspace altogether.

It was the night of the 2019 general election, the one many hoped would bring about a government that had the interests of the country and people at heart. I wanted to generate sounds that expressed just how much I longed for the election results to change things for the better, to deliver a powerful positive charge, but feared that the cards were stacked against my hopes, that the worst could happen. My feelings of doom foreshadowed what was to come. Despair, disbelief, disenfranchisement. A Tory victory on the back of corruption and lies, with my visions of another period of Thatcherism turning out to be far worse. Nevertheless, the festival event had been uplifting, bathing us in an atmosphere of positivity and warmth, great energies and diverse works, including the re-enactment of Vito Acconci's 1972 *Seedbed*. The artist lay in a space beneath a false floor, in this case a runway, and masturbated while fantasising to the sound of the people walking above him, voicing his progress to orgasm into a microphone that was fed to speakers in the gallery. We stood around talking and laughing as the hall was being cleared and the runway for the Acconci piece dismantled. There was a sudden halt to our chatter as we looked on the floor to see the pink dildo used for the masturbation action lying in the dust between the catwalk supports – discarded, job done, purpose fulfilled. I don't know what happened to it. Maybe it just got trashed or ended up in someone's personal collection.

27

Looking at Delia's drawings, reading through her handwritten notes and listening to her voice so many times had provided me with some sense of who she really was. Her BBC work jottings were incredibly fascinating as a window into her creative mind. Her schoolbooks took me back to my own high-school scribblings, triggering memories of taking notes in class ready to write up in neat essay form as part of my daily homework. Among her copious hurriedly scrawled notes were pages of different handwriting styles – carefully rounded letters, large, small, forward-sloping, backward, italic. In the 1950s we were told that our handwriting had to be exceptionally well crafted as that was how we would be judged. It would define us as educated and capable, and acceptable in society. It also gave an insight into our personality and as our 'mark' contributed to our sense of identity. I had the feeling that Delia was exploring, like I had, just how her 'mark' could represent her, searching for a style she felt comfortable with.

I tried out a number of styles, even copied those of my friends. I was fascinated by the smooth flow of the ink as it created a multitude of wonderful shapes that together formed a decipherable language – a valuable means of communication and aid to learning, and for me also another visually gratifying creative pleasure. Calligraphy was a thing back then and like many of my friends I received a calligraphy pen set for Christmas. It's a craft that requires time and precision, and I lacked the patience. Delia seemed to have mastered it, using it to write her name in a more visually symbolic form, with elegant decorative swirls and ornate flurries, over and over, stretching across adjoining pages. An exercise completely opposite in purpose to the hurriedly scribbled notes she used for her homework, which were super-large, at times spread just a couple of words to a line.

It crossed my mind that Delia would have benefited from learning shorthand and probably would have liked it. My sister was taught it and could do over 120 words per minute. It fascinated me to watch her making abstract squiggles. It's like a secret code. I'm not sure I could have mastered the skill. Too much to ask of me to keep those abstract shapes within the constraints of their meaning. I'd have started forming patterns of my own from them, riding roughshod over the rules and creating nonsensical words . . . which isn't such a bad idea. I love the look of words whatever the language and style, especially the beautiful medieval script in Margery's book.

Whether Margery's book is deemed an autobiography or hagiography, it is *her* story about how she asserted what she felt was her right to live her pious life, fashioned from many influences to suit her*self*. Her 'work' is herself, the book, the 'recording' of her *self*-defining transformation. Formed from her memories of the significant moments of her life, selected for a particular purpose, to hopefully inspire and comfort others as well as spread the word of God. No amount of subjective analysis by me or anyone else will ever provide the truths behind and within Margery's book. What matters is not whether she 'wrote' it herself or whether others had a hand in compiling it, or how well she 'succeeded' in her mission, but that she did it.

Thys boke is not wretyn in ordyr, every thyng aftyr other as it wer don, but lych as the mater cam to the creatur in mend whan it schuld be wretyn, for it was so long er it was wretyn that sche had forgetyn the tyme and the ordyr whan thyngys befellyn. [This book is not written in order, each thing after another as it was done, but just as the story came to the creature in her mind when it was written down, for it was so long before it was written that she had forgotten the timing and the order of when things happened.]

Reading Margery's book had me totally confused time and again. I was left piecing things together, wondering what happened when – and then asking myself why. The twists and turns frustrated me. My opinion of her kept changing the more research I did, as I tried to get a handle on her circumstances, the causes of her unconventionality and why she decided to write her book. Despite repeated requests for me to write my autobiography I didn't attempt it until the time felt right, and that was in my mid-sixties, like Margery. The reason for the long delay in her finally responding to God's command and the calls of clerics for her to write about her visions and life was very different to mine.

And so it was twenty yer and more fro that tym this creatur had felyngys and revelacyons er than sche dede any wryten. Aftyrward when it pleased ower Lord, he comawnded hyr and chargyd hir that sche schuld don wryten hyr felyngys and revelacyons and the forme of her levyngs that hys goodnesse myth be knowyn to all the world. [And so it was more than twenty years from that time this creature first had feelings and revelations before she had any of them written. Afterwards, when it pleased the Lord, He commanded her and tasked her to have her feelings and revelations and her manner of living written down, so that His goodness might be known to the whole world.]

There was a lot at stake for her to even consider it, and the way she went about it was everything. There were risks involved. Among other things it had a lot to do with the commands she received from God and with what was happening in England at that time. Joan of Arc had been executed in 1431 for heresy and witchcraft, among other charges, and Margery had personal experience of being tried by Lollard hunters. It would have been insanely unwise to place herself in the firing line as a possible heretic again. In 1429 and 1430 four men from Lynn, no doubt known to Margery, had been accused of heresy. During the 1428–31 Norwich heresy trials two outspoken local women, Margery Baxter and Hawise Mone, had been convicted. Mone recanted. Baxter got off lightly with public floggings on four consecutive Sundays. The mandatory penalty for unrepentant heretics was only too familiar to Margery – death by burning at the stake, which, if not in Lynn, could be carried out in Norwich's infamous Lollards Pit at the bottom of Gas Hill, a burial ground specially for heretics. Her decision to not put the name of the convicted heretic Lollard priest William Sawtrey in her book was a sensible move. It would have been seen as an admission of her interest in and association with Lollardy. So saving her story for another time was the best thing for Margery and for her scribes, who were understandably also concerned for their safety. It was dangerous to be involved with her, let alone seen to be colluding with her by writing down her words in English.

I'm no expert in religion or medieval history. It's impossible for me to place myself in Margery's shoes. As an atheist it's hard for me to relate to what she took as the (gospel) truth, the word of God. She based her life around her faith and belief in an intangible being. Why wouldn't she, just like everyone else back then? The idea of not believing in a greater spiritual power was inconceivable. Much as I have my issues with orthodox religion, and Catholicism in particular, I have to accept it as the most important element of Margery's story because it was her life, all she had to make any sense of the world, her situation, the only avenue open to her to address her problems and search for freedom. She fought from within systems that held her down, using them to establish a kind of 'alternative lifestyle' that afforded her some independence and safety without having to forfeit her religious beliefs, which were crucial to her spiritual awakening and hopes to be recognised as a visionary mystic. Completing her pilgrimages despite dire conditions, sickness and victimisation was a phenomenal achievement. I could see why she wrote about them. Her coping and overcoming abuse, turning the other cheek, was a testament to her as a holy woman. But matters of faith presented substantial challenges in writing her book, both for her and the scribes involved. Among many possible 'dangers', her references to sex and sexuality had to be on point. Non-productive sex, or sex for pleasure, was seen as a criminal act – in some cases it could even be punishable by death.

Her reunion with her son John could have been the impetus she needed to begin her autobiography. It's thought he could have been the scribe who wrote the first draft of her book in 1432. The description she gives seems to fit him – a man born in England, living in Germany and marrying a woman there, and who knew Margery well enough to live with her during the time he wrote down her recollections. Whoever the man was, he died before the book was completed, only managing to get as far as Part One, and his writing was a rough, almost illegible cross between English and German. For a fleeting indulgent moment I entertained the thought that it was Margery's own writing, and any misspellings could be a clue to that fantasy. She does actually mention writing a letter to her son, but the general opinion is that she was 'illiterate' – usually based on her saying that she wasn't '*lettryd*'. But that isn't the same thing as what we understand 'illiterate' to mean today. '*Lettryd*' to Margery meant 'schooled in Latin' – which she wasn't. Latin was for the Church and the rich and powerful, and writing was a skill taught separately (if at all) from reading. It's possible that as a merchant's daughter she would have been taught to read well enough for her religious studies, and she does mention that God said he was pleased with her '*whethyr thu redist er herist redyng*' ('whether you read or hear reading'). Even so, the fifteenth century was an oral culture, heavily reliant on memory, though Margery's seems to have been pretty exceptional. People were read to and preached to, with religious teachings reinforced by the mystery plays that travelled around from town to town, including Lynn. I feel sad that Margery had possibly never felt the power of externalising her thoughts through writing them down herself. The process of that pathway of thoughts from brain to hand to pen to paper is so special, such an expressive personal act.

The first priest Margery approached to copy out the badly written first draft couldn't make head nor tail of it and was simply too scared to get involved. Margery turned to another priest scribe but he was also unsure. But how things can turn on a sixpence. He had been sceptical about Margery because of her reputation, but this changed after he read a treatise on Marie of Oignies and realised how Margery's life of pilgrimage, chaste marriage and uncontrollable weeping mirrored Marie's. Margery suddenly looked like a safer bet. He began to think of her more respectfully and accepted the task. On 23 July 1436 he started transcribing the original German/English manuscript. He must have been committed and had some staying power because even though his eyesight was failing he carried on. It took him nearly two years. It was 28 April 1438 when he began writing down the second part of Margery's story.

As is typical of Margery, confusion surrounds the question of which priest originally transcribed her book. Some say it was her faithful confessor Robert Springolde. But it seems certain that the Benedictine monk Richard Salthows of Norwich Cathedral Priory was the scribe of the only surviving fifteenth-century copy – the one that now sits safely in the British Library in London. His name appears on a flyleaf: '*Jhesu mercy quod Salthows*' ('Thanks be to Jesus, says Salthows'). I thank *him* for devoting so much time and care to it, as well as whoever it was that oversaw the binding together of all the pages of Margery's story in the mid-1440s, years after her death. Without their mindfulness in preserving her work and creating a copy we might never have heard of her. The original manuscript it was copied from is missing – leaving me wishfully thinking that it's lying in some out-of-the-way place, and one day it will turn up just like Salthows's copy did in 1934. Until then the only point of contact with Margery is the manuscript in the British Library. Just a short train ride away, it was tantalisingly close to me but was understandably classified as an item of 'restricted access', viewable only under specific circumstances.

After studying Margery so intensely I felt such an emotional attachment to her that my desire and need to see her *Book* became more pertinent, verging on imperative. I took a chance and submitted my request to the British Library, and to my absolute joy was granted access. When I read the email I shouted out to Chris, 'I can see Margery's book!!' I was giddy with excitement. The date and time was confirmed and I took an early-morning train to King's Cross and walked up Euston Road to the library. I was met in the Manuscripts Reading Room by my assigned invigilator, who led me into a private room. In readiness for us a foam book support and snake beads for holding the delicate pages down had been placed at one end of a long table. I stood waiting and watching as the medium-sized archive box was placed on the table. The box was opened, and when I got my first glimpse of Margery's *Book* I was suddenly overcome by emotion, all choked up, tears welling up in my eyes. I never expected I'd feel so overwhelmed but I suppose tears were befitting for both such a special occasion and Margery.

I had some inkling of what to expect from the various images of the manuscript on websites and in books, but seeing it in the flesh was a totally different and incredible experience. Because it represented Margery's strength and power in my mind I'd thought it would be large and imposing. But the book was indeed small as described, just 215 by 140 millimetres, the same size as my old diaries that had formed my autobiography. Margery's *Book* was laid carefully on the support and I sat waiting in anticipation for my invigilator to open it. But he stepped away and told me that he was happy for me to handle the book myself. I couldn't quite believe I was going to actually touch Margery's *Book*. I was tentative as I didn't know how delicate it was. I took my time, taking in the look of it. It was bound in wooden boards covered in leather. The leather binding showed signs of wear and tear with small rips and scuff marks. The outer cover was mostly dark brown with beige mottled areas. It was hard to tell what the original colour had been. For a 580-year-old book it didn't smell musty and was in surprisingly good condition, probably helped by being shut away for centuries and protected by its chemise (which was in pieces and showed signs of having been nibbled by mice).

I gently took Margery's *Book* in my hands. Finally being able to hold it meant so much. It was a blissful moment, a physical connection between us. I carefully turned it over to take in its form, its 'being', and wanted to hug it to my chest. But of course I couldn't, and I needed to look inside, to hopefully satisfy my curiosity on a number of issues surrounding its form and history. I set the book back down on the foam support. The moment had come and I opened her *Book* for the first time.

The flyleaves were made of parchment and the rest of the book was of paper – the cheaper alternative to parchment, which was reserved for archival documents and the most important books. Recorded on the opening pages were the inscriptions of two owners of the manuscript, the Butler-Bowdon crest and the words 'this boke is of montegrace', the Mount Grace Carthusian charterhouse in north Yorkshire. One thing that puzzled me was how and why it had ended up so far away from King's Lynn. There is a clue bound into the end of the book, a folded letter on parchment dated 1440, addressed to William Bogy, the vicar of Soham, granting him permission to study at university. Soham was in the diocese of Norwich, and Margery talks of her numerous visits to the Franciscan nuns at Denny Abbey, very close to Soham, which was also closely associated with Pembroke College, Cambridge. The vicar possibly acted as spiritual guide to the nuns and he could have been given the first manuscript of Margery's book at the abbey, perhaps taking it with him when he left for university. Then somehow the manuscript found its way into the hands of the Carthusian monks, most likely at their monastery at Sheen, near London.

It's all supposition of course but not totally improbable. Margery had direct contact with Carthusian monks. In 1434 she visited Sheen and the Bridgettine abbey nearby at Syon, where she received the Lammas Day pardon. Carthusian monks were known for copying and correcting texts and had a preference for the practice of affective piety, like Margery's. They held women visionaries in high regard and were known for disseminating devotional and mystical manuscripts written in the vernacular. It was common for monks to move around and books were borrowed between charterhouses, so it's not impossible that if Margery's book was at Sheen it could have been taken to Mount Grace. It's been suggested (by Julie A. Chappell) that in 1533 the manuscript was taken by an as yet unknown route to the London Carthusian Charterhouse and most likely hidden away during the Dissolution of the Monasteries. According to Chappell, in 1538 it came into the possession of a former Carthusian monk, Everard Digby, who was related to the Butler-Bowdons, in whose house it was eventually found.

When I finally got to set my eyes on the first page of Margery's story I took a sharp intake of breath at the image before me – the sheer artistry of Salthows's exquisite penmanship, the consistency of shape and line spacing, with the words contained perfectly within a demarcated area in the centre of the page. How he managed to write so beautifully and so small with a quill pen and ink not only shows magnificent skill and patience but also that he (and the diocese of Norwich) valued and accepted Margery as a devout woman. Salthows filled the lines right up to the margin, with any half-lines ending with a three-dot triangle (symbolic of the Holy Trinity) to indicate that any further writing was not by him. The end of the *Book* was marked with six of these triangles. But two pages away next to the Soham parchment letter is a roughly written recipe for medicinal sweets used for curing the 'flux', a term for the dysentery that Margery had nearly died from, and which was attributed to the imbalance of humours, as were other ailments such as her fits of weeping. I wondered if Margery had got the recipe from consulting Nicholas of Lynn's book *Kalendarium*, which gave advice and treatments in relation to the phases of the moon. That the recipe was included in her book is significant and brings us closer to the earthly practicalities of addressing and coping with her many sicknesses and 'afflictions'.

The neatness of the writing made me think about when Margery dictated her stories to the first scribe and how demanding that process would have been in light of the available writing materials, which would have made it difficult to write fast enough to keep up with her. Maybe that was a reason why it was so hard to read. The scribe who eventually acted as her amanuensis must have been more proficient, possibly doing short sections at a time, checking with Margery before moving on to the next part of her story.

The annotations fascinated me as to what purpose they served. They were all made in red ink, scattered throughout the book, within the writing and in the margins – dots, dashes, words, under-scoring, embellishments of drawings, and numerous sacred hearts as figurative expressions of love of God. I thought the marks within the text may have been amendments to punctuation and grammar, or indications of places of specific interest and spiritual impor-tance. But it was far more than that. The scatterings of red ink were made by at least four different Carthusian monks and proved to be excitingly revealing. The key points of Margery's piety were all 'highlighted' in this way, to be noted by those reading her book for spiritual guidance – her weeping, her visions, her spiritual mar-riage, all practices acknowledged and recommended by the monks. Margery feeling the fire of God within her warranted a drawing of a crown with flames shooting from the top, and her white clothing an image of a 'dress'. A manicule with ermine cuff pointed to 'I am in you and you in me' to emphasise 'oneness' with God. What I really liked was the addition of a large initial letter 'O' to some paragraphs, which had been made into a face and gave me the impression of Margery looking out from her book. All the red-ink responses were religious in nature, made very clear by the first being the sacred monogram 'IHC' ('in the name of Jesus Christ'), placed at the top of the first page – above where Margery's words began.

It's not known who the annotators of Margery's manuscript were, but one of the Carthusian monks, James Grenehalgh, who annotated manuscripts including Julian of Norwich's *Revelations*, had similar struggles with sexual temptation to Margery. James was based at Sheen Charterhouse and was mentor to Joanna Sewell, a nun at the Bridgettine house of Syon. They developed a close friendship and were suspected of being 'intimate'. He used the annotations he made in devotional manuscripts she would read to communicate his affection for her, even intertwining their initials in a unifying monogram. With physical or 'inappropriate' contact between monks and nuns being forbidden but virtuous friendship encouraged, they found it difficult to know where to draw the line when meeting for readings and exchanges of manuscripts between their two neighbouring religious houses. James was demoted from monk to 'guest' and sent to Coventry Charterhouse, then to Hull Charterhouse, where he died in 1529.

Margery's affective piety, the source of so much anguish throughout her life, had ended up being the key to securing the preservation, survival and dissemination of her *Book*. The Carthusian mystics Richard Methley and John Norton of Mount Grace are referred to on a number of occasions. In Chapter 28, '*so fa* [Father] *RM & f* [Father] *Norton of Wakeness & of the passion*' is written next to Margery's description of her screaming and crying at the Lord's Passion. Men added their experiences, aligning themselves with Margery. Her *Book* was accepted as a valid and valuable endorsement of their own affective piety. A genderless experience and life of pious devotion as God's 'creatures'.

My hour's viewing had gone quickly. It was time to leave. Margery's *Book* was returned to its archive box. I thanked my invigilator for all his help, said goodbye and headed back to King's Cross to go home. As I sat on the train my mind was racing, going through everything I'd just experienced. I hurriedly made some notes, then relaxed, leaned back and looked out the window, letting my thoughts drift as I revisited and savoured the hour I'd spent with Margery's *Book*. I felt comforted by the physical evidence that so many people had read the book prior to it disappearing for so long. The traces of marks made by their touch on the pages showed that her words were cherished and respected. And I had now added a trace of myself, a mark of my physical contact with Margery. Viewing and handling her book had been so very special and had far exceeded my expectations.

All the trouble Margery went to to make sure her book got written is understandable. It was her legacy. Her reason for not wanting it to be read until after her death is obvious under the circumstances, but there may have been a subtext to it. To be regarded as a holy woman or saint, as Margery hoped, it was an advantage to have a book written about you posthumously. And it stood as a powerful symbol of endorsement if a male cleric did it – which Margery had made sure of. Margery 'writing' her story herself in her lifetime was a clever way of breaking with convention to ensure her voice was heard. The 'word' of God held such power. She used his words cleverly to justify her actions, to circumvent obstacles and to create situations that served her own purposes, her personal needs, to shift her 'place' to one of her own choosing. It gave *her* words power. Because no matter what opposition and criticism she faced, everyone knew that ultimately God's words were inviolable – and were a great weapon for attack and defence that she made much use of throughout her battles. She played the Church and other powerful men at their own game, using the Bible and reciting word for word from it to argue her case, always making it clear that she was guided by God through her visions and her prayers. As such his (*her*) word couldn't be questioned without invoking retaliatory accusations of heresy. She had constant clashes with men throughout her spiritual journey and in trying to get one to write her book for her. None of the run-ins she had with them deterred her from making herself heard – in life and in death. Her *Book* makes sure of that, loud and clear.

I've read many theses and books about Margery, and found some of them unfairly judgemental, particularly about her using a male amanuensis, claiming that her book, being filtered through a man, was therefore not *her* voice. For a start, like most women of the fifteenth century she used male scribes even for general letters to family and friends. Margery's life was centred on making her voice heard through her secular and religious activities – too loud and clear for her own good at times – but she ensured its presence continued after her death in the form of her book. As far as I'm concerned her book is *her* story in *her* voice. It echoes throughout, accompanied where necessary by the 'ecclesiastic voices' of her scribes acting on her behalf in a supporting protective role – with her approval. The fact that she says she didn't write it herself, even though she possibly could have done, was an act of self-defence as well as advantageous. The book is peppered with religious quotations and allusions, maybe even illusions, that all serve specific purposes, but I wouldn't call it a work of fiction. Going by other first-hand accounts of medieval life and historical documents it's plausible that the events of Margery's selected recollections had likely taken place when and in the ways she described. One thing for sure is that as a fifteenth-century woman Margery was in a position of perpetual reliance on the will of men, always having to seek their permission, and that included the common practice of dictating to male scribes. Ever wary, Margery had her scribe read back to her what he'd written to check it was a true representation of what she'd dictated to him. I still cling to the possibility that

Margery could read to some degree, enough to double-check what the scribe wrote if she felt it necessary. That her memories of what happened '*sche knew ryght wel for very trewth*'.

I came across some feminist writings on Margery that argued against her being regarded as a proto-feminist because she never succeeded in becoming independent, again because she used a male amanuensis, and because she never fully overcame her submissive female role. That she remained, body and soul, under the control of men in her complete devotion to Christ and in returning to her wifely duty of looking after her invalid husband. Does that mean any married woman who is devoted to her husband or who follows a religious doctrine controlled by men can't claim to be feminist? Margery struggled to be free of the expectations and constraints that were constantly pulling her back 'under' to set her in her place. Society and the Church dictated what she could and couldn't do based solely on her being a woman, and she had to negotiate her way through a minefield of rules to avoid being killed. She may not have managed to break completely 'free' but she did break away from her ascribed role and had an adventurous life, to say the least. More than that, her writing the book about her life is a tribute to and declaration of her belief in her *self*-worth as a woman.

Her 'recording' throws light on the plight of early-fifteenth-century women, what was demanded of them, the predicaments they faced and how they dealt with them, and what it was like to be ridiculed and persecuted because of the intolerance towards people who didn't 'fit'. She deliberately had her book written in the 'language' of her time, mid-fifteenth-century Norfolk East Anglian English, no doubt influenced by Julian of Norwich, who had written her book *Revelations of Divine Love* in English. By choosing the vernacular Margery 'speaks' to the people she wanted to address, making sure they understood how she wanted to be remembered. That she took so many risks and had the initiative and *self*-worth to record her life in the form of a book demonstrates the unyielding attitude of an incredibly strong, self-determined individual, uncowed by the powerful men who were equally determined to silence her.

The thing scholars and academics always mention is Margery writing about herself in the third person, as 'this creature'. She goes to great lengths to reiterate that she is susceptible to lechery and vanity like everyone else but wants to prove that she is an example of the possibility of redemption. Portraying herself as a 'creature' of God helped deter criticism that it was all about her and her own self-importance – vanity was only one of the many sins she was accused of. Calling herself 'this creature' has been interpreted by some as a sign of her feeling diminished. But it wasn't unusual for men and women of her time to refer to themselves that way. It doesn't mean 'animal'. It means 'created by God'. Writing in the third person as someone trying to make good their failings, to be worthy, was a wise move – and in my twenty-first-century opinion, placing herself on a par with all 'creatures' was an unwitting declaration of equality. It was something she also did when she'd been ordered by the Archbishop of York to swear never to preach publicly again. She refused. She had the right as a woman whom God had spoken to and she quoted the Bible as proof:

> . . . *the gospel makyth mencyon that, whan the woman had herd owr Lord prechyd, sche cam befor hym wyth a lowde voys and seyd, 'Blyssed be the wombe that the bar and the tetys that gaf the sowkyn.' Than owr Lord seyd agen to hir, 'Forsothe so ar thei blissed that heryn the word of God and kepyn it.' And therfor, sir, me thynkyth that the gospel gevyth me leve to spekyn of God.* [. . . the gospel mentions

that, when the woman had heard our Lord preaching, she approached Him with a loud voice and said, 'Blessed is the womb that bore thee, and the paps that gave thee suck.' Then our Lord said again to her, 'Yea rather, blessed are they who hear the word of God, and keep it.' Therefore, sir, I think that the gospel permits me to speak of God.]

Even though Margery's autobiography is focused on her faith, her struggles and hard-won spiritual achievements, as well as giving guidance to others and presenting a very particular perception of herself, there are so many situations she faced that echo those of women across the centuries to the present day. To some extent she succeeded in her aim of seeking recognition, because after her death not only did Salthows copy her book in full, obviously finding it worthwhile and useful for spiritual teachings, but selected extracts of her book were printed as religious pamphlets by Wynkyn de Worde in 1501 and in 1521 by a London publisher in a book, among other mystical works. So she must have got something right. But it came at the price of being edited out of her own book. The stories of all her hard work to overcome problems she encountered were removed, deemed 'unsuitable', but the 'useful' parts were appropriated and exploited. I feel she wanted people to know what she'd been through, the personal cost to a woman who fought tooth and nail to break away, who was knocked down and got up again every time. Removing Margery's voice, all her radicalism, was reprehensible, a sin in itself.

I like to think that Salthows met with Margery's approval, that he was an empathetic scribe, someone who was on the same page as her. That's of immense importance when the writing is intensely personal. I was so fortunate that was the case with the French translator of *Art Sex Music*. After reading my book, Fanny Quément approached my literary agent offering to translate it for a possible French edition. It wasn't the usual protocol but I was over the moon that it came about the way it did. Her request was driven by a sense of resonance with my approach to life and art – those connections I felt with Margery and Delia. Fanny was passionate and committed to getting a French version published, hoping whichever publisher took it up that she could be the translator. I hoped so too. Fanny emailed to tell me all about herself, pointing out that her name was 'no weird mirror effect', just a mere coincidence, but nevertheless a rather nice one. She described her feelings about my book, about herself and being part of the experimental multidisciplinary art collective La Méandre, putting on events, working and living in the partly abandoned industrial Port Nord in Burgundy. It all had echoes of life during my time in the COUM collective, which had struck a chord with her.

An autobiography is not about one person's experiences but also about all the other people involved and those who subsequently hear, read and relate in some way to the actions, themes, emotions and scenarios. It was obvious by what Fanny had said in her emails and the questions she asked me that she understood that. The 'right' publisher was found – Editions Audimat – with Fanny as the translator. I couldn't have asked for a better gathering of 'forces' working on my behalf. I'd felt Fanny was the perfect person to translate my words when I'd read what she said of her overriding intention: 'It is your voice I want to broadcast in my language.' Fanny was rigorously attentive to detail and the particular nuances in translating my words into French, checking with me about subtle differences in meaning. It was reassuring, admirable, respectful. I felt like Margery must have done when she and her scribe worked together for the same end – accuracy, being true to her word. As the publication of *Art Sex Musique* drew close

Fanny emailed me to check on a few more things. In my reply I mentioned I was writing a small section about our exchanges and asked her permission to include some of her words. The 'no weird mirror effect' coincidence recurred. She was also in the throes of writing an article about her work on the translation for the magazine *Panthère Première* and was about to ask my approval to use extracts from my emails to her. 'It was very funny to read you ask me if you could quote from my emails, because I was going to ask you exactly the same question!' We were mirroring each other, making our own recording of such a special encounter. A mutual moment of inspiration.

28

I finished the music for the 'Delia' soundtrack and delivered all the audio files to Caroline. Her film ended at the point where Delia left the BBC and went to live in Cumbria, but I was more than curious about what happened there and afterwards. That part of her life seemed to be a mystery to everyone. It was too irresistible not to look further into those 'missing' years.

Delia may have been out of the BBC in 1973 but she didn't stop making music. Her time at the RW had had its rewards and brought some awards, with her music having been an essential element in prize-winning collaborations. She was co-composer for Roberto Gerhard's *The Anger of Achilles*, which won the 1965 Prix Italia, and she personally got to receive the trophy for the educational broadcasting Japan Prize in 1971 for, of all things, giving voice to stones and trees for Ted Hughes's *Orpheus*. I wouldn't even know where to start with an assignment like that. It was one of those 'impossible' jobs Delia could do that others wouldn't even attempt. But out of the multitude of collaborations the most rewarding were those she worked on with women, notably the artists Madelon Hooykaas and Elsa Stansfield, with whom she enjoyed a long-lasting friendship. In the early seventies Elsa had got in touch with Delia through their connections with the London Arts Lab. She wanted a composer to work with her on the sound for Anthony Roland's 1972 film *Circle of Light: The Photography of Pamela Bone*. The images were like the music, made up of different layers to create moods. The film won the Short Art

Film section of the prestigious Cork Film Festival, which must have given Delia a special sense of achievement and encouragement that her work did indeed have a place and validity outside of the BBC. That there was another option open to her.

When Delia met Elsa's partner Madelon the three of them made two films together, *One of These Days* (1973) and *About Bridges* (1975). Madelon and Elsa's way of working was so different from what Delia had previously experienced. She was involved right from the start of the projects, and Madelon and Elsa insisted that Delia was present at the shooting of both films so she could get a feel of the rhythm of the city for the music. That sentient connection with space was part of Delia's character. Roger Limb, one of the original Radiophonic Workshop members, recalled her going to his house for dinner. When invited to sit down she declined and started walking around the room. 'I can't sit down until I've got to know the room,' she explained. It also applied to the acoustics of sound and how things affect them. Delia could interpret people's mood by their voices. In conversation with Roger over the phone she could 'hear' that he'd shaved off his beard.

Just to be with Madelon and Elsa, working in collaboration with their own independent methods and sensibilities, was a far cry and refreshing change from the exasperating times spent on some of her last BBC projects. Finally, she felt free of the restrictions that had dogged her creativity for years. She had input and as a result produced music that was inspired by the close artistic relationship between the three of them. This alternative way of working with like-minded women was enlightening and uplifting, especially because while Delia was in their warm company she was also at her lowest ebb.

Shortly after leaving the BBC Delia made her first trip as an independent artist to work in Amsterdam with Madelon and

Elsa. They thought she looked exhausted, worn down. A few years later, on the verge of leaving London, she made her second journey to Amsterdam to work with them on the film *About Bridges*. Amsterdam being a city of many, many bridges, the film was to reflect the experiences of the workers who built and maintained them, the locals and others who used them and the viewpoint of the artists involved. There's a wonderful Delia melody in the soundtrack with an unmistakable nursery rhyme feel, clearly audible in a brief, distinctive phrase from 'London Bridge Is Falling Down'. A nice example of Delia's sense of humour and, some might say, a subtle or intentional sign of her life in London crumbling away; time to move on. After all, the film was about the concept of bridges, what they represented in personal terms, metaphorically or in their functionality.

The actual filming was another revelation for Delia, seeing firsthand what was involved and the hoops they had to jump through in the film industry. Madelon told me that in order to fund the project they had to hire a male crew for one day who had to be credited on the film. As soon as they got to Amsterdam and had used the male crew for their contracted time they shot the rest of the film with their own equipment. Around that time I'd made films without funding or involving the male-dominated unionised film industry, avoiding 'official channels'. It made me wonder why they'd taken that route. Needs must, and I wondered if it also could have had something to do with Elsa, Madelon and Delia's situation and their artistic worlds being different from mine. I must have been further out on the fringes than I thought, moving in different artistic circles or mindsets, while they worked within institutions, Elsa and Madelon in the university system and Delia with the BBC. They were used to operating in and working out ways round the regulations of who was allowed to do what, how and when. I understood the unions were protecting their members, but it was well known that this often created difficulties with time, finance and missed creative moments for the artists. I had none of that to consider. I was involved with the Art Meeting Place artists collective in Long Acre, Covent Garden, which provided free means of access to shared or subsidised equipment and facilities. Delia was working just down the road from AMP, at Elsa's studio in Neal's Yard. Funny to think of us possibly passing by each other, preoccupied with our thoughts on our projects, heading to our 'free' work spaces.

I always felt that two tiers of unconventional artistic activity existed in Covent Garden: one that stayed within the established art world, which gave it kudos, and one that didn't give a damn about such things. I inhabited the latter. The art was what mattered, and that existed in its own right, not subject to 'fitting in' or meeting the criteria to qualify as 'art' and acquire the necessary value required by commercial galleries and institutions. I had no career path in mind, artistic or otherwise. I was merely 'creating' for its own sake. That remains the same. I think Delia was caught somewhere in the middle, until her move to Cumbria.

Delia's eccentricity extended to her home life, which was certainly not 'domestic'. She lived in chaos, surrounded by her boxes and suitcases from previous moves, which were mainly left unpacked. Whenever her possessions piled up to the point where it became impractical she took it as a sign to move on, as if that episode of her life had reached its conclusion, exhausted all possibilities, that there was nowhere else for things to go (literally). It was time to make space for whatever was next. Her life was contained in boxes, past activities stored away out of sight in readiness for a new phase. It was a pattern repeated for all the numerous places she lived, whether it was her place in Kensington Gardens

Square in Paddington, above the flower shop in Clifton Road, Camden Town or Powis Square in Notting Hill.

When eventually the complexities of Delia's life became too much for her, she escaped them by moving to Cumbria, where she worked in a disused quarry, in charge of three transmitters delivering the weather forecast in French each night, even though she couldn't speak French particularly well (she kept a French–English dictionary by her side). She was formidable, and the Scottish, English and French engineers and crews all respected and adored her. They knew her as the woman who wrote the *Doctor Who* theme tune and rightly assumed she'd gone to work there for some much-needed peace and space.

With the political landscape of the seventies being manifest on the streets of London, the contrast with the Cumbrian countryside must have been startling as much as a soothing antidote. Delia went from intense social and work lives to what would seem near-isolation. From the noise and crowds of people in London to a close-knit community of a few hundred with one post office, one general store, one phone box and a solitary bus stop. At least that was conveniently outside her house, but it only ran an hourly service to other villages and the small market town of Brampton, where you could then catch a connection to places further afield. That didn't matter so much. She was in her element working with radio. Despite that, she felt out of place, something she hadn't anticipated. Her distinctive upper-class voice made her immediately conspicuous and she could come across as hoity-toity. Her hippy dress sense, with layers of clothes, a hat sat atop cascades of her auburn pre-Raphaelite hair and a man's long overcoat, worn summer or winter, didn't fit in either, and although happy with her workmates the locals didn't take to her. They thought she was an eccentric Londoner, mistaking her confident demeanour for her being a bit up herself. In an effort to fit in more she took to playing darts in the local pub and was brilliant at it. She'd take a snort of snuff, a swig of Guinness, step up, take aim and 'bullseye'!

Delia had enough money to buy a small house built from the stone from Hadrian's Wall in the picturesque village of Gilsland. She moved into the first home she could call her own – the same routine as every previous move, stacking her 'nest' of boxes around her. She was settling in but still had a lingering feeling of being treated as an outsider. In an attempt at acceptance and in the hope of a long-term friendship she made the bizarre decision to marry a local miner's son and labourer for the gas pipeline, David Hunter, from nearby Haltwhistle. They got married in October 1974, he moved into her house and she began her first taste of married life. It all happened so fast, just over a year after leaving the BBC. They were the most unlikely couple. Delia was a Cambridge graduate, David was poorly educated and had been a troublesome child. She was creative, he had no interest in the arts. The contrast between them was emphasised by her sophisticated voice set against his strong Cumbrian accent, her beauty and refinement next to his unkempt, beer-bellied appearance and brutish manner. It could have been a purely sexual attraction, although according to one of her friends there was little sign of it when they were out together, only a sense that Delia was unhappy.

The bare-knuckle ride of working-class life can be very rough and ready and brought risks that had never crossed Delia's mind. The potential for violence may not have been uppermost in her thoughts when she chose to marry as a means of fitting in with the local people. Alcohol was what brought her and David together when they met for the first time in Gilsland's local pub, the Samson. It was a very rough drinking house, an eighteenth-century coaching inn that seemed stuck back in time, with many of its original features untouched. There were only two small, basic bars with bare, worn flagstone floors and no decoration, just a lone dartboard on the wall. One of the bars had a notably overbearing sense of it being a male space. It was mainly frequented by farm workers and labourers, while 'others' like Delia sat and drank in the smaller bar.

It turned out that alcohol was the only thing Delia and David appeared to have in common. By all accounts it was a troubled and confrontational marriage, with them both drinking in the pub each night. It became obvious that she had problems with the relationship. There were outward signs that Delia was falling apart, that she was struggling to keep herself together. Her appearance had deteriorated, as if she'd given up on herself, and the house was in such a neglected state no one was allowed inside. When things got too much and she needed to speak to someone she'd ring her friend and confidante Cath to meet up with her in a pub. She'd be there way ahead of time waiting for Cath, with her pint of Guinness and Cath's half-pint sat on the table ready for her. Delia was in such a quandary and desperately needed to get away. David wasn't good for her and she was looking for a way out. The marriage had helped to distract her from the depressing accumulation of interminable demands she'd had to deal with in London, but Delia and David were incompatible, and her feelings of disharmony and being 'out of place' persisted. The marriage inevitably failed and she left her job at Laing.

A possible way out of her marriage presented itself. Delia had found some semblance of affinity to a different way of life when she encountered Li Yuan-chia, a Chinese artist who had bought and renovated a sprawling row of farm outbuildings, converting them into his home and an art space he called the LYC Museum. It was at Banks, near Brampton, very close to Hadrian's Wall, and five miles from Gilsland. Li had bought the buildings from his friend and neighbour, the artist Winifred Nicholson, at a cut-down price because of their dilapidated state and took on all the work himself. He and Delia bonded as two creative artists and souls, and he offered her some work helping him at the museum, where she could live for free and be paid a small wage. Although she didn't get involved in the creative process, she wanted at that time to be in nature, among creative people, to be where things were happening. Li was supportive when her marriage was falling apart. That led to rumours that he and Delia were having an affair, which appeared to be correct when Delia moved out of her home in Gilsland to work and live with Li in a close relationship. That really set tongues wagging. David was furious, accusing Li of stealing 'his' wife, as if his rights as a husband had been violated. As if Delia belonged to him. Delia was unwavering. She ignored the gossip and her husband's demands for her to return and threw herself into LYC activities.

The studio managerial skills Delia had acquired at the BBC came in useful as she liaised with the artists and poets who frequently visited, worked and exhibited in the LYC galleries. She assisted in organising readings and exhibitions and oversaw some events, as well as access to the library, photographic darkroom and children's art room. It was a welcoming place where participation was encouraged, providing a space for performance, a communal kitchen and sculpture garden. The LYC was all about and for people, offering total freedom of artistic expression and experimentation. The doors were always open, with no entrance fee. It was as near to being on the fringes as Delia had been for years and the closest she was to what my life has been – Art is Life. Li had been closely involved with the experimental London-based art collective the Exploding Galaxy – the inspiration for COUM

Transmissions. His free approach to art mirrored my own, and so it seems did Delia's new lifestyle. The LYC offered her some tranquillity as well as a creative environment, with the added advantage of a more spiritual approach to life and art in Li's concept of 'the cosmic point' – the beginning and end of all things in the universe. That was at the centre of everything Li did. It applied to art, in all the differing forms it took. Sometimes for him the cosmic point could be a small solitary dot or it could expand to include objects and writing, to reflect and represent his life experiences.

Delia was enjoying life at the LYC, going on long walks, bathing in a nearby waterfall, picnicking in the fields and enjoying communal meals with artists and visitors. It was during one of the evening meals that there was a sudden violent hammering on the door and loud shouting. The diminutive Li answered the door to find an irate man, red in the face and clearly spoiling for a fight. David wanted to settle some scores, he wanted his wife back. The ruckus ran its course, with Delia's strapping husband pushing and shoving and throwing punches, and the peace-loving Zen Buddhist Li coping as best he could with being the target of his anger. The door was closed, Li's cut face was treated and the meal resumed. Presumably to avoid accountability, a rumour was circulated by the locals that a 'dark' stranger had beaten Li up, which then got embellished to it having occurred in the dead of night, as if some mystery man had done it. Li wouldn't discuss it. But it impacted badly on Delia.

Two eccentric personalities do not always make for a great mix. As a couple they looked odd, with Li a good two foot shorter than Delia. Their relationship was very unusual, described to me as 'covert'. There was no show of affection between them in company, so that some people never realised Delia and Li were a couple. They lived together in the flat in the new part of the museum. Delia being a night owl and Li the opposite, getting up at dawn and always early to bed, meant they each had their own room. As two private people they understood that they each needed their own space. In his own world, Li made no demands of her that would 'drain' her. But as two single-minded individualists with very different character traits and approaches to life, any expectation of a lasting partnership didn't bode well. It was Delia's drinking that was really problematic for Li. It disturbed him, caused tensions between them. Li was teetotal (as was Winifred Nicholson) and couldn't handle alcohol or the effect it had on Delia. It made things awkward, especially when Delia and Li held a special supper party for Winifred and her artist friends. The exotic fish and ginger concoction was delicious and they all sat playing word games amidst an uncomfortable atmosphere of disapproval at the amount of wine Delia was getting through. The stack of her empty wine bottles in and around the dustbin was an embarrassment to Li. If he noticed anyone had caught sight of them he'd walk away, not saying a word.

The museum never closed, not even on Christmas Day. There was no downtime and Delia's hopes of a release from relentless work met with disappointment. The work was non-stop, with the museum hosting up to four exhibitions a month, each with its own catalogue designed and printed at the LYC. The place was always busy, having in excess of twenty thousand visitors a year, and the workload began to resemble the overloaded BBC schedules Delia had wanted to escape from. She was idealistic but the reality of life at the LYC didn't live up to her expectations. She'd loved working with her friends Madelon and Elsa, and their visit to the LYC on New Year's Eve 1976 perhaps relit a spark in her or gave her the jolt she needed.

Madelon was into Zen Buddhism like Li and gave Delia a copy of her book *Zazen* as a gift. I like to think of it as a gesture of faith in Delia's courage and strength to find her way, an encouragement to refocus. Madelon had sensed Delia's disquiet, that she wanted to explore her newfound freedom, but that life in Cumbria wasn't working out that way for her. Madelon's inscription to Delia was a quotation from the book: 'Freedom isn't doing what you like, but liking what you do.'

Delia no longer had her old bicycle. She'd catch the local bus or on fine days walk to the nearby pub in Lanercost, a two-mile hike to buy her supplies of wine or meet with friends. Sometimes she'd cadge a lift or go by cab to the station to catch the train to London. She'd also begun taking night walks along the riverbank to visit Andy Christian, an artist she'd befriended who frequented the museum. He lived close by and worked with Winifred. They'd drink and talk into the small hours but never about her musical past, that was out of bounds – although her mind would often focus on music, when she'd make oblique references to her previous advertising work by blurting out extraordinary ideas she'd had, including one for an ad for Guinness, her favourite tipple at the time. It was obvious that her heart was still in music, her mind supremely sharp, her intellect intact, never affected by her intake of alcohol.

Delia knew no one when she moved to Cumbria and even after she'd been there a few years she hadn't made any very close friends. Li was the closest person to her. But if she was looking for someone to share her envisaged world, Li was not the person. What Delia hadn't foreseen was how their relationship would develop in ways she found uncomfortable. The LYC was Li's place, his world, his obsession, and there was no place within that bubble for 'Delia'; she would have to fit into *his* world. She must have felt she was yet again second and 'other', and alone even though it was clear he wanted her around. Although she had a number of friends she'd call or visit when she needed someone to talk to, things weren't going well. Another bout of depression was descending on Delia.

She arranged to meet up with her friend Cath in a pub four miles away. What she needed to say had to be said out of earshot of anyone at the LYC. She let her friend know that she was leaving Cumbria, that she couldn't stay at the LYC any longer. She was going to have to go because of Li. She didn't explain why in any detail, just that she'd had to keep a chair against her bedroom door because she didn't feel safe. She didn't want any help to sort out what was wrong. She was adamant: 'No, no, I'm going!'

It was time to move – again. When she told Li she was leaving he was incredibly upset; he really wanted her to stay. Their relationship was the only significant one he'd had for some time. But Delia had her reasons for going and nothing could change her mind. We'll never know whether it was her own personal issues or the 'call' of music that led to her leaving the LYC. Ironically in 1976 Desmond Briscoe had made a work based on Cumbria, *A Wall Walks Slowly*, which Delia had heard and loved so much she wrote to him to compliment him on how he had utterly captured the beauty and mood of the place. Maybe that contact and Madelon and Elsa's last visit triggered something in her.

There was a glaring gap in her life in Cumbria. Li's diverse interests and artistic activities lacked the one creative art that was Delia's soul: music. Her years at the LYC were largely barren of music. She lacked the means to record her ideas, while music played constantly in her head. Her income had also taken a substantial hit and she struggled to pay the mortgage on her house in Gilsland. She was hemmed in on all sides. Within a short time of Delia co-signing Li's *Artist Book No. 4* 'Wishing you PEACE and LUCK' in 1976, she had moved out, seemingly accepting and acting upon Madelon's view that her freedom lay elsewhere, with different people, doing other things. Most of her things were moved for her by a guy she'd met from the nearby artist community and whom she visited frequently to play chess. The only things she left behind were a piano and her cat, Horribles.

During Delia's time in Cumbria she contacted Brian Hodgson sporadically, only revealing what she wanted to about her situation, keeping her life compartmentalised. Brian had offered her work but she wasn't interested. She didn't want to be part of any organisation again, large or small.

She'd begun a relationship with Clive Blackburn after meeting him at various parties on her trips to London. There was no lightning bolt of love at first sight. In fact they'd often get into heated arguments. He was thirteen years younger than her and had no links to her past, knew nothing about her. Finding out months into their relationship that she had created the *Doctor Who* theme tune was a complete surprise. It must have felt like a fresh start for Delia, no 'baggage', nothing to live up to. They could just be themselves, together.

There was no divorce from David Hunter. Delia moved on as she always did, treating it as another chapter in her life to be boxed up and put aside. She sold the house in Gilsland at a knockdown price and invited friends and villagers to a leaving party on a sunny autumn Sunday. Everyone congregated outside – David was nowhere to be seen. Delia appeared from the kitchen with a tray of scones she'd baked for everyone. It was a most unusual, very un-'Delia' farewell gesture considering her dislike of domesticity – but turned out to be very 'Delia' as the scones were all burnt, the currants blackened to a crisp. All the things she didn't want were laid on the grass bank at the back of the house, a rather sad display of parts of her life she was leaving behind. Unlike previous moves, when she abandoned things she felt she didn't need, this time she was most insistent that everyone take one thing each to remember her by. There were silk scarves, jewellery, pictures and other trinkets and souvenirs she'd accumulated. She couldn't understand why no one took up her offer to claim her celebratory contraceptive coil, a symbol of her rebellion, her sexual liberation and a 'screw you' to Catholicism. What wasn't taken she either sold cheap at auction or stored in the houses of acquaintances from the thriving art community she'd met through the LYC. They became a kind of support network, letting her stay with them as she went on frequent train journeys to London with the aim of maintaining contact with her music colleagues while she contemplated a return to working there again.

She stayed with various friends in London and started enjoying the party life, once more being magnetic, entertaining Delia. At her first meeting in London with the artist Elisabeth Kozmian to talk about working on a soundtrack for her film *Two Houses* (1980), Delia came across as fascinating, cheerful and majestic. The timing was perfect. Elisabeth's film was about converting two houses, her own and an architect friend's. For Elisabeth, working on rebuilding from the ruins of the past represented the 'self', as in the Jungian theory of working on yourself to find the true self. Transformation and self-awareness would have matched well with Delia's state of mind. The only instrument and sound she chose to accompany the film harked back to the beginnings of her love of music, the piano.

The 1970s were tough and self-defining times for both Delia and myself. Neither of us knew just how much at the time. We were getting through as best we could, keeping our heads above water, and always fiercely maintaining focus on and protecting ourselves. It's hard to explain the inner strength that carries you through dark times, when for some strange reason you don't feel oppressed despite what's going on. It's as if you're a witness to muted babblings and demands, watching and hearing as if you're outside it all, behind an invisible protective shield, a tool of defence against all that's thrown at you. You see, hear and feel, but all the while knowing the true purpose of what is being said and done: that your role is to enable, to 'feed', support and act as an inspiration or source for someone else's creative pursuits. The so-called muse. The realisation that your place in someone's life is not what you thought it was is initially heartbreaking – swiftly followed by feelings of betrayal, that what you thought was a special bond in a close relationship wasn't that at all. It was always and only ever about them. Everything they did and said was a stream of calculated lies to produce a particular effect to suit their own needs. You are a paradox, secondary yet essential. Delia discovered this in relation to her work at the BBC, with David, with Li. I discovered that in my relationship with Genesis. I went into survival mode, conserved my energy for my*self* until I was ready to move on. That turning point was in 1978, the same as Delia. I left to be with Chris, Delia to be with Clive.

29

In January 1980 Delia bought a small two-bedroom terraced house near the centre of Northampton. It was cheap and also a convenient train ride to London or to visit her ageing mother in Coventry. Shortly after she moved in, Clive called her to see if he could pop round. She hated visitors but agreed and tidied up specially for him – although it was such a mess no one would have guessed she'd cleaned up at all.

Clive started staying with her at weekends and they'd drive all over the country like tourists. They grew closer and became a couple, and he moved in with her within months. There was still the matter of collecting her belongings from Cumbria. They hired a Transit van and made several trips over a whole week to retrieve her worldly possessions. Collecting the few things she'd left at LYC was upsetting. Li had smashed up her upright piano in anger. She and Clive stayed at Delia's friend Joy's house just across the river. Joy had taken over Delia's job at the LYC and they'd become fond of each other. Delia and Clive slept on the fold-out sofa bed in Joy's living room. In the morning as Joy passed them on her way to the kitchen she saw their feet poking out of the blankets, lovingly entwined. She's never forgotten that image of what she called their 'ecstatic feet'.

A new home brought about a new style of dress for Delia, much more low-key. Still she was all in brown from head to toe, as per usual to hide the snuff stains, except for her favourite navy donkey jacket, which Clive bought at her request after she'd loved wearing one during her time working for Laing. Her brown hold-all went everywhere with her. It held the essentials she needed, tins of snuff with specially prepared tissues cut into quarters for taking it, a couple of bottles of wine if she was visiting friends, and always pens, a notepad and graph paper for writing music – and a mechanical stopwatch. But the one thing she always made absolutely sure to carry with her was what she called her 'magic mittens', large black woollen gloves that were big enough to hide a small bottle of brandy in one and rum in the other. When one bottle ran out she'd drop it into her bag and put the other glove on, sipping from them when travelling by train or bus, or even in the pub in addition to the drink she'd bought. She was quite amused at her ingenuity in concealing her drinking, assuming she was fooling everyone and not even thinking that wearing a large black glove that was repeatedly being raised to her mouth was odd in itself. But overall, Delia drew little attention in her practical corduroy trousers, sensible shoes and baker-boy cap. And that's how she wanted it.

Delia got a job in a bookshop and began to lead a more sedate lifestyle, retreating and controlling who she saw. At first she had no television in the house, just the radio, listening to *The Archers* on Radio 4 but usually tuned to Radio 3 to hear classical music, sometimes turning it off halfway through a track to guess the composer, then turning it on to see if she was right. She invariably was. It was as if she was recreating the days when she felt most comfortable and unpressured, indulging herself in her lifelong love of radio. Eliminating the TV removed any negative associations with her work at the BBC. After a few years Clive bought a TV and Delia took to watching sitcoms, dramas and Formula 1 motor racing, finding Murray Walker's commentaries hilarious. More surprising to me was her love of snooker, and that she would go and watch her favourite player, Alex Higgins, when he competed in Northampton. Having a TV meant she could also indulge in watching some of her favourite films from her youth – films from the 1950s and 60s, anything with Marlon Brando in it, especially *On the Waterfront*, or French New Wave films like François Truffaut's *Jules et Jim*.

Delia and Clive lived and slept in the large room that took up the whole of the ground floor of their Northampton home, with most of Delia's hoard of boxes stored in the upstairs rooms and the attic. With the arrival from Cumbria of the vanloads of packing cases, furniture, her VCS3 and other musical equipment, a piano, electric piano and her trusty spinet, the house quickly filled up as Delia's nest of chaos once more formed around her (and Clive). Space was tight, not helped by her 'filing system' of keeping her papers and newspapers with music and notes written all over them on the floor in what seemed quite arbitrary fashion. It worked for her. Nothing was allowed to be touched; she was obsessive about keeping things where she'd put them, even though it was inconvenient and inconsiderate when living with someone else. Clive once, and only once, went to tidy up and throw away what he thought was a tatty old discarded newspaper. Delia flew into a rage and snatched it off him to show him important phone numbers she'd jotted down on one of the inside pages. He didn't touch anything after that. Likewise his one-time foray into composing music with Delia. Clive had worked on radio transmitters and was knowledgeable about electronics but he wasn't a musician and that had helped avoid conflict in their relationship. He kept away from music, except for the one time they decided to attempt a few songs. He wrote some lyrics and presented them to Delia, only to be greeted with a terse reprimand for encroaching on her musical territory. In her mind he must have 'sung' the lyrics in his head to a melody, therefore creating music without her input. Clive stayed clear of any further musical collaborations.

Delia was introverted but intense and would internalise much of her anger and disappointment. Clive could sense her energy, knowing instinctively at any given time whether she would speak to him or whether she'd decided not to for an unknown reason, sometimes for days. Confronting her wasn't an option; she'd go berserk because she was always right and wouldn't be challenged. The argument would go on and on, so he'd wait patiently until she'd come round. Her moods swung unpredictably from delightful to infuriating. She tried to deal with them by giving up drinking, but it made no difference. She hardly slept when sober and was highly excitable and manic, furiously writing pages and pages of music, then becoming totally depressed. After six months of sobriety she started drinking alcohol again. Clive persuaded her to lay off spirits because they had a tendency to make her volatile, so she stuck to sipping wine all day, which seemed to calm her.

Living with Delia and her eccentricities required a practical arrangement that gave each of them their own space and helped to limit misunderstandings and hassles. Clive mainly worked upstairs, leaving Delia to her own company downstairs, where they'd meet for dinner. But with Delia being so undomesticated there were no set meal times. She'd wake him at three in the morning to eat. Meals would not always appear on time, or at all. Sometimes she'd fry onions and garlic and the smell would permeate the house, giving Clive the impression that food was on its way, but it seldom materialised. She never cleaned or threw anything away. Eventually Clive found living with Delia unbearable and he bought his own house round the corner, but he never 'left' her – they remained a close and devoted couple in an unconventional relationship that worked for them both. The previous relationships Delia had invested herself in had failed. With Clive she was the happiest she'd ever been. She had always needed someone who understood her and loved her for herself, and Clive was happy for her to be 'Delia'. To Clive there was no one quite like her, even when she was difficult.

Accompanying Delia's mass of boxes stacked around the house were ever-increasing piles of papers, notes and books, and masses of large blue and gold snuff tins. She always maintained a good supply of snuff but never threw the empty tins away, using them to store small things like drawing pins and paper clips. She had a policy of no visitors in the house bar a few close friends who she knew wouldn't judge her for the state of the place. When postmen knocked to deliver packages she never answered the door, nor to the neighbours who had taken them in for her. The only time Delia relented and allowed 'outside' visitors through the door was to let workmen in when the leaking roof became in desperate need of repair – the living room was strictly out of bounds. Although she wanted to be left alone with her music in her space, there was an element of guilt about the mess she lived in. Her house-proud mother never visited – Delia always went to see her in Coventry. Their relationship was difficult, like some mother–daughter relationships can be. It was more through a sense of duty that Delia took care of her mother's needs when she became very ill. She spoke of her as being a religious fanatic, but when Brian Hodgson met her he found her very amiable and warm. She liked a drink and seemed rather exuberant, like Delia.

Those interested in Delia and her work have tended to assume that she gave up music when she left London. They couldn't be more wrong. Every day was given to music, it was her lifeblood, and she'd always have paper and pen at her side, writing notes while listening to the radio. But as far as the making and recording of music was concerned, technology had moved on, and she realised she needed to catch up. In 1983, in his role as the new director of the RW, Brian booked Delia on a weekend course on a desktop composing programme which he thought she'd find exciting. It had the opposite effect and brought home to her just how out of touch she was. She felt incapacitated by the new technology and the task of learning a different language of numbers, a new way of using mathematics in relation to music via the intermediary of a computer. The years she spent in Cumbria away from music had served the purpose of giving her 'time out' but had a cost as far as the practicalities of composing were concerned. Facing that realisation left her in tears throughout the course. She returned to Northampton disheartened, and the numerous requests she received from musicians and former colleagues to work on projects mostly got a polite reply of 'I'm not working any more.' Now she had the freedom to choose what to do, she only accepted projects that appealed to her, such as visiting Adrian Wagner's well-equipped studio to work on a commissioned theme for a programme on Stonehenge and to create and record her own new music.

A lot happened in the last four years of Delia's life. It was a rollercoaster of events. In 1993 an interview she'd given about her music appeared in *Doctor Who Magazine*. Then the following year her mother died. A few years later her RW colleague John Baker passed away, which seemed to prompt her to revisit her past, taking a trip to the Isle of Wight, where John had lived, and going to see and talk with Daphne Oram in her care home.

Interest in Delia and her work accelerated. She was in demand again, receiving and enjoying much-deserved respect and recognition, doing radio and magazine interviews. At the same time she was facing life-threatening health concerns, having been diagnosed with breast cancer in 1997. Delia underwent surgery for a double mastectomy. As a woman it sends shudders down my spine to write those words, to think about what they mean and the effect a mastectomy has on a deep emotional and psychological level. She spoke about it obliquely to Brian during one of their phone calls, telling him almost in passing, 'I've lost my twin peaks.' A traumatic experience uttered as a veiled acknowledgement of the loss of part of her femininity, her womanhood. It was hugely affecting. So much so that Delia, usually so private about her personal life, talked about her experience on BBC Radio 4's *Woman's Hour* in October 1998.

The same week she'd been persuaded by Mark Ayres to attend as a guest on the Radiophonic Workshop panel at the *Doctor Who* convention, PanoptiCon in Coventry. It was a challenge for her to talk in public about *Doctor Who* after all those years, not least because of the crowds, which she always found difficult to handle. Wine and snuff helped and she enjoyed herself, but not without people noticing how nervous, rather fragile and tearful she was during the panel discussion, especially when Ron Grainer was mentioned. Despite what had happened she still held a soft spot for him. Some people thought her unease and being a little overwhelmed was partly due to receiving so much attention for what she'd achieved all those years ago. An additional clue was the pink breast cancer awareness ribbon she proudly wore. She was probably still in a state of shock and trying to deal with the effects of her recent cancer treatment, as well as coping with so many questions and people wanting a piece of her. At the same time, she was so happy to be appreciated and to see how much her music meant to people.

In 2000 Delia was approached about releasing a compilation album of her selected works. She was back in tune with herself.

But when she asked the BBC for permission to license a number of thirty-second tracks they said each one would cost her £500. That made the album unaffordable and ended her aspirations to reconnect with her BBC compositions. It hurt her to go back there.

I've put it all behind me. It's the doing of it that was the pleasure really. I can still hear beautiful things in my mind, and I know how I can make more beautiful things too, that's the important thing.

The majority of Delia's socialising was done by telephone, though sometimes she'd travel outside Northampton or arrange to meet people in a nearby pub. As acknowledgement of her work and its importance to the development of electronic music grew she was approached by numerous younger musicians. She became a bit of a guru and was flattered, though a little shy and reticent about reconnecting with 'work' in music, remaining wary of being exploited. Around the time of her illness the singer and record producer Peter Kember (aka Sonic Boom) had contacted her, being a huge admirer of her work. She became his mentor, spending hours on the phone teaching him all about the harmonic series and sound structure, and in return he informed her about new technology and how sampling could fit her way of working. After realising there was a way to adapt and use them as tools rather than just ready-made preset sound machines, she bought herself some second-hand electronic equipment, including a Digitech S200 effects unit and a Yamaha DX200 synth. I've always stayed well clear of synth presets myself, for the same reasons as Delia. They can be a good starting point in triggering an idea or mood but used on their own they're too recognisable and an easy option. The challenge of creating my own music is everything – as it always was for Delia.

Hooking up with Peter reawakened her motivation to begin making pure electronic music again, free of any limitations. 'Now without the constraints of doing "applied music", my mind can fly free and pick up where I left off,' she said. On occasions she visited Peter in his studio, taking some of her equipment with her, including her VCS3. She enthused on the phone to Brian about being 'rediscovered' and how getting together with Peter was so exhilarating. True to her capricious nature, she was hyper-excited at the prospects – then seemed to suddenly rail against Peter, saying she wasn't getting much out of the collaboration and was becoming increasingly suspicious of people's motives, and worried about being ripped off. It was all too reminiscent of her past dealings with the music business. There had been talk with Peter of setting up a Delia Derbyshire website. Then, apparently to her utter surprise, it appeared, launched without her consultation or permission. She was furious. She felt 'used' – that her name and her life had been borrowed by other people to make them look good.

Delia wanted to end the collaboration with Peter and asked him for her equipment back. She intended to set up her own home studio after being excited at the prospect of getting an Apple Mac to explore the mathematical method of FM synthesis. Peter refused to return it. Brian was surprised, having heard how wonderfully things were working out with her newfound musician friend, only for Delia 'to ring myself and also Mark Ayres a few months later to say the guy had stolen all her equipment and was not to be trusted'. Peter's understanding was that Delia had gifted it to him. Their friendship was over, having made just one short piece of music together, *Synchrondipity Machine*.

Putting your trust in people can lead to dark places and conflict. Precious 'relics' of my own have suffered the same fate. In my case, a friend of Sleazy's had been entrusted with some of his belongings, which included historic archive materials and artworks related to my work with COUM and TG that Sleazy was temporarily holding on to for me. After Sleazy's death I asked his friend to return the items. The friend had no legal entitlement to sell what was in his 'care' but belonged to me. Unfortunately, I had no affordable recourse in terms of legal action or energy, and despite my numerous pleas for what was mine I had to watch as item after item appeared for sale on eBay, swelling his bank account at the expense of my archival 'recordings'.

Delia's occasionally contrary recollection of things and her erratic behaviour could be confusing for those involved with her. Not least for her old friend Angela Rodaway, when Delia broke off their thirty-year friendship, offering her no reason. When Delia started visiting Daphne Oram she was full of praise and sympathy for her not having been fully recognised for her contribution to music, then she abruptly changed her mind, denouncing Daphne as nasty and devious. There was also an occasion when Delia objected to the published version of an interview she'd done, saying it was all lies. The transcript revealed it to be an accurate record of the very words uttered from her own lips.

Looking back at the last few years of Delia's life, it was as if she knew time was running out and wanted to fit as much into her life as possible. Besides her association with Peter Kember as musical sounding board and adviser, as late as early 2001 she'd been working with him on a project that had always been close to her heart: an organisation to promote awareness of electronic music. She'd also begun her own ambitious research into the musical application of shapeshifting alloys. The future was promising to be creatively productive for her. She now knew about the technology that could help her realise her conceptual musical ideas. There was even talk of the RW getting together again with the help of Mark Ayres to collaborate on a soundtrack for Rory Hamilton and Jon Rogers's 2002 Generic Sci-Fi Quarry project. The thought of performing in public had never suited her temperament; she just wasn't a public person. There were long phone calls with Mark, who tried to persuade Delia about the idea. The very last call he had with her about it stuck in his mind. Almost in passing, as when Delia told Brian about her breast cancer, she mentioned that she wasn't well, that she was bleeding but didn't want to worry Clive about it. Mark told her to see a doctor straight away. Their phone call ended with talk of them driving to Peter Kember's to collect her gear after she had seen a doctor, and Delia asking Mark to set out the details of the music project in a letter to her. He did as she asked. It was returned to him unread, found in a pile of other unopened letters when her house was cleared.

I've repeatedly mentioned Delia being a private person, and what epitomises that is that during those first months of 2001, while she was still coping with having breast cancer, she was also undergoing tests on her liver, suspecting her drinking had caused some damage. The results showed nothing conclusive, but a few months later her liver failed and she was rushed to intensive care at Northampton General Hospital. When Delia was nearing her end Clive contacted some of her friends, including Jane, who'd known her since university days in Cambridge, and Brian. Both of them went immediately to be with her, Jane flying all the way from New York. Delia died on 3 July 2001. Clive was devastated.

After having put her trust in so many people and being let down, Delia knew she could rely on Clive. He saw that her wishes were carried out and she was laid to rest in the family plot with her mother, father and sister Benita. The inscription on the gravestone lists each of their names and the word 'REUNITED'. Delia left everything she owned to Clive, except one painting by Winifred

Nicholson, which she'd bought during her stay at the LYC. She left that to Jane, who donated it to Cambridge University. Clive cleared Delia's house himself and drove to London to deliver the 267 tapes and all RW-related papers from the attic to Brian, who passed them to Mark Ayres. The many necessary house repairs hadn't been done so the structural condition was poor, and with the inside being in a filthy state Clive had to sell it off cheap.

As sole beneficiary of Delia's estate Clive approached Peter Kember, as did Mark Ayres, both requesting that he return Delia's equipment so that it could be placed within her archive. Frustratingly they met with refusal, for the same reason given to Delia when she'd asked. Delia's VCS3 was sold, and as far as I'm aware no one knows where it ended up. That saddened Clive, making him regret he'd not fought harder to get it back.

One thing that Delia mentioned to Clive in the last years of her life was that she thought no one would remember her. He always assured her that they would, and he was so right, not only in terms of all the articles, films and music inspired by and dedicated to her, but in the posthumous honorary doctorate from Coventry University he accepted on her behalf in 2017. She would have appreciated and burst out laughing at that, and to see the blue plaques put up outside both the Coventry houses she'd lived in – and the street named after her. Or to see me and Caroline on one of our trips to Coventry being photographed beside the life-size 'Delia' stencil by the artist Stewy, which had been sprayed on one side of Coventry University's music, media and performing arts building on International Women's Day 2018.

Far from being a tragic figure, Delia wasn't at all embittered or downtrodden. Her resilience was phenomenal. She was angry yet resigned to all the things that had happened to her and magnanimous when it came to discussing them, saying that she'd made her own choices and had no regrets about them. It was the choices others had made in how they treated her that were the source of some of her problems. The people who used her by taking advantage of her ingenuity and generosity hurt her the most.

I find it so very sad that Delia's ventures into music collaborations later in her life ended in disappointment for her. That she felt a sense of unfairness and betrayal so close to the end of her life at yet another act of exploitation using her cultural significance, and at the loss of her equipment, an act of cultural vandalism. Thankfully Delia's beloved spinet didn't suffer from such exploitation when it found its way back into the world, probably because it had been stored away, inaccessible and partly broken. Clive sold it to someone who was unaware of its provenance – a fresh start, free to be enjoyed again by someone new. Delia spoke the absolute truth when she said, 'I gave my whole life to my music.' To as near the end as she was able, her life was music, music, music.

30

On 30 January 2020 I was taken by surprise by the *Art Sex Music* film being announced by *Screen Daily* as 'a biopic about Cosey Fanni Tutti, the outrageous and controversial UK performance artist, stripper and musician'. Hmmm, I thought. I wasn't overly happy (or surprised) by the journalist's choice of words to describe me when I'd have been OK with 'controversial artist'. But that wouldn't do as good a job of drawing people's attention – which I was hoping this wouldn't, as the official announcement had yet to be written and sent out. Nevertheless, after having to keep quiet about the film for nearly three years I felt a surge of relief that it was out there. A joint statement saying the *ASM* film was now in development was written by Andrew, Christine and myself and put out via social media. The reaction was incredibly exciting, with people speculating on who would be cast as me and Chris, even putting themselves forward. I must say that for me it was a great celebratory, counter-historic moment to 31 January being the official date of the UK breaking away from the EU.

With my work on the 'Delia' soundtrack completed, all that was left to do for the film were my last scenes, which were to be shot in Coventry. It had been scheduled for January but had to be postponed because Chris had been so ill. We didn't know the cause of his illness. We thought it was a bad bout of flu or a severe chest infection. He was coughing constantly, going purple in the face. Any pressure on his back seemed to trigger a coughing fit, so he was having to sleep sitting up, leaning forward. I was thrust into a world of fear as I watched him deteriorate. All the pre-scribed medications seemed to work only in the short term or have adverse effects of delirium, fainting, rashes and vomiting. After the third course of antibiotics and steroids he seemed to be improving. Then he had an alarming relapse. I found him laid on the floor of the studio fighting for breath. He couldn't speak. Under doctor's orders I didn't wait for an ambulance and drove him straight to A&E in our car, while he vomited into a bucket between gasps for air. Our GP had alerted the hospital so they would be expecting us and Chris was immediately put on oxygen, monitored and given medication. Then he was sent home for me to nurse him.

Chris responded well to the medication, so the filming was rescheduled for 8 and 9 February. After a week of warnings of Storm Ciara, predicting catastrophic conditions with 80 mph winds and torrential rain that could cause flooding and 'threat to life', it was decided to carry on regardless and hope to catch some windows of calm, seeing as some scenes were being shot in sheltered places, beneath bridges and underpasses. I was to be filmed driving around Coventry and walking about gather-ing field recordings of the ambience in various parts of the city. The most important scene was my placing Delia's name alongside the 'Derbyshire Way' street sign. There had been a campaign led by Peter Chambers, the director of Coventry Music Museum, to have a road named after Delia in recognition of her being born there and her incredible achievements. The museum has a display dedicated to Delia and signatures were collected from its many visitors. The campaign succeeded. At first the name was to be 'Derbyshire Road', but Peter pushed to change it to 'Derbyshire Way', to reflect Delia's individuality. But the council had been immovable on its decision to exclude her Christian name, so Caroline had written what seemed the 'proper' signage into the script, a scene to correct the omission of Delia's name. It was a significant moment, that on behalf of Delia we could 'sign' her, an acknowledgement she deserved even if only for the purposes of the film, which of course would be out in the world with the true origins of the street name that might otherwise be unknown to those who hadn't heard of her.

Chris and I had decided to drive there on the Saturday, the day before scheduled filming, when the crew were also arriving to do other things. That was a good decision as the day was sunny and the winds and rain hadn't yet arrived, bar a few gusts courtesy of the weather front preceding Ciara. So my Delia signage scene was brought forward, which meant I had to be filmed driving into Derbyshire Way. I hadn't driven a manual car for twenty-five years, so that was an experience. I stalled it on the second run, when it went all Benny Hill and *Carry On*, with the wipers going at full speed and the boot swinging open. I creased up with laughter – not professional but I couldn't help myself. Within an hour the shots were in the can and Delia had been duly served.

The underpass was our next location for some scenes of me making ambient recordings of Coventry. A great underpass was chosen – very J. G. Ballard (in fact many parts of Coventry are), black-and-white-striped paving and glossy white tiled walls. It was deserted, with just debris and a stray empty box of Viagra tablets lying about. The camera was set and just about to film my walking towards it when the producer Andy shouted, 'We have three friends approaching.' With that, three hooded, rather skanky-looking guys turned the corner heading my way, but Andy had already come to meet me and walk me back. No eye contact. It felt uneasy, like we had dared to intrude on their patch – for whatever purpose they used it for. One guy started a dialogue with Nick the cameraman, raising objections to him filming, asking if it was a documentary piece on homeless people. Nick explained he wasn't filming the guy, it wasn't about him, but the guy wasn't to be pacified; in fact he seemed on the verge of telling us to fuck off or else. It was a vibe of unspoken threat. We moved away from the underpass to the huge car park to decide whether to stay and carry on filming, but one guy followed us with his backpack and large bag, placing them against the wall, putting his hood up with his black scarf masking his face, just his eyes staring at us, making an unmistakable statement – that we had invaded his territory and were unwelcome. It was clear there would be no point in trying to negotiate; the threat was tangible and may well have accelerated if we didn't just heed the message and leave. We'd missed the weather window for the day's shoot in the underpass.

We drove to the ruins of Coventry Cathedral for more filming. I hadn't seen it since the summer of 1962, when I visited with my sister, mother and grandmother. We had all stood on the steps of the new cathedral looking up at the twenty-five-foot sculpture that I assumed was Christ crucified on the cross – at a glance the shape suggested that and I've always retained that impression. Sixty years later I again stood on the steps looking at the same statue and realised it's not Christ or a crucifixion. I was informed that it's St Michael defeating the devil. As an irreligious ten-year-old I obviously hadn't taken much notice or found it all that interesting, nor that the building of the Cathedral Church of St Michael was begun in 1951, the year I was born. Within a hundred yards of the ruins was Bayley Lane, which had once been the ditch (bailey) that surrounded the former twelfth-century Coventry Castle. I walked past tall, rusting iron plates commemorating some of the houses that had stood there before they were bombed in the Second World War. Vertical metal sheets etched with the history of each house dating as far back as Margery's time. In 1410 numbers 38 and 39, The Priory House, had been the family home and business premises of Robert Allesley, girdler. Now all the houses were marked as 'Destroyed by the blitz'. The war had wiped them out as it had the cathedral and assigned them a different place in history.

I was filmed making my way alongside the cathedral ruins, up the steps to the side gate and down, walking the narrow cobbled street, a wonderful atmosphere, a true sense of walking back in time. I could hear the rhythmic clip-clopping of my footsteps on the stones and stooped down to record them. I came to the iron church gates and recorded my tapping and scraping them with sticks and metal keys, the sound of the wind howling through the porch stinging my face and taking my breath away with the force of it. The ambient elements of old Coventry captured for me to download and add to my 'Delia' sound library for use in any additional music that Caroline might need later for the soundtrack.

When we returned to the underpass the following day it was pouring with rain, swathes of it being whipped up by the forecast 80 mph gusts of wind. There was no sign of our previous 'friends'. Nonetheless filming resumed in far from ideal conditions. It's amazing what determination and creativity can achieve. We did the car scene, now with Andy driving as I'd somehow managed to sprain my ankle the night before. The magic of film got around that problem. We all ploughed on getting the necessary shots done, and by mid-afternoon suddenly the sun appeared and the dark sky was now a beautiful blue. Chris and I took that opportunity to drive home. A direct line across country back to Norfolk, blue skies all the way and the company of a huge full moon low on the horizon. Within half an hour of getting home the winds started up again. We'd slipped into that window of calm before Ciara blasted us. Watching the news reports on the havoc wreaked by the storm, we heard them mention that the wartime sirens had been used in the North.

Chris's illness, which had delayed the Coventry film shoot, suddenly took on a new significance when images of the full horror of the COVID-19 virus were televised. Chris and I realised how lucky he'd been. It was like watching his ordeal from two months earlier. He was now on yet another course of antibiotics and coping with the residual effects of lung damage and fatigue, and was told his illness had most definitely been COVID. The virus was sweeping the globe and taking many of the frailest as well as the seemingly healthy, with all the associated initial disbelief, confusion about what to do, how to defend against it, how to fight the spread, how to cope with the grief surrounding the mounting death rate, followed by increasing fear, self-preservation, callous defeatism and complacency, selfishness and arrogance, conspiracy theories, and the UK government being accused of ineptitude and unscrupulous pandemic-related financial transactions. As COVID spread, access to all that the 'free' world had to offer was shrinking by the day, with people self-isolating, shielding and being quarantined, and countries around the world in lockdown and closing their borders. It wasn't dissimilar to the fifteenth century, when the walled town of Bishop's Lynn, where Margery lived, closed its gates at night to ward against villains and military invasion as well as the plague; or the 1950s, when the two gates of Hull were closed during the poliomyelitis outbreak. Delia and I both experienced the fear of catching the polio virus, her during the first wave in 1947.

Parallels prevail despite the progress made over the past six hundred years – and not only when it comes to the lives of women. The Black Death was delivered by fleas and lice into households across Europe, and COVID, it seemed, could possibly be delivered to your very door by home deliveries of essential supplies, or by asymptomatic family and friends. Echoes across the centuries and decades, whether of invisible infectious diseases or bombs – all unpredictable but deadly dangers that loom in the background of everyday life. Threats and large-scale loss and death affect our life choices. Delia and I had to deal with the aftermath of the war that devastated her home town of Coventry and my own of Hull, the looming threat of the end of the world during the Cuban Missile Crisis, and no vaccines or effective cures for some deadly diseases. For Margery it was wars, religious persecution and plague. Now it is still wars and religious issues, with the addition of all the effects associated with climate change and the continuing real-time threat of the COVID pandemic.

When we're faced with the ultimate threat of death there seems little point in 'treading water'. It makes sense to me that we'd want to get as much as we can out of life while we can, if time is of the essence. I remember my mother talking about the Second World War and people 'living for today', hoping there'd be a tomorrow and an end to the incessant feeling of dread, the grief of bereavement, not knowing when the horror would end. Sexual freedom during the war and the abandonment of some social mores provided a release, but women had to be discreet, aware of being judged as 'loose', a term not readily used against men (then or now) who likewise happily adopted the same approach to enjoying themselves before it was too late. Faced with life on the edge there seemed no point in planning for the future – the future was uncertain, there was only 'now', and what to do with that time was a matter of urgency. That attitude to life, resulting from difficult and dangerous circumstances, played a part in defining and inspiring myself and Delia. Margery faced the prospect of death so many times: as punishment for heresy, taking the last rites after difficulties in childbirth, when suffering from severe dysentery and also fearing recurrences of the plague. That such desperation can bring about something positive and uplifting is what underpins the determination that all three of us share in making life not only bearable but fulfilling.

31

You never really know the true scale of who has seen your work or what influence it's had. My working on the development of the *Art Sex Music* film was a revelation to me in that regard.

#CASTING FEATURE FILM
Looking for actors/performance artists/musicians to play
#CoseyFanniTutti

On 6 November 2020 the casting call for the film *Art Sex Music* went out and was picked up by the press and social media. The response was unexpectedly overwhelming. I had no idea that the hundreds of people who applied even knew who I was, let alone that so many women would cite my work as inspirational. My first reaction was how wonderful it felt that we all shared a view of life and art anchored in our *free self*. Not so wonderful were the hassles we'd all encountered, revealed in the answers to the questions posed in the brief for the audition. Talking directly to camera, those who applied were asked to say why they wanted the role of 'Cosey'. The film was about personal freedom. With one of the themes being sex, each person was asked to express their feelings on sex and nudity on camera and invited to ask questions of the film-makers about any issues they might have about the film itself. They also had the choice, if they wanted, to 'Talk about taboos' – which subjects were off limits and why – and how they felt about the hypocrisy of society, and tackling it personally and publicly.

The answers given by those who chose to speak about these topics caught me totally by surprise. I wept as I watched some of the casting tapes, at the openness in sharing their thoughts. The emotion reflected in their eyes, facial expressions, hand gestures and voices was incredibly compelling and heart-rending. Their individual stories touched a nerve. I knew exactly the feelings they were describing. My experiences were shockingly similar. Not only in some of their accounts of sexism, dealing with coercion and control at the hands of men, but their emotional responses, how they'd chosen to deal with the things that had happened and were still happening to them. Pushing the hurt down deep inside, always feeling its presence and knowing that at certain times it would work its way to the surface, but possessing the strength and determination to deny its power over them – to use it to their advantage. I'd like to say it astounds me that in the twenty-first century young women are still going through the same misogyny and abuse I and countless others have come up against. But it doesn't. What does is the rebellious spirit of women, their indomitability, their absolute refusal to be held back or pinned down. Fierce in their fight for freedom for the *self*.

My unanticipated reaction to these very powerful personal 'conversations' may have had an effect on my response to the improvised scenes the actors were asked to do. One was about the dread of the violent reaction when telling a boyfriend you're leaving him. Another was based on the phone conversation I had with my mother after the ICA *Prostitution* exhibition furore (over my exhibiting my soiled tampons and pornographic magazine artworks), when she said she'd have nothing more to do with me. I'd expected to find these difficult to watch but I found myself strangely and comfortably distanced, watching 'me' from outside, as an observer. I looked and listened to another 'Cosey', appraising the recreation of 'myself', analysing the accent, language and body language to see if it was 'me'. It was early days but I was elated by how the film was already promising to enrich and expand my artistic and personal views and my*self.* The casting tapes had afforded me the privilege of witnessing the impact of my work and of getting to see and hear such honest personal and artistic exchanges with people I'd never met, yet who clearly understood first-hand my approach to life and art and the challenges I and so many 'others' face.

I was heartened by the positive reactions to my book and the film. But the battle to be heard is never over. In February 2021 what I can only describe as a grenade lobbed from beyond the grave threatened the plans for the *ASM* film project. The estate of Genesis P-Orridge forbade the use of any Throbbing Gristle music in the film. My initial response was tempered, then a level of anger rose that I'd not felt for years – that history was repeating itself in my having to deal with the unreasonable controlling and obstructive behaviour of Genesis by proxy. My disclosure and honest accounts in my autobiography of the abuse I received from Genesis was allegedly the reason behind the estate's refusal. Questions ran through my mind. Why should I be punished in this way for telling my life story? Why should I be expected to be silent about the bad things that happened to me and thereby allow the perpetuation of what I knew to be myths and falsehoods about Genesis?

That a film which included the founding of industrial music and Throbbing Gristle couldn't feature the very music that defined the genre and TG seemed preposterous. Especially because during the time we were working on finding a solution to the problem we were receiving requests for the use of TG music in other people's projects. The Genesis estate granted all of them. It was absurd and incredibly frustrating to think that anyone else could use the TG music I had co-created, but not me. Chris and I refused permission for other TG synchronisation proposals until the dispute over music for the *ASM* film was sorted out. I had to bear in mind it was the revelations about Genesis in my book that were the main factor. But there was the real possibility that the strategy of excluding TG music could easily backfire and draw more attention to his misdeeds, with further adverse effects on his reputation. The press could have a field day, and I was prepared to think about taking that route if necessary.

After considering how best to tackle the issue I realised it maybe wasn't such a problem. In fact the attempt to throw a spanner in the works had done me a favour. It triggered a rethink that brought about exciting new ideas. Who would have thought that what I'd taken as a vindictive act could have had such a positive creative effect? My enraged knee-jerk reaction had turned from a 'fuck you' to a 'thank you' . . . with a victorious 'fuck you' cherry on top. But I knew, as did Chris, the representative of the record label and publisher for the TG catalogue and those acting on behalf of the estate, that there could be calamitous ramifications for the TG legacy if things escalated or were left unresolved. The will to make the decision of the estate have some semblance of rightness never wavered. Making sense of and trying to work around what seemed like an illogical and foolhardy decision by the estate took six months of negotiating and great patience, until thankfully an agreement of sorts was reached. As far as I was concerned the whole debacle should never have arisen, but why would I assume that when so much else concerning Genesis had always been such a struggle, a fight against tyranny.

Regardless of this interference, work on the *ASM* film had continued. The selection from the hundreds of casting tapes had been made and in April 2021 screen tests were set up in London for five actors. Because of COVID restrictions everyone had to be tested to help ensure they were safe. Some had expected me to be there, but I wasn't able to attend – which in retrospect I think was probably a good thing. I didn't want to distract anyone or make them feel uncomfortable in any way. All five screen tests were watched independently by Andrew, Christine and myself and Chris, and we all reached the same decision. The actor who would play 'Cosey' was chosen. The schedule was reassessed, and permission for the use of TG's music was now in place. *Art Sex Music* the film could proceed and I could re-engage with Delia and Margery.

32

Having followed Margery's life through to its end I was left with a lingering question. What lay behind the outrageously theatrical, singular style of prayer and devotion that caused her so much trouble and personal angst? I came to my own conclusion that it was a combination of factors. Her eccentric form of piety was the combined result of the medieval biological understanding of the body, the myriad of religious teachings, and the models of spirituality, imagery, music and theatre she'd come into contact with daily. Christian mysticism was a known practice so Margery's visions of Christ weren't that unusual. There was a Franciscan friary close to where she lived and the friars who preached and taught in the community encouraged affective piety, a highly charged form of emotional religious devotion that involved picturing themselves taking part in the scenes of Christ's Passion, to experience his pain and understand just what he suffered for them. It was a model that Margery seemed to have followed, but in her own over-the-top way. Her visions weren't magical or caused by sickness but by the practice of using her imagination to project herself into biblical scenes as an onlooker, a participant – as well as to have 'conversations'.

What was unusual about Margery (other than her howling) was her view that her personal revelations bypassed male intermediaries and that God had directly told her to do all the things she was being criticised for. This shielded her, cleverly making God responsible for her actions. She wasn't unique in what she said and did. Margery was very much aware of other well-known holy women. She took inspiration and strength from revered and canonised female martyrs and saints, as well as from the Virgin Mary, 'Mother of Christ', and Mary Magdalene – the so-called repentant sinner and 'Christ's Bride'. Mary Magdalene was second to the Virgin in popularity, and Margery adopted and cited in her book the practices associated with her: *'terys of compunccyon, devocyon, and compassion'*. Margery could align herself with both in terms of 'motherhood' and her 'marriage' to Christ. But knowing chastity was seen by the church as a way to heaven, Margery mourned the loss of her virginity: *'For becawse I am no mayden, lak of maydenhed is to me now gret sorwe.'*

Reinstating her chaste status became the focus of Margery's life. Being a wife, a mother and from a wealthy family, her visions, episodes of ecstasy, being in a 'relationship' with Christ, wanting and later daring to wear white, wanting and later achieving a chaste marriage, her life of penance, pilgrimages and weeping all mirrored the lives and writings of holy women familiar to her. Marie of Oignies and St Bridget of Sweden, and her book *Revelations* (recordings of her visions and communications with God, Jesus and Mary), alongside St Katharine the virgin martyr, who also had a mystical marriage to Christ, all influenced Margery's chosen 'alternative' lifestyle. They suffered and sacrificed so much in their lifetime, only being fully recognised for their spirituality after their deaths. It seems that not many people readily accepted or expected that Margery, the woman up the road, was perhaps a saint in the making. It takes time and the unrelenting persistence shown by Margery and those she emulated.

Time has been good to Margery. Her words now extend further than spirituality; they are used for degree courses and are scattered across the internet, with her *Book* receiving due recognition as a seminal work. For me this is not only because it is considered the first autobiography written in the English language but because it is by a woman, and is unlike other books written by women of her time, which focused on spirituality. Margery used their format but skilfully put her*self* at the centre, revealing *her* life experiences and those of other women in the fifteenth century. She set a precedent. Her *Book* signals to women that they had a right to be heard, their voices had value and a valid place in the world, and her 'recording' could possibly also be considered as one of the first moves towards equality in *self*-expression through the written word.

—⁓—

When my writing about Delia's life was drawing to a close I started stalling, had trouble focusing, lost motivation. I was suffering from what I'd describe as something similar to Delia's 'reverse adrenaline'. A reluctance to come to a 'full stop'. I didn't want to 'end' Delia. It was like denying her presence in my life, as if she was no more than part of the act of my writing, when it felt like so much more than that. I felt the same about Margery. I'd enjoyed being 'in' their lives so much.

Delia was exceptional by the very definition of the word, noticeably so in her character and music. She was an anomaly and flouted the rules at a time when men had full access to all areas and were instrumental in granting her that 'right', just as Margery was subjected to the control and whim of men. Always having to go through men, being in a constant battle, is fatiguing and wears you down. Breaking through the glass ceiling wasn't acknowledged until the 1980s. For Delia, Margery and myself it was more like being surrounded by four walls, a solid floor and a cciling, with a door opened at men's behest, allowing our entry into places chosen for us. We all wanted and needed more and were unhappy about being trapped in a system that favoured men (and still does). It was imperative for us to break out in order to pursue our desires, our individuality. And that meant defying the notion of 'permission', finding unsuspected ways, manipulating systems of control to worm our way into places we weren't supposed to go, saying and doing things women weren't meant to, whether that was through religion or creativity.

Whenever people ask me about why I make music and art, my answer is the same as Delia's: 'It's in my blood, it's just my instinct. Absolutely. That's all I can say.' It's an innate, irrepressible compulsion and desire – like Margery, we can't help ourselves. My art and music is about my life, about others' lives, the events of the world we inhabit, those elements are the beating heart of my work. It's how I communicate my feelings, to share with those who come across my 'recordings'. Whether they get that is not important. As Delia said about her *Doctor Who* tune, 'it's that it was done at all'. If I hadn't, or she hadn't, or Margery hadn't done what she did, there would be no 'recording' for others to refer to or possibly be inspired by in their own quest for freedom to express and be themselves. It's our actions and the consequential residual 'echoes' from the process of 'being' that are important. We three responded to the 'echoes' of others from before and during our lifetimes. Whether directly or indirectly, negative or positive, they played a significant part in why we chose to do what we did. As Delia said to Brian in a moment of melancholy (and foresight) as they stopped in the middle of Putney Bridge on the way home after a fruitful session at Peter Zinovieff's studio:

> What we are doing now is not important for itself, but one day someone might be interested enough to carry things forwards and create something wonderful on these foundations.

Delia, Margery and myself took on the world, each making our mark in history. Others have analysed, critiqued, sometimes lauded and exalted our lives and works through theses, books, music and films, increasing our imprint from the humble beginnings of our own 'voices'. We all fought hard for our freedom and our own place in the world. We all had the strength of will to defeat the odds stacked against us as women in our eras. Relentless and determined in our pursuit to be ourselves, defying categorisation – not misfits, wreckers, witches or heretics but individualists prepared to 'voice' our presence by our actions within societies intolerant of such behaviours. I feel the most appropriate way to end is with Delia's 'last word', which seems to sum up our defiant spirit. On looking for her will among all the paperwork scattered about her house, her partner Clive came across the document in a brown manila envelope. It was clearly marked in large black lettering not with 'WILL' but with the word 'WON'T'.

Afterword

Caroline's film, *Delia Derbyshire – The Myths and the Legendary Tapes*, was screened at the SXSW Festival and won the 'Visions' category of the Adam Yauch Hornblower Award: 'In honor of a filmmaker whose work strives to be wholly its own, without regard for norms or desire to conform.' The 'Visions' category was so apposite and completed the circle of intent that underpinned the whole project – to create an individualistic, unapologetically unconventional 'vision' of Delia.

Acknowledgements

My heartfelt thanks to Delia Derbyshire and Margery Kempe. Without their fearsome spirit this book would not exist. Thanks and gratitude to Caroline Catz for inviting me to be part of her film about Delia. Our working together was an exceptional experience in so many ways and played such a huge role in this 'recording'.

Special thanks to David Butler for his invaluable assistance and generosity in helping me through the complexities of Delia's 'recordings', and to Mark Ayres, the Delia Derbyshire Estate, the University of Manchester Library, the John Rylands Research Institute and Library, Dr Janette Martin, Jessica Smith, Jane Donaldson.

Huge thanks for sharing your memories of and thoughts about Delia with me: Clive Blackburn, Brian Hodgson, David Vorhaus, Robert Wyatt, Madelon Hooykaas, Joy Dee, Cath Foxon, Andy Christian, Peter Kember, Jo Hutton.

Thank you, Andy Stark, Anti Films, Martin Pavey, Nick Gillespie, Felicity Hickson, Ed Dowie, Callum Hickey, for the great time I had working with you all on the 'Delia' film.

Thank you, Professor Anthony Bale and Susan Maddock, for your generosity and guidance. I'm especially grateful to Anthony for his kind permission to quote from his translation of Margery's *Book*. My thanks and gratitude to the British Library for allowing me access to her book.

Thanks to my wonderful editor Alexa von Hirschberg for her dedication and enthusiasm for immersing herself in the multi-layered world of myself, Delia and Margery. Thanks to the amazing Eleanor Rees. Also to my agent Matthew Hamilton for his advice and much-appreciated positive and uplifting response to the manuscript drafts. Thank you, all at Faber, especially Luke Bird, Hannah Knowles, Mo Hafeez, Dan Papps, Joanna Harwood, Jack Murphy and Pedro Nelson. Thanks to Lee Brackstone, who was there at the very beginning.

Thanks to Andrew Hulme, Christine Alderson, Jason Lim, Robin Wood for building my Synthi A, Fanny Quément, Skot Armstrong.

Most of all thank you to my lover, my life, Chris Carter, for his enduring support, boundless patience, humour and encouragement throughout the process of writing this book.

Notes

CHAPTER 2

I wanted to do music. Austen Atkinson-Broadbelt, 'Soundhouse: Delia
   Derbyshire', *Doctor Who Magazine* 199 (1993), pp. 14–16.
I will not make a pavilion. Le Corbusier quoted in Oscar Lopez, 'AD
   Classics: Expo '58 + Philips Pavilion/Le Corbusier and Iannis
   Xenakis', *ArchDaily*, 26 August 2011, https://www.archdaily.
   com/157658/ad-classics-expo-58-philips-pavilion-le-corbusier-
   and-iannis-xenakis.

CHAPTER 5

I was told in no uncertain terms. John Cavanagh, *Original Masters*,
   BBC Radio Scotland, October 1997.
he reduced me to a very small height. Quoted in Ned Netherwood, *An
   Electric Storm: Daphne, Delia and the BBC Radiophonic Workshop*,
   Obverse Books, 2015, p. 15.
I joined in 1962. Austen Atkinson-Broadbelt, 'Soundhouse: Delia
   Derbyshire'.

CHAPTER 6

I mean Negative Capability. John Keats, letter to George and Tom
   Keats, December 1817, https://www.poetryfoundation.org/
   articles/69384/selections-from-keatss-letters.
It was music. Jo Hutton, 'Radiophonic Ladies', 2000, https://www.
   sonicartsnetwork.org/ARTICLES/ARTICLE2000JoHutton.html.
The term 'radiophonics'. BBC Engineering Monograph No. 51:

Radiophonics in the BBC, November 1963, Delia Derbyshire Archive, DDA/3/11.

Even after the success of Doctor Who. Austen Atkinson-Broadbelt, 'Soundhouse: Delia Derbyshire'.

People seem to think. Kirsten Cubitt, 'Dial a Tune', *Guardian*, 3 September 1970, https://www.theguardian.com/music/2014/sep/03/radiophonic-workshop-delia-derbyshire-interview-1970.

I find myself much more bass-sensitive. Delia Derbyshire in an interview rebroadcast on *Woman's Hour* on BBC Radio 4, 2008, https://wikidelia.net/wiki/Woman%27s_Hour_2008-07-25.

Yes! It went out. Sonic Boom [Peter Kember], interview first published in *Surface* magazine, May 2000, http://www.delia-derbyshire.org/interview_surface.php.

It was a magic experience. John Cavanagh, *Original Masters*.

CHAPTER 8

Music, once admitted. School exercise book, Delia Derbyshire Archive, BDD/1/1/1/2.

If music be the screen. Delia Derbyshire Archive, BDD/1/1/1/2.

Music is the real universal. School exercise book, Delia Derbyshire Archive, BDD/1/1/1/2.

CHAPTER 9

No, serys, I am neither. The Book of Margery Kempe, 1440. All quotations from Margery are taken from *The Book of Margery Kempe*, with a new translation by Anthony Bale, Oxford World's Classics, 2015.

CHAPTER 10

Dear Sirs, Further to your recent letter. Quoted by Clive Blackburn in correspondence with the author, 22 August 2019.

a very versatile girl. Quoted in Matthew Sweet, *Sculptress of Sound: The Lost Works of Delia Derbyshire*, BBC Radio 4, 2010, https://www.bbc.co.uk/programmes/b00rl2ky.

I only saw certain aspects. Brian Hodgson, interviewed by the author, 17 March 2020.

CHAPTER 11

putting on an act. Nathalie Léger, *Suite for Barbara Loden*, Les Fugitives, 2015, p. 66.

I've never wanted to be. Austen Atkinson-Broadbelt, 'Soundhouse: Delia Derbyshire'.

The conjugal debt. The Book of Margery Kempe, trans. Anthony Bale, p. 15.

The more mockery you get. The Book of Margery Kempe, trans. Anthony Bale, p. 33.

CHAPTER 12

I go back to first principles. John Cavanagh, 'Delia Derbyshire: On Our Wavelength', *Boazine* 7 (1998), http://www.delia-derbyshire.org/interview_boa.php.

everything in the music shop. Delia Derbyshire, 'Little Willie's Sneeze', Delia Derbyshire Archive, BDD/1/1/1/2.

You did not know. Delia Derbyshire, 'Little Willie's Sneeze', Delia Derbyshire Archive, BDD/1/1/1/5.

when we were having our or . . . Sonic Boom, interview for *Surface* magazine.

CHAPTER 13

I have a very strange mind. Desmond Briscoe and Roy Curtis-Bramwell, *The BBC Radiophonic Workshop: The First Twenty-Five Years*, BBC, 1983, p. 86.

Delia and I used to say. James Gardner, 'Interview with Brian Hodgson', *These Hopeful Machines*, New Zealand Radio, 19 April 2010, https://www.rnz.co.nz/concert/programmes/hopefulmachines/20131008.

CHAPTER 14

translating notes on the page. Austen Atkinson-Broadbelt, 'Soundhouse: Delia Derbyshire'.

That's why I'm so fond. Austen Atkinson-Broadbelt, 'Soundhouse: Delia Derbyshire'.

Doctor Who *was my private delight.* Austen Atkinson-Broadbelt, 'Soundhouse: Delia Derbyshire'.

The music itself was sacred. *Masters of Sound*, BBC Worldwide documentary, 2006.

CHAPTER 15

Directors who came to see me. John Cavanagh, 'Delia Derbyshire: On Our Wavelength'.

Musical innovation is full of danger. Plato, *The Republic*, Book IV.

Freedom does not exist. Maria Alyokhina, *Riot Days*, Penguin, 2017.

CHAPTER 16

Take 'rorate'. Delia Derbyshire Archive, DDA/1/1/4/1.

Arrange sections. Delia Derbyshire Archive, DDA/1/1/4/1.

CHAPTER 17

So the camels rode off. Brian Hodgson, 'Delia Derbyshire: Pioneer of Electronic Music Who Produced the Distinctive Sound of *Doctor Who*', *Guardian*, 7 July 2001, https://www.theguardian.com/news/2001/jul/07/guardianobituaries1.

And then she went and arranged. The Book of Margery Kempe, trans.
  Anthony Bale, p. 74.
Daughter, I will have you married. The Book of Margery Kempe, trans.
  Anthony Bale, p. 79.

CHAPTER 18
I got so addicted. Jo Hutton, 'Radiophonic Ladies'.

CHAPTER 19
I've got an open attitude. John Cavanagh, 'Delia Derbyshire: On Our
  Wavelength'.

CHAPTER 21
End Doctor Who *slow.* Delia Derbyshire Archive, DDA/1/1/15/3/9/4.
Countdown to lift off. Delia Derbyshire Archive, DDA/1/1/15/3/7/3.
Apollo & blast off. Delia Derbyshire Archive, DDA/1/1/15/3/7/2.
early bird via synthi. Delia Derbyshire Archive, DDA/1/1/15/3/9/4.
our old friend. Desmond Briscoe, 'Radiophonic Workshop in
  Concert' (*IEE 100*), 1971, p. 3, Delia Derbyshire Archive,
  DDA/1/1/15/3/6.
without parallel. Desmond Briscoe and Roy Curtis-Bramwell, *The
  BBC Radiophonic Workshop.*
This device. Desmond Briscoe, 'Radiophonic Workshop in Concert'.

CHAPTER 22
too sophisticated. John Cavanagh, *Original Masters.*
too lascivious. Sonic Boom, interview in *Surface* magazine.
I think I must have reverse adrenaline. Brian Hodgson, 'Delia
  Derbyshire: Pioneer of Electronic Music'.
DOCTORS!! Delia Derbyshire Archive, DDA/1/1/19/3/3.

pressures of today cause drama. Delia Derbyshire Archive,
   DDA/1/1/19/3/3.
Something serious happened. John Cavanagh, 'Delia Derbyshire: On
   Our Wavelength'.
I still haven't worked out. Jo Hutton, 'Radiophonic Ladies'.

CHAPTER 23

people that are just interested. John Cavanagh, 'Delia Derbyshire: On
   Our Wavelength'.
It often happens. Austen Atkinson-Broadbelt, 'Soundhouse: Delia
   Derbyshire'.
Ms Derbyshire was, crucially. Robert Wyatt, email correspondence
   with author, 26 and 27 February 2020.
her almost childlike enthusiasm. Robert Wyatt, email correspondence
   with author.
Perhaps a man with her ideas. Robert Wyatt, email correspondence
   with author.

CHAPTER 24

she was always afraid. The Book of Margery Kempe, trans. Anthony
   Bale, p. 218.

CHAPTER 26

they will hear. Latin homework book, Delia Derbyshire Archive,
   BDD/1/1/5.

CHAPTER 27

This book is not written in order. The Book of Margery Kempe, trans.
   Anthony Bale, p. 6.
And so it was more than twenty years. The Book of Margery Kempe,
   trans. Anthony Bale, p. 5.

whether you read. *The Book of Margery Kempe*, trans. Anthony Bale, p. 265.

the gospel mentions. *The Book of Margery Kempe*, trans. Anthony Bale, p. 115.

It was very funny. Fanny Quément, email correspondence with the author, 24 March 2021.

CHAPTER 29

I've put it all behind me. Jo Hutton, 'Radiophonic Ladies'.

Now without the constraints. Written by Delia before she died, http://www.delia-derbyshire.org.

I gave my whole life to my music. Austen Atkinson-Broadbelt, 'Soundhouse: Delia Derbyshire'.

CHAPTER 30

a biopic about Cosey Fanni Tutti. Geoffrey Macnab, *Screen Daily*, 30 January 2020, https://www.screendaily.com/news/andrew-hulme-to-direct-art-sex-music-about-uk-performance-artist-cosey-fanni-tutti-exclusive/5146685.article.

CHAPTER 32

It's in my blood. Sonic Boom, interview for *Surface* magazine.

it's that it was done at all. Austen Atkinson-Broadbelt, 'Soundhouse: Delia Derbyshire'.

What we are doing now. Brian Hodgson, 'Delia Derbyshire: Pioneer of Electronic Music'.

Sources

Delia Derbyshire

BOOKS AND THESES

Breege Brennan, unpublished Master's dissertation on Delia
Derbyshire, National University of Ireland, Maynooth, 2008

Desmond Briscoe and Roy Curtis-Bramwell, *The BBC Radiophonic
Workshop – The First Twenty-Five Years*, BBC, 1983

Jonathon Green, *Days in the Life: Voices from the English Underground
1961–71*, Heinemann, 1988

Ned Netherwood, *An Electric Storm: Daphne, Delia and the BBC
Radiophonic Workshop*, Obverse Books, 2015

Louis Niebur, *Special Sound: The Creation and Legacy of the BBC
Radiophonic Workshop*, Oxford University Press, 2010

James Percival, 'Delia Derbyshire's Creative Process', Master's thesis,
University of Manchester, 2013, https://wikidelia.net/images/d/
d1/Delia_Derbyshire%27s_Creative_Process.pdf

*Riches of the Rylands: The Special Collections of the University of
Manchester Library*, Manchester University Press, 2015

Geoffrey Rivett, *The Development of the London Hospital System 1823–
2020*, Nuffield Trust, 2021, https://www.nuffieldtrust.org.uk/files/
development-of-the-london-hospital-system-navigable-version.pdf

Angela Rodaway, *A London Childhood*, Virago Press, 1985

Teresa Winter, 'Delia Derbyshire: Sound and Music for the
Radiophonic Workshop, 1962–1973', Doctoral thesis, University
of York, 2015

Ben Allen, 'Doctor Who Theme Co-composer Honoured with Posthumous PhD', Radio Times, 21 November 2017, https://www.radiotimes.com/news/tv/2017-11-21/doctor-who-theme-co-composer-honoured-delia-derbyshire-honorary-phd/

'Anorak', 'In Photos: What World War Two did to Coventry', Flashbak, 2012, https://flashbak.com/in-photos-what-world-war-two-did-to-coventry-14271/

Austen Atkinson-Broadbelt, 'Soundhouse: Delia Derbyshire', Doctor Who Magazine 199 (1993), pp. 14–16

Richard Anthony Baker, 'John Baker Biography', Trunk Records, https://www.trunkrecords.com/releases/john_baker_08/john_baker.php

Rob Baker, 'Sex, Drugs, Jazz and Gangsters – The Disreputable History of Gerrard Street in London's Chinatown', Flashbak, 12 July 2020, https://flashbak.com/sex-drugs-jazz-and-gangsters-the-disreputable-history-of-gerrard-street-in-londons-chinatown-430639/

Jacqueline Banerjee, 'John Rylands Library, Manchester, by Basil Champneys (1842–1935). 2: Interior', The Victorian Web, 5 August 2012, https://victorianweb.org/art/architecture/champneys/2.html

'BBC World Service: 1940s', BBC World Service, https://www.bbc.co.uk/worldservice/history/story/2007/02/070122_html_40s.shtml

'Bebe Barron: Co-Composer of the First Electronic Film Score, for "Forbidden Planet"', obituary, 8 May 2008, https://www.independent.co.uk/news/obituaries/bebe-barron-cocomposer-of-the-first-electronic-film-score-for-forbidden-planet-822755.html

Madeline Bocaro, 'Getting to the Bottom of Yoko Ono's Film', 22 July 2016, http://madelinex.blogspot.com/2016/07/getting-to-bottom-of-yoko-onos-film-no.html

Kate Brown, 'Surrealism Was a Decidedly Feminine Movement. So
Why Have So Many of Its Great Women Artists Been Forgotten?',
Artnet, 18 February 2020, https://news.artnet.com/art-world/
kunsthalle-schirn-surrealist-women-1779669

James Bulley, 'Still Point by Daphne Oram', 2018, http://www.
jamesbulley.com/still-point

David Butler, '"Way Out – of This World!" Delia Derbyshire,
Doctor Who and the British Public's Awareness of Electronic
Music in the 1960s', *Critical Studies in Television* 9:1 (spring
2014), pp. 62–76

David Butler, 'Delia Derbyshire', in *History of the BBC: Pioneering
Women*, 2018, https://www.bbc.com/historyofthebbc/100-voices/
pioneering-women/women-of-the-workshop/delia-derbyshire/

David Butler, 'Whatever Happened to Delia Derbyshire? Delia
Derbyshire, Visual Art and the Myth of Her Post-BBC Activity',
British Art Studies 12 (2019), http://britishartstudies.ac.uk/issues/
issue-index/issue-12/whatever-happened-delia-derbyshire

David Butler, 'The Origins of Certain Lives: The Development,
Reception and Influence of the "Inventions for Radio" by Barry
Bermange and Delia Derbyshire', *Historical Journal of Film, Radio
and Television* 40:4 (2020), pp. 823–46

Caro C, 'Electric Storm 50', interview with David Vorhaus for Delia
Derbyshire Day 2019, https://deliaderbyshireday.com/david-
vorhaus-interview-dd-day-2019/

John Cavanagh, interview with Delia Derbyshire for *Original
Masters*, BBC Radio Scotland, 1997, transcript at https://
wikidelia.net/wiki/Radio_Scotland_interview

John Cavanagh, 'Delia Derbyshire: On Our Wavelength', *Boazine* 7
(1998), https://www.delia-derbyshire.org/interview_boa.php

John Cavanagh, sleeve notes for *Electrosonic* album (1972), 2006,
https://www.discogs.com/release/2798941-Don-Harper-

2-Li-De-La-Russe-Nikki-St-George-Electrosonic/image/
SW1hZ2U6MzI2Mjc1Mzg=

Lauren Clarke, 'Road to Be Named after Coventry Music "Pioneer" Delia Derbyshire', *Coventry Observer*, 28 November 2016, https://coventryobserver.co.uk/news/road-to-be-named-after-coventry-music-pioneer-delia-derbyshire/

Fidelma Cook, article about Delia Derbyshire based on an interview with Clive Blackburn, *Mail on Sunday*, 20 March 2005, reproduced at https://wikidelia.net/wiki/Mail_on_Sunday_article

'Coventry – Your Memories', https://www.historiccoventry.co.uk/memories/memories.php

'Creating the Music and Sound Effects of Forbidden Planet', *Soundworks Collection*, 14 March 2013, https://soundworkscollection.com/post/creating-the-music-and-sound-effects-of-forbidden-planet

Kirsten Cubitt, 'Dial a Tune', *Guardian*, 3 September 1970, https://www.theguardian.com/music/2014/sep/03/radiophonic-workshop-delia-derbyshire-interview-1970

Hugh Davies, 'Daphne Oram', *Guardian*, 24 January 2003, https://www.theguardian.com/news/2003/jan/24/guardianobituaries.artsobituaries

Delia Derbyshire, 1939 register entry, www.ancestry.com

Edward Derbyshire, 1911 census record and 1965 probate record, www.ancestry.com

Patrice Devincentis, 'Pioneers of Electronic Music: Oram, Anderson, and Dudley', *Synth and Software*, 2 July 2020, https://synthandsoftware.com/2020/07/pioneers-of-electronic-music-oram-anderson-and-dudley

Bob Dormon, 'Delia and the Doctor: How to Cook Up a Tune for a Time Lord', *The Register*, 19 November 2013, https://www.

theregister.com/Print/2013/11/19/doctor_who_theme_elements_
examined/

Christine Edge, 'Morse Code Musician: How Delia Crashed the
Sound Barrier', *Sunday Mercury*, 12 April 1970

David Ellis, 'David Vorhaus and Kaleidophon Studio', *Electronics
& Music Maker*, June 1981, http://www.muzines.co.uk/articles/
david-vorhaus-and-kaleidophon-studio/2670

James Gardner, 'Interview with Brian Hodgson', *These Hopeful
Machines*, Radio New Zealand, 19 April 2010, https://www.rnz.
co.nz/concert/programmes/hopefulmachines/20131008

Charlotte Perkins Gilman, 'What is "Feminism?"', *Atlanta
Constitution Magazine*, 10 December 1916, reproduced at https://
www.newspapers.com/clip/39281446/what-is-feminism-by-
charlotte/

Chloe Glover, 'Manchester Honours the Woman Behind the
Pioneering Music of *Doctor Who*', *Guardian*, 10 January 2013,
https://www.theguardian.com/uk/the-northerner/2013/jan/10/
blogpost-delia-derbyshire-electronic-music-dr-who

Elizabeth Gow, 'What's in a Name?', *Rylands Blog*, 31 May 2021,
https://rylandscollections.com/2021/05/31/whats-in-a-name/

Jennifer Harby, 'The Coventry Blitz: "Hysteria, Terror and
Neurosis"', BBC News, 13 November 2015, https://www.bbc.
co.uk/news/uk-england-coventry-warwickshire-34746691

Graham Harris, 'Delia Derbyshire: A Personal Tribute', March 2005,
http://delia-derbyshire.net/harris_tribute.html

Phil Hebblethwaite, 'Classic Photos from the Golden Days of the
BBC Radiophonic Workshop', BBC, 20 July 2018, https://
www.bbc.co.uk/music/articles/e71ca197-4808-4132-b1cc-
0078d8066fee

David Hendy, 'The Secret War', *History of the BBC*, https://www.bbc.
com/historyofthebbc/100-voices/ww2/secret-war

'The History of the John Rylands Library', the John Rylands Library, University of Manchester, 2013, https://docplayer.net/36603036-Contents-introduction-the-history-of-the-building-a-beautiful-building-the-collections-the-jewel-in-the-rylands-crown-unlocking-the-rylands.html

Brian Hodgson, 'Delia Derbyshire: Pioneer of Electronic Music Who Produced the Distinctive Sound of *Doctor Who*', *Guardian*, 7 July 2001, https://www.theguardian.com/news/2001/jul/07/guardianobituaries1

John Hodgson, 'Carven Stone and Blazoned Pane: The Design and Construction of the John Rylands Library', *Bulletin of the John Rylands Library* 89:1, https://doi.org/10.7227/BJRL.89.1.3

Tom Howells, 'How Daphne Oram's Radical Turntable Experiments Were Brought to Life after Seventy Years', *Factmag*, 13 July 2016, https://www.factmag.com/2016/07/13/daphne-oram-still-point-turntables-orchestra-performance/

Kenneth Hoyt, 'Library Description', John Rylands Library, 8 May 2012, http://johnrylandsstudy.blogspot.com/2012/05/library-description.html

Charlie Hulme, 'John Cassidy: Manchester Sculptor', 2013, https://www.johncassidy.org.uk/johnrylands.html

David Hunter, marriage registration, November 1974, www.ancestry.com

Jo Hutton, 'Radiophonic Ladies', interview conducted in 2000, published by Sonic Arts Network 2002, https://www.sonicartsnetwork.org/ARTICLES/ARTICLE2000JoHutton.html

'The John Rylands Library', *Hidden Architecture*, 12 May 2016, http://hiddenarchitecture.net/the-john-rylands-library/

Josh Jones, 'The Fascinating Story of How Delia Derbyshire Created the Original *Doctor Who* Theme', *Open Culture*, 7 January 2016, https://www.openculture.com/2016/01/the-fascinating-story-of-how-delia-derbyshire-created-the-original-doctor-who-theme.html

Acalya Kiyak, 'Describing the Ineffable: Le Corbusier, le Poème Electronique and Montage', thesis, Bauhaus-Universität Weimar, 2003, https://e-pub.uni-weimar.de/opus4/frontdoor/deliver/index/docId/1268/file/kiyak_pdfa.pdf

Benji Lehmann, 'The Story of the Oramics Machine', *Resident Advisor*, 12 October 2011, https://www.residentadvisor.net/features/1305

John Leonard, 'The Rise and Fall of Delos: The "Visible" Island', 20 September 2017, https://www.greece-is.com/rise-fall-delos-visible-island/

Oscar Lopez, 'AD Classics: Expo '58 + Philips Pavilion/Le Corbusier and Iannis Xenakis', *ArchDaily*, 26 August 2011, https://www.archdaily.com/157658/ad-classics-expo-58-philips-pavilion-le-corbusier-and-iannis-xenakis

Susan Mansfield, 'Variations on the *Doctor Who* Theme', *Scotsman*, 25 September 2004

Steve Marshall, 'The Story of the BBC Radiophonic Workshop', *Sound on Sound*, April 2008, https://www.soundonsound.com/people/story-bbc-radiophonic-workshop

Steve Marshall, 'Graham Wrench: The Story of Daphne Oram's Optical Synthesizer', *Sound on Sound*, February 2009, https://www.soundonsound.com/people/graham-wrench-story-daphne-orams-optical-synthesizer

Gareth Millward, 'A Matter of Common Sense: The Coventry Poliomyelitis Epidemic 1957 and the British Public', *Contemporary British History*, 31 October 2016, https://www.tandfonline.com/doi/full/10.1080/13619462.2016.1247701

Gareth Millward, 'Poliomyelitis', in *Vaccinating Britain*, Manchester University Press, 2019, https://www.ncbi.nlm.nih.gov/books/NBK545991/

Hammad Nasar, 'Cumbrian Cosmopolitanisms', 26 February 2018, https://www.paul-mellon-centre.ac.uk/about/news/lycmuseum

Hammad Nasar, 'Cumbrian Cosmopolitanisms: Li Yuan-chia and Friends', *British Art Studies* 12 (May 2019), https://www.britishartstudies.ac.uk/issues/issue-index/issue-12/cumbrian-cosmopolitanisms

'Old Town South Appraisal', Hull City Council, 2005, available via https://www.hull.gov.uk

'The Oramics Machine – Created by Daphne Oram', *Clash*, 11 September 2011, https://www.clashmusic.com/features/the-oramics-machine-created-by-daphne-oram

Rob Orland, 'Some Blitz Statistics', https://www.historiccoventry.co.uk/blitz/blitz.php?pg=stats

Rob Orland, 'Coventry's Blitz – Moonlight Sonata', 2021, https://www.historiccoventry.co.uk/blitz/blitz.php?pg=blitz

'Otter Spotter', 'Daphne Oram of Tower Folly', *Stansted and Fairseat: Yesteryear and Today*, 13 March 2012, https://stanstedandfairseat.blogspot.com/2012/03/daphne-oram-of-tower-folly-fairseat.html

Jonathan Patrick, 'A Guide to Pierre Schaeffer, the Godfather of Sampling', *Factmag*, 23 February 2016, https://www.factmag.com/2016/02/23/pierre-schaeffer-guide/

Damion Pell, 'This Insanely Rare Synthi 100 Analogue Synthesizer Can Be Yours on eBay for Just a Mere £70,000', *Decoded Magazine*, 12 October 2015, https://www.decodedmagazine.com/ems-synthi-100-insanely-rare/

Helen Pidd, '*Doctor Who* Theme's Co-Creator Honoured with Posthumous PhD', *Guardian*, 20 November 2017, https://www.theguardian.com/music/2017/nov/20/delia-derbyshire-doctor-who-theme-co-creator-posthumous-phd

'Plinius' [Andrew Ray], 'Circle of Light', 2016, https://some-landscapes.blogspot.com/2016/08/circle-of-light.html

'Radiophonic Workshop', *Electronic Sound* 43 (2018)

Dan Reich, 'The Fibonacci Sequence, Spirals and the Golden Mean', Temple University, 2017, https://math.temple.edu/~reich/Fib/fibo.html

'Remains of the West Front, Nave and Aisles of Coventry Priory', Historic England, 2021, https://historicengland.org.uk/listing/the-list/list-entry/1076588

James Riley, 'Breaking the Sound Barrier', *The Year 2019*, Girton College Cambridge, https://issuu.com/girtoncollege/docs/the_year_2018-19_final_sc/s/156778

Jude Rogers, 'Back to the Future: The Continuing Legacy of the BBC Radiophonic Workshop', Red Bull Music Academy, 6 December 2011, https://daily.redbullmusicacademy.com/2011/12/bbc-radiophonic-workshop

Drew Schlesinger, 'Pioneers of Electronic Music: Delia Derbyshire, Maryanne Amacher, and Suzanne Ciani', *Synth and Software*, 9 March 2020, https://synthandsoftware.com/2020/03/pioneers-of-electronic-music-delia-derbyshire-maryanne-amacher-and-suzanne-ciani/

'The Secret Millionaire', BBC Manchester, 26 March 2008, http://www.bbc.co.uk/manchester/content/articles/2008/03/20/200308_enriqueta_rylands_feature.shtml

'Shiva Feshareki Will Perform Oram's Lost Piece . . .', *Resident Advisor*, July 2018, https://ra.co/news/42118

Sonic Boom [Peter Kember], 'Delia Derbyshire Interview', first published in *Surface* magazine, May 2000, http://www.delia-derbyshire.org/interview_surface.php

Elsa Stansfield, *Alchetron*, https://alchetron.com/Elsa-Stansfield

David Stubbs, 'A Storm in Heaven: David Vorhaus of White Noise Interviewed', *The Quietus*, April 2015, https://thequietus.com/articles/17531-david-vorhaus-white-noise-interview

Matthew Sweet, 'Queen of the Wired Frontier', *Observer*, 17 March 2002, https://www.theguardian.com/theobserver/2002/mar/17/featuresreview.review

Phil Taylor, 'Delia Derbyshire: Recording the Future', Effectrode, 2017, https://www.effectrode.com/knowledge-base/delia-derbyshire-recording-the-future/

'Tower Folly', *Geograph*, https://www.geograph.org.uk/photo/778149

Simon Trask, 'History of the Future: Kaleidophon Studios/David Vorhaus', *Electronics & Music Maker*, September 1986, http://www.muzines.co.uk/articles/history-of-the-future/1828

'Unit Delta Plus', *Delia Derbyshire: Electronic Music Pioneer*, http://www.delia-derbyshire.org/unitdeltaplus.php

'Voronoff', 'The Minaretic Octave', 30 July 2009, https://octagonmystic.wordpress.com

Watermill Theatre, programme for UDP Concert of Electronic Music, 10 September 1966, https://www.delia-derbyshire.org/unitdeltaplus.php

Paul White, 'David Vorhaus: Electronic Music Pioneer', *Sound on Sound*, February 2002, https://www.soundonsound.com/people/david-vorhaus

Ray White, *BBC Radiophonic Workshop* 2004–21, https://whitefiles.org/rwi/index.htm

FILM, AUDIO AND VIDEO

Kara Blake, *The Delian Mode*, 2009, https://www.youtube.com/watch?v=nXnmSgaeGAI

'Delia Derbyshire/Blue Veils and Golden Sands', https://www.youtube.com/watch?v=OyUkmxy5VMI

'Dick Mills, Interview at Whooverville 5 (Part One)', 2 September 2013, https://www.youtube.com/watch?v=9COYiD9VZ0I

'For Interest Only: An Introduction to the Delia Derbyshire Archive', Belle Vue Productions, 3 May 2017, https://www.youtube.com/watch?v=pPIqq7_RjnA

'Madelon Hooykaas Talking about Her Work and Collaborations with Elsa Stansfield', 26 November 2010, https://www.youtube.com/watch?v=3VRp3eV8OUQ&t=19s

Ian Marchant, '*Doctor Who* Theme Singles – Eric Winstone and His Orchestra', 14 August 2018, https://www.youtube.com/watch?v=93aKlhb8Y3Q

Masters of Sound, documentary featuring Delia Derbyshire, Brian Hodgson and Dick Mills, BBC Worldwide, 2006

Jenn Mattinson, 'Out of Place: Delia Derbyshire in Cumbria', 2017, https://soundcloud.com/delia-derbyshire-day/out-of-place-delia-derbyshire-in-cumbria

'The New Sound of Music (Part 1)', BBC documentary, 1979, https://www.youtube.com/watch?v=6MsyOe7xCqg

Oscar Sala, live concert on the Trautonium, 1991, https://www.youtube.com/watch?v=-tQQEChMq1A

Michele Soraperra, 'Philips Pavilion – Le Corbusier and Xenakis – Expo 58 (Part 01)', 1 November 2008, https://www.youtube.com/watch?v=_3cKxLxq-Xw

Matthew Sweet, *Sculptress of Sound: The Lost Works of Delia Derbyshire*, BBC Radio 4, 2010, https://www.bbc.co.uk/programmes/b00rl2ky

'Time on Our Hands', BBC documentary, 1963, https://www.youtube.com/watch?v=AYGt_UN0DpM

Woman's Hour interviews about Delia Derbyshire, BBC Radio 4, 25 July 2008, https://www.bbc.co.uk/radio4/womanshour/01/2008_30_fri.shtml

Iannis Xcnakis, 'Orient–Occident', 1960, https://www.youtube.com/watch?v=g7N2-nuZbxY

INTERVIEWS AND PERSONAL CORRESPONDENCE

Clive Blackburn, meeting with the author, 21 August 2019, and
  email correspondence, August 2019 and September 2020
Andy Christian, interview with the author, 9 October 2020
Joy Dee, interview with the author, 30 October 2020
Cath Foxon, interview with the author, 23 October 2020
Madelon Hooykaas, interview with the author, 9 January 2020
Brian Hodgson, interview with the author, 17 March 2020, and
  email correspondence, 2 and 13 June 2020
Jo Hutton, interview with the author, 14 April 2021
Peter Kember, email correspondence, September–October 2020 and
  August 2021
David Vorhaus, interview with the author, 27 July 2019
Robert Wyatt, email correspondence, 26 and 27 February 2020

Margery Kempe

BOOKS AND THESES

John Aberth, *The Black Death: The Great Mortality of 1348–1350*,
  Bedford/St Martin's, 2005
John H. Arnold and Katherine J. Lewis, *A Companion to* The Book of
  Margery Kempe, D. S. Brewer, 2004
Francis Bacon, *The New Atlantis*, 1627
Anthony Bale, *Margery Kempe: A Mixed Life*, Reaktion Books, 2021
H. S. Bennett, *Six Medieval Men and Women*, Cambridge University
  Press, 1955
Karen Elizabeth Berrigan, '"Woman, Why Weepest Thou?": The
  Influence of Mary Magdalene on *The Book of Margery Kempe*',
  Master's thesis, Dalhousie University, Canada, 1999
Louise Collis, *Memoirs of a Medieval Woman: The Life and Times of*

Margery Kempe, Harper & Row, 1964

Charles Creighton, *A History of Epidemics in Britain*, Cambridge University Press, 1891, https://www.gutenberg.org/files/42686/42686-h/42686-h.htm

Rose-Lynn Fisher, *The Topography of Tears*, Bellevue Literary Press, 2017

Anthony Goodman, *Margery Kempe and Her World*, Longman, 2002

Karen Harris and Lori Caskey-Sigety, *The Medieval Vagina*, Snark Publishing, 2014

Jack Hartnell, *Medieval Bodies: Life, Death and Art in the Middle Ages*, Profile Books, 2018

Courtney Rosali Higgins, *The Venetian Galley of Flanders: From Medieval (Two-Dimensional) Treatises to 21st Century (Three-Dimensional) Model*, Master's thesis, Texas A&M University, 2012, https://oaktrust.library.tamu.edu/handle/1969.1/ETD-TAMU-2012-05-10762

Henry J. Hillen, *History of the Borough of King's Lynn*, vol. 2, East of England Newspaper Co., 1907

Rosemary Horrox, *The Black Death*, Manchester University Press, 1994

Helen Kavanagh, 'The Topography of Illicit Sex in Later Medieval English Provincial Towns', Master's thesis, Royal Holloway, University of London, 2020

Margery Kempe, *The Book of Margery Kempe*, trans. Anthony Bale, Oxford World's Classics, 2015

Charles Kightly, 'The Early Lollards: A Survey of Popular Lollard Activity in England, 1382–1428', Doctoral thesis, University of York, 1975

Martin D. Locker, 'Landscapes of Pilgrimage in Medieval Britain', Doctoral thesis, University College London, November 2012

Elizabeth MacDonald, *Skirting Heresy: The Life and Times of Margery Kempe*, Franciscan Media, 2014

Ian Mortimer, *The Time Traveller's Guide to Medieval England*, Vintage, 2009

Toni Mount, *The Medieval Housewife and Other Women of the Middle Ages*, Amberley, 2014

Toni Mount, *Medieval Medicine: Its Mysteries and Science*, Amberley, 2015

Laura Pujolràs Borrut, '*The Book of Margery Kempe* (1501): The Construction of Women's Authority in a Proto-Feminist Context', thesis, Universitat Autònoma de Barcelona, 2016

Michael Schmoelz, 'Pilgrimage in Medieval East Anglia', Doctoral thesis, University of East Anglia, 2017

Brian C. Vander Veen, 'The *Vitae* of Bodleian Library MS Douce 114', Doctoral thesis, University of Nottingham, 2007

Christine Winter, 'Prisons and Punishments in Late Medieval London', Doctoral thesis, Royal Holloway, University of London, 2012

ARTICLES AND ONLINE RESOURCES

Esther Addley, 'Mass Grave Shows How Black Death Devastated the Countryside', *Guardian*, 18 February 2020, https://www.theguardian.com/society/2020/feb/18/mass-grave-shows-how-black-death-devastated-the-countryside

Linda Alchin, 'Sumptuary Laws of the Middle Ages', *The Middle Ages*, https://www.lordsandladies.org/sumptuary-laws-middle-ages.htm

Stephen Alsford, *Medieval English Towns*, 1998–2021, http://users.trytel.com/~tristan/towns/towns.html#menu

Stephen Alsford, *Florilegium Urbanum* [resources and commentaries on medieval life and religion], 2001–19, http://users.trytel.com/~tristan/towns/florilegium/flor00.html

Benjamin Arbel, 'Daily Life on Board Venetian Ships: The Evidence of Renaissance Travelogues and Diaries', *Rapporti mediterranei*, Instituti Veneto di Scienze, 2017, pp. 183–219, https://www. academia.edu/34333403/Daily_Life_on_Board_Venetian_Ships_ The_Evidence_of_Renaissance_Travelogues_and_Diaries

Rachel Arnold, 'Clothing as a Reflection of Economic Status, Familial Association, and Religious Affiliation in *The Book of Margery Kempe*', *Mapping Margery Kempe*, 1999, https://college. holycross.edu/projects/kempe/town/whiteclo.htm

Anthony Bale, 'Jerusalem, Geometry, and Medieval Germany', *Remembered Places*, 21 November 2013, https://rememberedplaces. wordpress.com/2013/11/21/jerusalem-geometry-and-medieval-germany/

Anthony Bale, 'What Was Life Like for a Middle-Class Medieval Woman?', Oxford Academic, 19 February 2015, https://www. youtube.com/watch?v=SJJ_kXS6kxE

Anthony Bale, 'Richard Salthouse of Norwich and the Scribe of *The Book of Margery Kempe*', *The Chaucer Review* 52:2 (2017), pp. 173–87, https://doi.org/10.5325/chaucerrev.52.2.0173

Anthony Bale and Kathryne Beebe, 'Pilgrimage and Textual Culture', *Journal of Medieval and Early Modern Studies* 51:1 (January 2021), http://read.dukeupress.edu/jmems/article-pdf/51/1/1/854611/0510001.pdf

'Bedford, Earls and Dukes of', *Encyclopaedia Britannica* 1911, https://en.wikisource.org/wiki/1911_Encyclopædia_Britannica/ Bedford,_Earls_and_Dukes_of

Goran Blazeski, 'Off to the "Holy Places": Pilgrimages During the Middle Ages', *The Vintage News*, 14 April 2017, https:// www.thevintagenews.com/2017/04/14/off-to-the-holy-places-pilgrimages-during-the-middle-ages/

Francis Blomefield, 'Freebridge Hundred and Half: Lynn', in *An Essay Towards a Topographical History of the County of Norfolk: Volume 8*

(London, 1808), pp. 476–533, *British History Online*, http://www.
british-history.ac.uk/topographical-hist-norfolk/vol8/pp476-533

'Bone Pen', *Medieval London*, Fordham University, 2017, https://
medievallondon.ace.fordham.edu/collections/show/99

The Book of Margery Kempe: Book 1, Part 1, ed. Lynn Staley,
University of Rochester, 1996, https://d.lib.rochester.edu/teams/
text/staley-book-of-margery-kempe-book-i-part-i

The Book of Margery Kempe, first page, manuscript of 1440, http://
english.selu.edu/humanitiesonline/kempe/showcase/webapp.php

'The Borough of King's Lynn: Charters, Letters Patent, etc.', HMSO
(1887), *British History Online*, https://www.british-history.ac.uk/
hist-mss-comm/vol11/pt3/pp185-209

Sarah Bryson, 'Childbirth in Medieval and Tudor Times', the Tudor
Society, 2015, https://www.tudorsociety.com/childbirth-in-
medieval-and-tudor-times-by-sarah-bryson/

Sarah Bryson, 'Travel Tips for the Medieval Pilgrim', Medievalists.net,
June 2016, https://www.medievalists.net/2016/06/travel-tips-for-
the-medieval-pilgrim/

John Capgrave and Karen A. Winstead, 'Introduction', *The Life
of St Katherine*, University of Rochester, 1999, https://d.lib.
rochester.edu/teams/text/winstead-capgrave-life-of-saint-katherine-
introduction

Martha Carlin, 'The Black Death in the British Isles', https://sites.
uwm.edu/carlin/the-black-death-in-the-british-isles/

Jennie Cohen, 'Seven Surprising Facts about Joan of Arc',
History.com, 28 January 2013, https://www.history.com/news/7-
surprising-facts-about-joan-of-arc

Anne Curry, 'Participants in the Battle of Agincourt', *Oxford
Dictionary of National Biography*, 4 October 2008, https://doi.
org/10.1093/ref:odnb/95588

Danièle Cybulskie, 'Medieval Pilgrimages: It's All About the Journey',

Medievalists.net, 2021 https://www.medievalists.net/2015/08/ medieval-pilgrimages-its-all-about-the-journey/

Caitlin Dempsey, 'A Brief Look at Medieval Maps and Travel Guides', *Geography Realm*, 26 November 2018, https://www.geographyrealm. com/a-brief-look-at-medieval-maps-and-travel-guides/

'Dukes Head Hotel', *Norfolk Public Houses*, https://www. norfolkpubs.co.uk/kingslynn/dkingslynn/kldhh.htm

'Erotic Badges', The Religious and Profane Medieval Badges Foundation, http://www.medievalbadges.org/mb_erotisch_tekst_ UK.php

'Fourteenth Century 1349: The Plague Years', Visit Norwich, 2018, https://www.visitnorwich.co.uk/article/14th-century-1349-the-plague-years/

Alison Flood, 'Archive Find Shows Medieval Mystic Margery Kempe's Autobiography "Doesn't Lie"', *Guardian*, 8 May 2015, https:// www.theguardian.com/books/2015/may/08/archive-find-shows-medieval-mystic-margery-kempes-autobiography-doesnt-lie

Tessa Frank, 'Margery Kempe: A Study in Urban Spirituality', https://www.theway.org.uk/Back/491Frank.pdf

Rosalie Gilbert, 'Medieval Births and Birthing', *Rosalie's Medieval Woman*, https://rosaliegilbert.com/births.html

'Hanseatic King's Lynn', Visit West Norfolk, http://www. visitwestnorfolk.com/wp-content/uploads/2016/03/1390-46_ Hanse_trail_leaflet_web.pdf

Katherine Harvey, 'Episcopal Emotions: Tears in the Life of the Medieval Bishop', *Historical Research* 87:238 (November 2014), https://onlinelibrary.wiley.com/doi/full/10.1111/1468-2281.12077

Katherine Harvey, 'The Salacious Middle Ages', *Aeon*, 23 January 2018, https://aeon.co/essays/getting-down-and-medieval-the-sex-lives-of-the-middle-ages

'History of King's Lynn Town Hall', https://www.kingslynntownhall.
  com/townhall/history/

'History of Markets', Borough Council of King's Lynn and
  West Norfolk, https://www.west-norfolk.gov.uk/info/20186/
  markets/407/history_of_markets

Julia Bolton Holloway, 'The Mystics' Internet: Julian of Norwich',
  http://www.umilta.net/mystics.html#JulianNorwich

'Hospitals: Hospitals in Lynn', in *A History of the County of Norfolk:
  Volume 2*, ed. William Page (London, 1906), pp. 441–2, *British
  History Online*, http://www.british-history.ac.uk/vch/norf/vol2/
  pp441-442

'How the King's Lynn Mart Was Placed in Peril by Past Plagues',
  King's Lynn News, 13 February 2021, https://www.lynnnews.
  co.uk/news/how-the-kings-lynn-mart-was-placed-in-peril-by-past-
  plagues-9156411/

Laura L. Howes, 'On the Birth of Margery Kempe's Last Child',
  Modern Philology 90:2 (November 1992), pp. 220–5, https://www.
  jstor.org/stable/438753

Jonathan Hsy, '"Be More Strange and Bold": Kissing Lepers and
  Female Same-Sex Desire in *The Book of Margery Kempe*', *Early
  Modern Women: An Interdisciplinary Journal* 5 (2010), pp. 189–99

Mike Ibeji, 'Black Death', BBC, 10 March 2011, https://www.bbc.
  co.uk/history/british/middle_ages/black_01.shtml

Danuta Kean, 'Recipe Found in Medieval Mystic's Writings Was
  Probably for "Dragges"', *Guardian*, 28 February 2017, https://
  www.theguardian.com/books/2017/feb/28/recipe-found-in-
  medieval-mystics-writings-was-probably-for-drugges-margery-
  kempe

Hilton Kelliher, 'The Rediscovery of Margery Kempe: A Footnote',
  British Library Journal 23:2 (1997), https:// www.jstor.org/
  stable/42554480

Tim Lambert, 'A History of King's Lynn', 14 March 2021, https://localhistories.org/a-history-of-kings-lynn/

Kathy Lavezzo, 'Sobs and Sighs Between Women: The Homoerotics of Compassion in *The Book of Margery Kempe*', in *Premodern Sexualities*, eds Louise Fradenburg and Carla Freccero, Routledge, 1996

'Littleoldboy', 'Southgates', *King's Lynn Forums*, 8 November 2006, https://www.kingslynn-forums.co.uk/viewtopic.php?f=14&t=1821

'Lollards Pit – A Grim Tale of Persecution!', *Norfolk Tales, Myths and More*, 10 March 2019, https://norfolktalesmyths.com/2019/03/10/lollards-pit-a-grim-tale-of-persecution/

Elona K. Lucas, 'The Enigmatic, Threatening Margery Kempe', *Downside Review* 105:361 (1987), pp. 294–305, https://journals.sagepub.com/doi/abs/10.1177/001258068710536104

'Margery Kempe', *Norfolk Women in History*, https://norfolkwomeninhistory.com/1300-1499/margery-kempe/

'Margery Kempe', *School of Divinity*, https://www.animatedmaps.div.ed.ac.uk/Divinity2/pilgrimages.html

'Margery Kempe and Julian of Norwich', King's Lynn Minster, https://kingslynnminster.org/history/margery-kempe/margery-kempe-and-julian-of-norwich/

'Margery Kempe Studies in the 21st Century', conference, University of Oxford, 18 March 2018 https://margerykempeconference.wordpress.com/programme/

'Margery of Kempe: Laywoman and Autobiographer', Encyclopedia.com, 6 December 2020, https://www.encyclopedia.com/history/news-wires-white-papers-and-books/margery-kempe

Joshua J. Mark, 'Margery Kempe', *World History Encyclopedia*, 6 June 2019, https://www.worldhistory.org/Margery_Kempe/

Laura Martisiute, 'Ten Surprising Facts about Pilgrimage in the Middle Ages', *Listverse*, 5 November 2016, https://listverse.

com/2016/11/05/10-surprising-facts-about-pilgrimage-in-the-middle-ages/

'Materials and Techniques of Manuscript Production', http://web.ceu.hu/medstud/manual/MMM/paper.html

'Medieval Hull', *A History of the County of York East Riding: Volume 1, the City of Kingston Upon Hull*, Victoria County History, 1969, *British History Online*, https://www.british-history.ac.uk/vch/yorks/east/vol1/pp11-85

'Medieval Prisons', York Museums, http://www.historyofyork.org.uk/themes/1000-years-of-justice-at-york-castle/medieval-prisons

Maurice Mikkers, 'The Journey of Imaginarium of Tears', *Micrograph Stories*, 7 January 2016, https://medium.com/micrograph-stories/the-journy-of-imaginarium-of-tears-5f70c8fb6f53

Tracey Monger, 'Norfolk Witchcraft – Executions – Ritual Objects', 2 January 2013, https://tracymonger.wordpress.com/2013/01/02/norfolk-witchcraft-executions-ritual-objects/

'Mudlark121', 'Today in London's Religious History: Lollard William Sawtrey Questioned for Heresy at St Paul's, 1401', *Past Tense*, 12 February 2018, https://pasttenseblog.wordpress.com/2018/02/12/today-in-londons-religious-history-lollard-william-sawtrey-questioned-for-heresy-at-st-pauls-1401/

Marie Nelson, 'From *The Book of Margery Kempe*: The Trials and Triumphs of a Homeward Journey', *Oral Tradition* 19:2 (2004), pp. 214–35

Lisa Padden, 'Locating Margery Kempe: An Examination of the Meaning of Space and Sexuality in *The Book of Margery Kempe*', *The AnaChronisT* 16 (winter 2011), pp. 1–17

'Paradise Lane, King's Lynn', *While There Is Light*, 6 September 2019, https://whilethereislight.co/feature/paradise-lane-kings-lynn/

Dan Pariser, 'Felix Fabri on Galleys, 1483', https://sites.google.com/site/shipwrightsfaq/smf-researchnotes/smf-RN-Galley

'Prisons and Gallows', *A History of the County of York*, ed. P. M. Tillott, Victoria County History, 1961, *British History Online*, https://www.british-history.ac.uk/vch/yorks/city-of-york/pp491-498

Virginia Raguin and Sarah Stanbury, *Mapping Margery Kempe* (introduction, outline and chapter summary of *The Book of Margery Kempe*, with glossary and discussions), https://college.holycross.edu/projects/kempe/text/welcome1.html

'Reglimpsing Norwich's "Lollards Pit"', *Norfolk Tales, Myths and More*, 5 November 2017, https://norfolktalesmyths.com/2017/11/05/a-glimpse-into-lollards-pit/

'Revealing the Past of Southgates', Historic England, 2020, https://historicengland.org.uk/whats-new/in-your-area/east-of-england/kings-lynn-research/southgates/

David Ross, 'King's Lynn Minster (St Margaret's) Church', *Britain Express*, https://www.britainexpress.com/counties/norfolk/churches/kings-lynn-minster.htm

'St Margaret's Area, Conservation Area Character Statement', Borough Council of King's Lynn and West Norfolk, 2003, revised 2008, available via https://www.west-norfolk.gov.uk

'St Margaret, King's Lynn', *Churches of Norfolk*, http://www.norfolkchurches.co.uk/lynnstmargaret/lynnstmargaret.htm

Charity Scott Stokes, 'Margery Kempe's Family Background and Early Years, 1373–1393', *Mystics Quarterly* 25 (1999), https://college.holycross.edu/projects/kempe/text/familybg.html

Charity Scott Stokes, 'Piety and Works of Mercy in Lynn', *Mystics Quarterly* 25 (1999), https://college.holycross.edu/projects/kempe/text/piety.html

'Sex in the Middle Ages', Medievalists.net, 2020, https://www.medievalists.net/2013/02/sex-in-the-middle-ages/

John Simkin, 'The Tudors: Tudor Heretics, John Wycliffe and the

Lollards', 1997, updated 2020, https://spartacus-educational.com/TUDheretics.htm

'Sir Roger Pilkington, II, Knight', Geni.com, https://www.geni.com/people/Sir-Roger-Pilkington-II-Knight/6000000000700963354

Sebastian Sobecki, '"The Writyng of This Tretys": Margery Kempe's Son and the Authorship of Her Book', *Studies in the Age of Chaucer* 37 (2015), pp. 257–83, https://doi.org/10.1353/sac.2015.0015

Sebastian Sobecki, 'From Ping-pong Cupboards to Gdańsk Archives: Finding Margery's Voice', *Women's Literary Culture and the Medieval Canon*, 19 May 2015, https://blogs.surrey.ac.uk/medievalwomen/2015/05/19/from-ping-pong-cupboards-to-gdansk-archives-finding-margerys-voice/

Jean Sorabella, 'Pilgrimage in Medieval Europe', Heilbrunn Timeline of Art History, Metropolitan Museum of Art, New York, April 2011, https://www.metmuseum.org/toah/hd/pilg/hd_pilg.htm

'Stones of King's Lynn', GroundWork Gallery, https://www.groundworkgallery.com/groundwork_projects/stones-of-kings-lynn/

Heather Teysko, 'Pregnancy and Childbirth in Renaissance England', Renaissance English History Podcast, 19 April 2017, https://www.englandcast.com/2017/04/englandcast-024-pregnancy-and-childbirth-in-renaissance-england/

Josephine K. Travers, 'The Alleged Illiteracy of Margery Kempe: A Reconsideration of the Evidence', *Medieval Perspectives* 11 (1996), pp. 113–24, https://www.academia.edu/7908265/

Rosalynn Voaden, 'Travels with Margery: Pilgrimage in Context', in Rosamund Allen (ed.), *Eastward Bound: Travel and Travellers 1050–1550*, Manchester University Press, 2004, pp. 177–95

Nikolaus Wachsmann, 'Review: Oxford History of the Prison: The Practice of Punishment in Western Society', *Reviews in History*, November 1996, https://reviews.history.ac.uk/review/14

David Wallace, 'Margery Kempe in Gdansk, 1433', William Matthews Memorial Lecture, Birkbeck College, 2005

Kathleen Walsh, 'The Deconstruction of the Protofeminist Lens When Applied to Margery Kempe', *Medium*, 19 January 2016, https://medium.com/@kathleenjuliamary/the-deconstruction-of-the-protofeminist-lens-applied-to-margery-kempe-5218d6dd1875

'The Witches of Lynn', Norfolk Record Office blog, 31 October 2018, https://norfolkrecordofficeblog.org/2018/10/31/the-witches-of-lynn/

Naoë Kukita Yoshikawa, 'Margery Kempe's Mystical Marriage and Roman Sojourn: Influence of St Bridget of Sweden', *Reading Medieval Studies* 28 (2002), pp. 39–57

Naoë Kukita Yoshikawa, 'Marian Virtues and Margery Kempe: The Influence of Carmelite Devotion to the Virgin', *Carmelite Studies*, 2003, https://www.carmelite.org/sites/default/files/documents/Heritage/yoshikawamargerykempe.pdf

Index

Initial articles ('The', 'An', 'Le') in titles of works are ignored for the purpose of alphabetical order, e.g. *The Book of Margery Kemp* will be found at 'Book'. Abbreviations: CFT = Cosey Fanni Tutti; DD = Delia Derbyshire; MK = Margery Kempe; RW = Radiophonic Workshop; TG = Throbbing Gristle

Art Sex Music

A Sunday Times, Telegraph, Rough Trade, Pitchfork and Uncut Book of the Year

Shortlisted for the Penderyn Music Book Prize

Shocking, wise and life-affirming, *Art Sex Music* is the captivating memoir of an inspirational woman.

'A remarkable autobiography . . . Inspiring.' *Sunday Times*

'Extraordinary . . . Darkly funny [and] consistently fascinating . . . Forever accustomed to life as an outsider, Tutti has never sought approval, but now it's here whether she likes it or not.' Fiona Sturges, *Guardian*

'An essential read . . . Fearless, powerful, humorous, warm and intelligent.' Simon Tucker, *Louder Than War*

'Compelling . . . Tutti's clarity and conviction cuts through.' Victoria Segal, *Sunday Times*

'I love Cosey Fanni Tutti. Simple as that.' Nick Cave

'An extraordinary life.' Alexis Petridis, *Guardian*

faber